365 AIRCRAFT YOU MUST FLY

365 AIRCRAFT YOU MUST FLY

The most sublime, weird, and
outrageous aircraft from the past 100+ years

... HOW MANY DO YOU WANT TO FLY?

ROBERT F. DORR

ZENITH
PRESS

First published in 2015 by Zenith Press, an imprint of Quarto Publishing Group USA Inc., 400 First Avenue North, Suite 400, Minneapolis, MN 55401 USA

Zenith Press titles are also available at discounts in bulk quantity for industrial or sales-promotional use. For details write to Special Sales Manager at Quarto Publishing Group USA Inc., 400 First Avenue North, Suite 400, Minneapolis, MN 55401 USA.

To find out more about our books, visit us online at www.zenithpress.com.

Library of Congress Cataloging-in-Publication Data

Dorr, Robert F.
    365 aircraft you must fly / Robert F. Dorr.
        pages cm
    ISBN 978-0-7603-4763-8 (pb)
    1. Antique and classic aircraft—Popular works. 2. Airplanes—Piloting—Popular works.
        I. Title. II. Title: Three hundred sixty five aircraft you must fly.
    TL515.D66 2015
    629.133'3—dc23
                            2014048852

Acquisitions Editor: Erik Gilg
Project Manager: Madeleine Vasaly
Art Director: James Kegley
Cover Designer: Simon Larkin
Layout Designer: Rebecca Pagel

On the front cover: Plane, Steve Collender/Shutterstock; Sky, Mau Harng/Shutterstock
On the frontis: Serg64/Shutterstock

Printed in China

10 9 8 7 6 5 4 3 2 1

CONTENTS

Introduction: Before Takeoff 7

Austria-Hungary 8

Canada 9

France 15

Germany.. 27

Israel... 36

Italy.. 38

Japan.. 42

The Netherlands................................... 48

Russia and the Soviet Union............................ 49

Spain 63

Sweden 64

Switzerland... 66

The United Kingdom 69

The United States................................. 89

International Aircraft 305

Planes by Maker.................................316

Postscript: After Landing.................. 320

Before Takeoff

S trap in. Welcome to the wonders of aviation. Get comfortable in the cockpit and get ready.

On the pages ahead are aircraft of all sizes and shapes, from the straightforward to the sublime. You'll find big planes and small helicopters, some simply wonderful and others seriously weird. Outstanding, outlandish, outrageous—they're all between these covers.

You'll hate some. You'll love some. A few will arouse both reactions at the same time. The idea is for you to get into the air and to restore your long-held belief that flying is fun.

This is a book. If you're open to the idea, a book can take you anywhere. In our daily lives where we all scratch out a living, raise families, and struggle with one issue or another, you may never get a real-world opportunity to handle the controls of the Wright Flyer, a B-17 Flying Fortress, or the mind-boggling SR-71 Blackbird.

In a book, you can fly them all.

In this book, you're the pilot.

Because you're already an aviation nutcase—hey, that was obvious when you cracked the cover—this volume is not an attempt to compete with the reference works already on your shelf that contain all the specs of all the world's aircraft.

This isn't a reference work.

This is a time machine, meant to take you in several directions— but first and foremost to take you back to those glorious days of youth, when flying was a new and wondrous thing.

When flying was fun.

Remember?

Some of the flying machines on the pages that follow were designed for recreation and sport. Some were intended for racing. Many have the primary function of transporting passengers from Point A to Point B.

And, yes, some of the airplanes and helicopters in this book have a military mission. No one likes war, but warplanes and their restored civilian cousins— warbirds—hold a special fascination for all of us. Having received orientation flights in military aircraft ranging from the F-15E Strike Eagle to the B-52 Stratofortress, I can testify that even aircraft intended for deadly duties can give you moments of fun.

So, again, make sure those seat straps are cinched tight, do a visual check around the ramp, and reach for the starter button.

It's time to get into the air.

And enjoy.

Robert F. Dorr, 2015

1.24.1917
AVIATIK D.I

AN OBSCURE BUT POTENT
SHOOTER FROM WORLD WAR I

The Aviatik D.I was the first fighter designed in the Austro-Hungarian Empire. Also known as the Berg D.I after its designer, Julius von Berg, it fought on the Italian front in the Great War of 1914 to 1918. Despite structural weaknesses and being prone to engine overheating, the D.I performed well and some pilots preferred it to the better-known German Albatros D.III. The open-air cockpit had only a token windscreen, so the D.I was a "cool" plane to fly in more ways than one. Pilots praised its excellent climb rate but lamented its lack of synchronized armament.

Engine: 1 Austro-Daimler water-cooled inline engine
Horsepower: 200
Maximum speed: 18,000 mph in orbit
Wingspan: 26 ft. 3 in.

- First flight: January 24, 1917
- Number built: About 700
- Displayed at the Museum of Flight, Seattle, and Vienna Technical Museum

11.14.1935

NOORDUYN NORSEMAN

THE AIRPLANE FOR THOSE ACHING FOR ADVENTURE

For anyone wanting to respond to the call of the wild and be a bush pilot, this is the right plane. Designed by Robert Noorduyn, the rugged Norseman was meant from the start to have interchangeable wheel, ski, or twin-float landing gear and to serve Canadian pilots hauling people and supplies into the frozen north. Military versions, including the American UC-64, served all over the world, including the Arctic and Antarctic. This is a great aircraft for hauling passengers and cargo to difficult places. Pilots rave over its ability to get into and out of almost any location.

Engine: 1 Pratt & Whitney R-1340-AN1 Wasp radial piston engine
Horsepower: 600
Cruising speed: 150 mph
Wingspan: 51 ft. 6 in.

- First flight: November 14, 1935
- Number built: 904
- Produced from 1935 to 1959
- 749 built as US Army UC-64s
- A Norseman carrying bandleader Glenn Miller disappeared near England in 1944

5.22.1946

DE HAVILLAND CANADA DHC-1 CHIPMUNK

"I FLING THIS THING AROUND THE SKY FOR FUN"
—Paul Miller, Chipmunk owner

In the years after World War II, this was the training plane that introduced young Canadian, British, Belgian, and Portuguese military pilots to the joy of flying. In the twenty-first century, civilian student pilots in many countries are still cutting their teeth on the de Havilland DHC-1 Chipmunk. This tandem two-seater is a lightweight, no-frills, highly maneuverable basic trainer that forgives mistakes and encourages good piloting. It is so popular that an owner is rarely willing to part with one, so very few are on the aircraft sales market at any time. To put it another way, the popular Chipmunk is a keeper.

Engine: 1 de Havilland Gipsy Major Mk 1C engine
Horsepower: 145
Maximum speed: 140 mph
Wingspan: 34 ft. 4 in.

- First flight: May 22, 1946
- Number built: 1,283 in Canada, Britain, and Portugal, 1947–1956
- Cost: About $16,000 in 1947; typically $65,000 to $135,000 today
- About 500 are airworthy today
- Still used as a military trainer in Portugal

AVRO CANADA CF-100 CANUCK

AN EFFECTIVE INTERCEPTOR REMEMBERED WITH AFFECTION

With a pilot in the front seat and a radar observer in back, the CF-100 Canuck was Canada's equivalent to the Northrop F-89 Scorpion or Lockheed F-94. The job: defend North America from attack. The CF-100 was a much-loved aircraft, from a great Canadian military aircraft industry that never again produced a military plane in significant numbers. In addition to homeland defense, the CF-100 supported Canada's forces in Western Europe and served in the Belgian air force. Five versions or "marks" were produced, each with minor improvements on the basic, straight-wing, two-crew, twin jet design. Pilots liked the stable ground handling on ice-slickened surfaces, and the short takeoff run and rapid climb that made the Canuck an effective interceptor.

Engines: 2 Avro Canada Orenda 11 turbojet engines
Thrust: 7,300 lb. each
Maximum speed: 552 mph
Wingspan: 57 ft. 2 in.

- First flight: January 19, 1950
- Number built: 692
- Nicknamed "the Clunk" by crews
- Served in two Belgian squadrons, 1957 to 1964
- About a dozen are in museums today; none flying

11

11.12.1959

AVRO CANADA VZ-9 AVROCAR

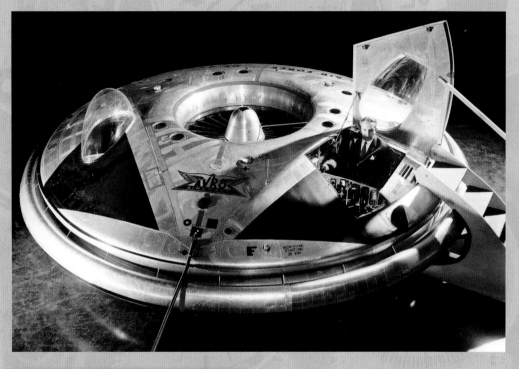

Engines: 3 Continental J69-T-9 turbojet engines
Thrust: 660 lb. each
Maximum speed: 27 mph
Diameter: 18 ft.

- First flight: November 12, 1959
- Number built: 2
- Found to be unstable in flight
- Logged 40 hours of low-level hovering
- 1 survives today

UFO: UNSUCCESSFUL FLYING OBJECT

No little green men from another galaxy are inside this flying saucer, but the US Air Force did invite speculation by calling it Project Silver Bug. The Avro Canada VZ-9 Avrocar was the work of a team of maverick engineers, headed by British aircraft designer "Jack" Frost, who were studying new ways to use a ducted fan to channel jet power and enable aircraft to take off and land vertically. It might have looked like a flying Frisbee, but as a joint air force–army program, the VZ-9 represented a serious effort based on Korean War lessons to find new ways to take off and land in tight places. The answer, it turned out, was more obvious—the UH-1 "Huey" helicopter—and the Avrocar, which contributed to aeronautical knowledge but was essentially unworkable, is now a museum display.

BOMBARDIER CHALLENGER 600 SERIES

"THE CAPABILITIES OF A JETLINER WITHOUT THE HIGH COST" —Bombardier

Strongly influenced by US aircraft developer Bill Lear, and built by Canadair before a company name change, the Bombardier 600 series offers corporate executives as much cabin space as an airliner, transcontinental range, and a high standard of comfort and efficiency. The 600 series also comes in civilian freight, military patrol, and military transport versions, including the US Coast Guard's VC-143 Challenger. The 8.2-foot-wide cabin is unmatched in the bizjet world and the pilot-handling qualities of the 600 are superb.

Engines: 2 General Electric CF34-3A turbofan engines (typical)
Thrust: 9,100 lb. each
Cruising speed: 529 mph
Wingspan: 64 ft. 4 in.

- First flight: November 8, 1978
- Cost: Used 600s selling for $1.2 million in 2015
- Capacity: Up to 19 passengers
- Named LearStar 600 in its design stages

6.20.1983
BOMBARDIER E-9A WIDGET

NO FLYING SAUCERS, PLEASE—
IT'S FOR WEAPONS-RANGE CLEARANCE

The E-9A Widget is a military version of the Bombardier Dash Eight commuter airliner. Because it is so little known as a US Air Force plane, the E-9A draws the attention of conspiracy theorists who place it at the mysterious Area 51 transporting those little green men seized from a UFO. The truth isn't half as macabre, but it's still unusual: the E-9A is a watchdog. It ensures that Gulf of Mexico waters remain clear of boat traffic during live weapons launches and other potentially hazardous military activities. Equipped with AN/APS-143(V)1 radar, the E-9A provides 360-degree radar coverage and datalink relay information and can detect a person on a life raft twenty-five miles away.

Engines: 2 Pratt & Whitney Canada PW120A turboprop engines
Horsepower: 2,000 each
Cruising speed: 310 mph
Wingspan: 81 ft. 11 in.

- First flight: June 20, 1983 (Dash Eight)
- 2 in service
- Operated by 82nd Aerial Target Squadron
- Stationed at Tyndall Air Force Base, Florida

BLÉRIOT XI

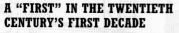

A "FIRST" IN THE TWENTIETH CENTURY'S FIRST DECADE

Just thirty-six minutes to cross the English Channel on July 25, 1909! What an extraordinary achievement on the part of Louis Blériot in those pioneering days when the pilot was in the element and the wind was in the wires! Underwritten by Blériot and designed by Raymond Saulnier, the Blériot XI used unique flight-control surfaces including an all-flying vertical tail. It was a monoplane—the first to make repeated flights successfully—in an era when most aircraft had two wings. The two restored examples flying today perform just as brilliantly as this aircraft did in 1909.

Engine: Anzani 3-cylinder semi-radial engine (and others)
Horsepower: 25
Maximum speed: 46 mph
Wingspan: 25 ft. 7 in.
Propeller diameter: 6 ft. 10 in.

- First flight: January 23, 1909
- Capacity: Up to 3 passengers
- Built in single and two-seat versions
- Considered the first successful monoplane
- 2 restored examples are the oldest flyable aircraft in the world today

1912
DEPERDUSSIN MONOCOQUE

PLANNED FOR PERFORMANCE, BUILT FOR SPEED

The Deperdussin *Monocoque* was a development of a 1911 racing aircraft designed by Louis Béchereau that became the first plane to exceed 100 miles per hour in level flight. Its fuselage was made of bonded tulip wood, its wings covered in linen. As a monoplane, it was decades ahead of the generations of biplanes that came after it. Compared to other early aircraft it was sleek, almost bullet shaped, with a flush propeller spinner at its nose. It was not the first with its unique features, but its name has become a generic term: *monocoque* now refers to a type of construction in which the outer skin carries all or a major part of load bearing. It was a new idea in the time of Deperdussin but has been the usual method of aircraft construction ever since.

Engine: 1 Gnome Lambda air-cooled rotary engine
Horsepower: 160
Maximum speed: 130 mph
Wingspan: 12 ft. 10 in.

- First flight: 1912
- Built by what was then called the Société pour les Appareils Deperdussin (SPAD)
- Won the Gordon Bennett Trophy Race in both 1912 and 1913
- Set a world speed record of 126.7 mph
- Aviation pioneer Armand Deperdussin was once a cabaret singer
- Though one of the fastest aircraft in the world, it did not attract enough orders to prevent Deperdussin from going bankrupt

"DEPERDUSSIN" MONOPLANE.　　　　　MAYS, ALDERSHOT.

1915
CAUDRON G.4

A WORKMANLIKE DESIGN IN A WAR MACHINE

Large, sturdy, functional if not fashionable, the Caudron G.4 twin-engine biplane reconnaissance bomber reflects the efforts of René and Gaston Caudron, brothers who created one of France's first planemaking companies. Optimized for bombload and defensive armament, the G.4 was a solid weapon of war used to good effect in the 1914–1918 conflict not merely by France but by Britain's Royal Navy and several other air arms. For its era, this was a remarkably dependable aircraft and a stable platform for its pilot.

Engines: 2 Le Rhône C radial engines
Horsepower: 80 each
Maximum speed: 80 mph
Wingspan: 56 ft. 5 in.

- First flight: 1915
- Number built: 1,358 (France), 51 (Italy), 12 (Britain)
- Cost: About $21,000 in 1916
- Crew: 2 (pilot, observer/gunner)
- Pioneered night bombing techniques

NIEUPORT 17

Library of Congress

A FAMOUS FRENCH FIGHTER WITH AN ATTITUDE

The Nieuport 17 was an improvement on earlier "fighting scouts" from this planemaker, including the earlier Nieuport 11, which had been France's answer to the so-called Fokker Scourge in 1916—outclassing and outgunning vaunted German fighters with relative ease. Nieuport fighters were noted for their simplicity, maneuverability, and endurance. They were also sassy, in a manner of speaking, always willing to be at the forefront of the action. Equipped with a single machine gun and eventually (in the Nieuport 17*bis* model) with a synchronizer that allowed the gun to be on the centerline in front of the pilot, the Nieuport 17 was a formidable weapon in early use but eventually met its match when newer German fighters demonstrated comparable performance.

Engine: 1 Le Rhône 9Ja 9-cylinder rotary engine
Horsepower: 110
Maximum speed: 130 mph
Wingspan: 26 ft. 9 in.

- First flight: January 1916
- Armament: One of the first warplanes to be armed with rocket projectiles
- 18 countries flew Nieuport 17s
- Inspired the Nieuport 17 Restaurant in Tustin, California
- Designed by Gustav Delage
- Many replicas flying today

1919

FARMAN FF 65 SPORT

THE PRESTIGE PLANE FOR
THE POSTWAR PRIVILEGED

The well-heeled gentleman of France (no ladies invited, please) needed a touring aircraft in the heady, sporty era that came after the Great War. What better than the Farman FF 65 Sport, introduced in single- and two-seat models—a handy biplane ideal for that weekend jaunt from Paris to the Mediterranean. And, of course, because the upper crust enjoys a good contest, the Farman Sport had to be modified (by removing its engine) to participate in a gliding contest. Remarkably, about ten of these sport planes were imported by a US agent in Kansas City and were sold and flown in North America.

Engine: 1 Le Rhône rotary engine (typical)
Horsepower: 60
Maximum speed: 88 mph
Wingspan: 23 ft. 4 in.

- First flight 1919
- Number built: About 36
- First displayed at a Brussels trade show, 1921
- 1 is on display at the Smithsonian National Air and Space Museum today

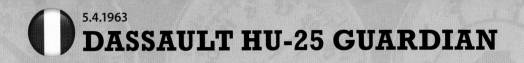

5.4.1963

DASSAULT HU-25 GUARDIAN

Engines: 2 Garrett ATF3-6 turbofan engines

Thrust: 5,440 lb. each

Maximum speed: 566 mph

Weight: 32,000 lb. (Maximum takeoff weight)

Wingspan: 53 ft. 6 in.

- First flight: May 4, 1963 (Falcon 20)
- Number built: 41
- Typical mission: 3½ hours
- Operated from 1982 to 2014

"NOT A DRY EYE IN THE PLACE"
—Capt. Samuel Creach, HU-25 retirement ceremony, September 23, 2014

The HU-25 Guardian was the US Coast Guard's popular and effective medium-range surveillance fixed-wing aircraft. Also dubbed the Falcon, the HU-25 was a military derivative of the Dassault Falcon 20 business jet, five hundred of which were built for civilian use, initially as Mystère 20s. The HU-25 performed search and rescue, law enforcement, and military readiness duties. Several HU-25As were modified to HU-25B standard for pollution control, including oil-slick detection duties in the Persian Gulf following the 1991 war. Nine HU-25As were modified to become HU-25Cs for drug interdiction duty, and later became HU-25Ds with new radar. The only jet ever to be part of the air fleet of the coast guard, the HU-25 was retired with much fanfare on September 23, 2014.

AIRBUS HELICOPTERS AS350 ÉCUREUIL

A POPULAR UTILITY HELO WITH NO BAD HABITS

Known abroad as the *Écureuil* (Squirrel) and in the United States as the AStar, the Airbus Helicopters AS350 is a supremely versatile light rotorcraft with a wide range of uses, from tourist flights to naval patrol duty. It exists in more than a dozen civil, military, and law-enforcement versions and has strong potential for future production and improvement. It offers good visibility and maneuverability and a comfortable perch for its pilot.

Engine: 1 Lycoming LTS101-600A-3A turboshaft engine
Horsepower: 800 shaft
Cruising speed: 152 mph
Rotor diameter: 35 ft. 1 in.

- First flight: June 26, 1974
- Cost: About $2 million new today
- On May 14, 2005, an AS350 touched down on the top of Mount Everest at 29,030 feet
- Military users include Australia, Brazil, and Jordan
- Described by actor-pilot John Travolta as "A super ship."

9.1977

AIRBUS HELICOPTERS AS532 COUGAR

A MUSCULAR LIFTING MACHINE

The AS332 Super Puma and AS532 Cougar are beefed-up cousins, civilian and military respectively, of the familiar Puma helicopter, which has been performing yeoman service in dozens of countries for decades. Trademark of the Super Puma and Cougar: robustness. These are tough, hardy helicopters that can handle almost any climate or terrain. The flight deck could use more elbowroom and easier access, but otherwise the cockpit of these hardworking helicopters is a treat to the touch for even the most temperamental pilot.

Engines: 2 Turbomeca Makila 1A1 turboshaft engines
Horsepower: 1,589 shaft each
Cruising speed: 154 mph
Rotor diameter: 51 ft. 2 in.

- First flight: September 1977
- Capacity: Carries 20 to 25 fully armed troops
- Armament: Naval versions carry mines and missiles
- Built in 7 basic versions

DASSAULT RAFALE

A MULTI-ROLE FIGHTER FROM A SINGLE EUROPEAN NATION

Introduced in 2001, the Dassault *Rafale* (Squall) equips the French Air Force and conducts carrier-based operations in the French Navy. It's a high-tech, multirole warplane that can handle a variety of missions while retaining the capability to win a dogfight with the best of them. The delta-wing, canard flight surfaces make the *Rafale* extremely maneuverable, while a cannon and a variety of missiles make it potent. The cockpit is ergonomic, tailored for pilot efficiency and comfort.

Engines: 2 Snecma M88-2 turbofan engines
Thrust: 17,000 lb.
Maximum speed: 1,180 mph (Mach 1.8)
Wingspan: 50 ft. 1 in.

- First flight: July 4, 1986
- Number built: 130 as of June 2014
- Cost: $124 million in 2009
- Only current European fighter built entirely in one country

7.14.1988

SOCATA TBM 700

AN EXECUTIVE RIDE WITH MUSCLE

The TBM 700 is a single-engined, turboprop, six- to seven-seat executive transport constructed mainly of aluminum and steel but with tail surfaces made of Nomex honeycomb. It's a beefy, powerful aircraft with a spacious, well-designed flight deck and passenger compartment. The design originated with the US firm Mooney, which was purchased by French owners in the city of Tarbes in 1985. (TBM stands for Tarbes-Mooney.) Also marketed as the TBM 850 and TBM 900, this is a great ride for a VIP and a treat for a pilot.

Engine: 1 Pratt & Whitney PT6A-66D turboprop engine
Horsepower: 850
Maximum speed: 290 mph
Wingspan: 41 ft. 7 in.

- First flight: July 14, 1988
- Cost: About $4 million in 2014
- First marketed in 1990
- 125 in service in 2014

10.17.1988
AIRBUS HELICOPTERS EC135

FAT BUT FIT, FAST, AND FUN TO HANDLE

A beautifully functional flying machine even if known for being portly rather than pleasing to the eye, the Eurocopter EC135 is a pilot's delight, whether serving as a civilian ambulance or hauling military troops into battle. It's also widely used for offshore support of the oil and gas industries, and for law enforcement. It has been through multiple name changes, beginning as the Messerschmitt-Bölkow-Blohm Bo 108 but having its company name changed first to Eurocopter and then to Airbus Helicopters. Crew members like the oversized sliding doors and rear clamshell doors that permit easy loading and unloading of passengers and equipment. Pilots like the EC135's superb visibility, and its reliability and safety record.

Engines: 2 Turbomeca Arrius 2B2 or 2 Pratt & Whitney PW206B turboshaft engines
Horsepower: 621 to 633
Cruising speed: 158 mph
Main rotor diameter: 33 ft. 6 in.

- First flight: October 17, 1988
- Number built: About 1,100 as of 2014
- Capacity: Typically 1 pilot plus 6 passengers
- Uses the Fenestron system, with an enclosed tail rotor
- Considered friendly to mechanics and maintainers

10.25.1991

AIRBUS A340

A THROWBACK TO ANOTHER TIME

Look at it from a distance and the Airbus A340 resembles the first-generation jetliners that preceded it by three decades: in an era when all (well, nearly all) have two engines, the A340 has four, just like the Boeing 707 and Douglas DC-8. When it was designed, rapid increases in turbofan thrust still lay in the future, so four engines seemed right for the large, versatile aircraft that offered long range and would be built in four versions. The A340 is a great aircraft for both pilots and passengers, with Airbus's signature flight controls that function almost automatically, but the A340 is considered a gas-guzzler, which is why Airbus announced in 2011 that it would discontinue production. Some commercial carriers are retiring A340s, while others use them on long-haul routes where fuel consumption rates are lowest.

Engines: 4 Rolls-Royce Trent turbofan engines
Thrust: 58,000 lb. each
Cruising speed: 543 mph
Wingspan: 208 ft. 10 in.

- First flight: October 25, 1991
- Capacity: Up to 475 passengers in high-density configuration
- Flies some of the world's longest nonstop routes, such as Singapore to Los Angeles
- A340-600 has the longest fuselage ever built by the Airbus family (247 ft. 1 in.)
- Used by a handful of purchasers as the world's largest executive VIP transport

ALBATROS D.III

AN IMPERFECT FIGHTER FOR THE RED BARON AND OTHERS

Designed by Robert Thelen, the Albatros D.III was the principal fighter used by German and Austro-Hungarian forces during the Great War of 1914 to 1918. It became the personal mount of great German aces such as Manfred von Richthofen and Ernst Udet. The Albatros ruled the skies during the short interval when German airpower dominated during "Bloody April" in 1917. A tailwheel sesquiplane biplane (the lower wings shorter than the upper), the Albatros appeared in several versions, including some with different propeller-spinner designs. The pilot peered into the wind over two .31-caliber Spandau 08/15 machine guns. It was trouble-plagued, with wing-spar failures as well as handling and reliability issues, but the Albatros was also the point of the spear—one of the earliest aircraft designed for the sole purpose of shooting down others.

Engine: 1 Mercedes D.IIIa inline water-cooled engine
Horsepower: 180
Maximum speed: 110 mph
Wingspan: 29 ft. 6 in.

- First flight: August 1916
- Number built: 1,866
- Derived from the successful Albatros D.I
- Served in 37 Imperial German Army Air Service squadrons
- Albatros engineers were influenced by the French Nieuport; unfortunately, they did not solve the Nieuport's structural wing issues for their aircraft

San Diego Air and Space Museum Archives

FOKKER DR.I DREIDECKER

THE MOST FAMOUS FIGHTER OF WORLD WAR I

"It climbed like a monkey and maneuvered like the devil," said the Red Baron, Manfred von Richthofen. The Fokker Dr.I *Dreidecker* (Triplane), designed by the prolific Anthony Fokker, was inspired by (but by no means copied from) Britain's three-winged Sopwith. When it entered service in April 1917, it immediately began shooting down Allied aircraft. Despite its small numbers and some manufacturing flaws, the Dr.I—often portrayed in Richthofen's color choice of blood red—became one of the most recognized aircraft of its era.

Engine: 1 Le Rhône 9J or Oberursel UR.II radial engine
Horsepower: 110
Maximum speed: 115 mph
Wingspan: 23 ft. 7 in. (top wing)

- First flight: July 5, 1917
- Number built: 320 by Fokker during World War I
- Armament: 2 synchronized 8mm Spandau machine guns
- Used a tail skid, not a tail wheel
- A full-sized replica is available as a kit in the United States

FOKKER D.VII

A FORMIDABLE FIGHTER WITH FRIENDLY HANDLING

The Fokker D.VII was a German World War I fighter aircraft designed by Reinhold Platz of the Fokker firm. Germany's best-known ace pilot, Baron Manfred von Richthofen, evaluated the D.VII and pronounced it ready for battle. It became one of the most familiar combat aircraft over the Western Front. Not plagued with the mechanical flaws or handling problems that hindered other pursuit ships on both sides, the D.VII was both a formidable aerial weapon and a super ship to fly. It was a latecomer to the war that might have had greater impact had it been rushed into service. The armistice that ended the Great War explicitly required Berlin's forces to surrender all D.VIIs to the Allies at the end of hostilities.

Engine: 1 Mercedes D.IIIa engine (early versions)
Horsepower: 160
Maximum speed: 189 mph
Wingspan: 29 ft. 2 in.

- First flight: January 1918
- Number built: About 3,300 in 1918
- Armament: 2 of Germany's ubiquitous Spandau machine guns
- Very agile in a close-quarters dogfight
- Several replicas flying today
- 1 is displayed at the Smithsonian; 1 sat unnoticed in a barn in Germany from 1918 to 1948 and is now displayed at the Deutsches Museum in Munich

4.27.1934
BÜCKER BÜ 131 "JUNGMANN"

"THE MOST FUN YOU CAN HAVE WITH YOUR CLOTHES ON"
—Jim Ring, present-day Bü 131 owner

Designed by Carl Bücker, a German who lived part of his life in Sweden, the Bü 131 *Jungmann* (Young Man) was the first aircraft flown by thousands of future Luftwaffe pilots in the 1930s and during World War II. The sturdy, agile, open-cockpit Bü 131 made it easy to learn the basics of stick, throttle, and rudder, and seemed capable of forgiving almost any mistake by a fledgling flyer. Today, it is a vintage sport plane much in demand by those who don't have one and a source of sheer pleasure for those who do.

Engine: 1 Hirth HM 504 inverted inline engine
Horsepower: 100
Cruising speed: 110 mph
Wingspan: 24 ft. 3 in.

- First flight: April 27, 1934
- Production was resumed in the 1990s
- About 200 flying today
- Built under license in several countries, including Japan

5.29.1935

MESSERSCHMITT BF 109

A CLASSIC, BUT KEPT IN PRODUCTION TOO LONG

A world-beater in 1935, painfully obsolete in 1945, the Messerschmitt Bf 109 fought in every battle from the Spanish Civil War until the end of the conflict in Europe. Willy Messerschmitt and Robert Lusser designed the Bf 109 to be fast and maneuverable. Early in its career, it was a match for early versions of the British Spitfire. However, the Bf 109 underwent very few changes during its decade in the sun, and as the war deteriorated for the German side, newer and better fighters eclipsed it. It was difficult to take off and land, and the cockpit of every version of the Bf 109 was sorely lacking elbowroom. Visibility was far from ideal. Yet some air aces preferred the Bf 109 to newer fighters. One claimed that if he could master the Bf 109, he could defeat anything the Allies had.

Engine: 1 Daimler-Benz DB 605A-1 liquid-cooled, inverted V-12 pistol engine (typical)
Horsepower: 1,480
Maximum speed: 400 mph
Wingspan: 29 ft. 7 in.

- First flight: May 29, 1935
- Number built: 33,984—the most produced fighter in history
- Accounted for 57 percent of German fighters built during World War II
- A "muscle car of the air," with a very small frame and a very big engine
- Small, narrow-tread landing gear made taxiing a challenge
- Less than half a dozen are airworthy today

FIESELER FI 156 STORCH

**Engine: 1 Argus As 10 air-cooled
inverted V-8 engine**

Horsepower: 240

Maximum speed: 109 mph

Wingspan: 46 ft. 9 in.

- First flight: May 24, 1936
- Number built: About 2,900
- Designed by Reinhold Mewes and Erich Bachem
- Manufactured in 5 countries

THE STOL PIONEER

Test pilot Hanna Reitsch landed one of these in the streets of bombed-out Berlin near Adolf Hitler's underground bunker in 1945 (although the Führer declined her offer to evacuate him). The Fieseler Fi 156 *Storch* (Stork), it seemed, could take off and land almost anywhere. In part because of leading-edge slats on its huge wing, it was one of the first fixed-wing aircraft able to shoehorn in and out of tight spaces—an early example of the short takeoff and landing, or STOL, aircraft. The *Storch* was valuable for VIP transport, liaison, artillery spotting, and other front-line duties. Field Marshal Erwin Rommel, the "Desert Fox," used *Storch* aircraft to conduct personal surveillance of the North African battlefield. More than a dozen are still flying today.

6.1.1939

FOCKE-WULF FW 190 WÜRGER

A THOROUGHBRED WITH A TIGHT TURNING RADIUS

German designer Kurt Tank called other fighters racehorses but said he wanted his Fw 190 to be a *Dienstpferd*—a charger, or cavalry horse. He succeeded. He created one of the true immortals, a fighter that could operate from ill-prepared front-line airfields, could be flown and maintained by men with only a little training, and could absorb severe battle damage and bring its pilot home. The Fw 190 *Würger* (Shrike), also called the "Butcher Bird," may have been the most maneuverable combat aircraft of World War II. It was one of the most capable all-around fighters and one of the easiest for a pilot to master.

Engine: 1 BMW 801D-2 14-cylinder radial engine
Horsepower: 1,700
Maximum speed: 408 mph
Wingspan: 29 ft. 5 in.

- First flight: June 1, 1939
- Allied bomber crews dreaded a head-on attack by an Fw 190 with guns blazing
- The long-nosed Fw 190D, or "Dora," performed superbly when introduced in 1944
- Wide-track landing gear gave the Fw 190 superb handling characteristics on the ground
- Otto Kittel, history's fourth-ranking ace, scored most of his 267 kills in Fw 190s

FOCKE-ACHGELIS FA 330 BACHSTELZE

Engine: No powerplant (rotors turned by wind)

Maximum speed: 25 mph

Main rotor diameter: 24 ft.

Fuselage length: 14 ft. 7 in.

- First flight: 1940
- Number built: About 200
- Maximum altitude: 795 feet
- Equipped with a parachute

DON'T GET TOO COMFORTABLE BACK THERE!

Often called a helicopter, Nazi Germany's Focke-Achgelis Fa 330 *Bachstelze* (Wagtail) was actually a rotary-wing kite, or gyroglider, towed astern by a submarine and used to search for naval threats. Adolf Hitler expressed interest in the Fa 330 during a military staff meeting. Blasted by the elements and tossed around like an acorn on the wind, the rider of this weird machine was an observer more than a pilot, assigned to cling for dear life and search. It was a wild, scary ride. The Fa 330 assisted in only one ship's sinking, when a U-boat used one to spot and destroy the Greek steamer *Efthalia Mari* on August 6, 1943. The typical wolf-pack skipper preferred to stay submerged when possible, leaving the Fa 330 stowed in a watertight compartment in the conning tower—and unused.

MESSERSCHMITT ME 262

STORMBIRD IN SERVICE TO THE SWASTIKA

The Messerschmitt Me 262, known in different variants as the *Schwalbe* (Swallow) and the *Sturmvogel* (Stormbird), was the world's first operational jet fighter. When the plane was displayed to Adolf Hitler at Insterburg, Germany on November 26, 1943, the Führer said that having a jet would help Germany win the war. Hitler's interest in using the Me 262 as a bomber is often cited as a mistake—had they been available earlier, jet fighters might have swept Allied bombers from Europe's skies—but a bigger problem was the poor manufacturing quality and unreliability of early jet engines. In the end, however, the Me 262 was a "might have been." Fully 20 percent faster than the Allied fighters it came up against, capable of reliable performance once it reached operating altitude, highly maneuverable, and heavily armed, the Me 262 was a lot to handle even when a skilled pilot was at the controls, and it never overcame obstacles created by poor leadership, technical glitches, and the vicissitudes of war.

Engines: 2 Junkers Jumo 004B-1/3 turbojets
Thrust: 2,000 lb. per engine
Maximum speed: 521 mph
Wingspan: 40 ft. 11½ in.

- First flight with propeller: April 18, 1941
- First flight using jet power: July 18, 1942
- First flight with tricycle landing gear: October 17, 1943
- Number built: About 1,400, but only 200 were in service at any one time
- Credited with shooting down 509 Allied aircraft
- About 150 were lost in combat

IAI KFIR

THE LION CUB THAT ROARED

The *Kfir*, or Lion Cub—pronounced *fear*—is the sleek hot-rod fighter every gung-ho pilot wants to fly. It's also an ideal role-player as a mock enemy (aggressor) and was used that way by the US Navy as the F-21A. Strongly influenced by French designs from the French Dassault *Mirage* family, yet emblematic of Israel's quest for an independent role in planemaking, the *Kfir* is light, nimble, and lethal. Like all J79-powered aircraft it is loud, but unlike most it offers the pilot a comfortable fit and a willingness to be flung all over the sky. It makes a good "aggressor" because it's so responsive and so maneuverable.

Engine: 1 Bedek-built General Electric J79-J1E turbojet engine with afterburner
Thrust: 12,000 lb.
Maximum speed: 1,516 mph (Mach 2.1)
Wingspan: 27 ft.

- First flight: June 1, 1973
- Number built: About 220
- 24 were leased to the US Navy as F-21As, 1985 to 1989
- One pilot called it "the fighter pilot's race car"

3.19.1984

IAI C-38A COURIER

"IT FILLED AN IMPORTANT NICHE AND DID A GREAT JOB"
—Lt. Col. Linda McTague, C-38A pilot

The Israel Aircraft Industries C-38A Courier was the US Air Force version of the Astra SPX long-distance executive jet. Years after the Pentagon purchased two for air national guard use, the design was sold to famous US planemaker Gulfstream and re-named the G100 in its civilian incarnation. The C-38A replaced the C-21 Learjet in the District of Columbia Air National Guard at Andrews Air Force Base, Maryland, beginning in April 1998. After many years of excellent service in executive transport and medical evacuation, the Pentagon announced in 2014 that it would retire the two C-38As as a cost-saving measure.

Engines: 2 Honeywell TFE731-40R-200F turbofan engines
Thrust: 4,250 lb. each
Maximum speed: 530 mph (Mach 0.84)
Wingspan: 54 ft. 7 in.

- First flight: March 19, 1984
- Number built: 2
- Capacity: Typically 8 passengers or 2 medical litters
- Range: 3,390 miles

1914

CAPRONI CA.20

A FIGHTER FROM GIOVANNI CAPRONI

The Caproni Ca.20 monoplane is considered the world's first fighter. It was far ahead of its time with speed, maneuverability, and a forward-firing machine gun mounted above its propeller arc; a complex, eye-level gun sight enabled the pilot to aim the .303-caliber Lewis machine gun positioned high above his head. Test flights proved that the Ca.20 was an exceptional performer—faster than military aircraft being made in France and Germany—but the Italian government placed its priority on bomber aircraft. Lacking official support in Rome, Caproni built just one Ca.20, which resides today at the Museum of Flight in Seattle.

Engine: 1 Le Rhône rotary engine
Horsepower: 110
Maximum speed: 102 mph
Wingspan: 26 ft.

- First flight: 1914
- Designer Giovanni "Gianni" Caproni (1886–1957) was trained as an electrical engineer
- Was stored by Caproni family in Italy for 85 years—in a monastery!
- Displayed in original condition, scars, stains and all

1916
CAPRONI CA.36

Engines: 3 Isotta-Fraschini V.4V water-cooled radials
Horsepower: 150 each
Maximum speed: 87 mph
Wingspan: 74 ft. 7 in.

- First flight: 1916
- Crew: 4
- Retired: Remained in service until 1929
- The huge wing was assembled in five sections
- The ultimate in an early series of large bombers
- The ultimate strategic bomber of 1914–1918
- A restored Ca.36 is displayed at the National Museum of the US Air Force, Dayton, Ohio

ONE OF THE FIRST BIG BOMBERS

In 1914, Italian engineer Gianni Caproni designed his Ca.36 as the ultimate in his series of multi-engined heavy bombers used in Italy, France, Britain, and the United States. In Italian hands, these sky giants bombed Austria beginning in 1917. The Caproni design was more advanced than any big bomber on drawing boards in the United States, so the Ca.36 became an important part of the US Army Air Service.

MACCHI C.205 VELTRO

A GREAT WARPLANE THAT DESERVES RECOGNITION

This was Italy's best fighter of World War II. The Macchi C.205 *Veltro* (Greyhound) was a match in speed, maneuverability, and firepower for any fighter the Allies could put up against it. Alas, it arrived late in the war and many suffered from poor assembly standards at the factory. Still, it was popular for its fighting ability, and for the visibility and comfort it offered the pilot. German officers liked it so much they formed a *Gruppe* of C.205s as part of their air arm after Italy was no longer a belligerent. German ace Dieter Schaub said the C.205 was superior to both the Messerschmitt Bf 109 and the North American P-51 Mustang!

Engine: 1 Fiat (Daimler-Benz) RA.1050 RC58 *Tifone* liquid-cooled piston engine
Horsepower: 1,475
Maximum speed: 400 mph
Wingspan: 34 ft. 9 in.

- First flight April 19, 1942
- Number built: Only 262
- One Italian pilot scored 14 kills in the C.205
- 3 survivors today, 1 airworthy

ALENIA C-27J SPARTAN

A "MINI-HERCULES" WITH LIFTING POWER

The Alenia C-27J Spartan was designed to transport cargo and ammunition into front-line battle zones where the larger C-130 Hercules won't fit or isn't economical. An international success, the C-27J has a checkered history in the United States, having been purchased but later rejected by—in succession—the army, air force, and air national guard before a few Spartans ended up in the coast guard and in special-operations units. Interest in other countries remains healthy. Pilots love the flexibility and agility of this tactical hauler, and say handling the controls is a treat.

Engines: 2 Rolls-Royce AE 2100D2A turboprop engines
Horsepower: 4,640 each
Maximum speed: 374 mph
Wingspan: 94 ft. 2 in.

- First flight: September 24, 1999
- Cost: $3 million in 2012
- Gunship version, used by Italian forces: the MC-27J Praetorian
- Ordered by air units in 8 countries

41

4.1.1939

MITSUBISHI A6M ZERO

REIGNED SUPREME IN THE PACIFIC—BUT NOT FOR LONG

The Zero couldn't be the best fighter in the world in 1941, Americans said, so they made up a myth: they claimed chief engineer Jirō Horikoshi had stolen the blueprints for a US fighter. It was sheer nonsense, and at the time Zeros appeared high over Pearl Harbor, this fast, lightweight plane may indeed have been the best fighter in the world. It had little growth potential, however, and initially did not have self-sealing fuel tanks or pilot armor. As early as mid-1942, new tactics and the introduction of better equipment enabled Allied pilots to engage the Zero on equal terms. By 1945, the Zero was obsolescent but still widely in service, some of them flown by *kamikaze*—suicide pilots.

Engine: 1 Nakajima Sakae 12 radial engine
Horsepower: 950
Maximum speed: 410 mph
Weight: 5,313 lb. (a real lightweight)
Wingspan: 39 ft. 4 in.

- First flight: April 1, 1939
- First air combat: September 13, 1940, in China
- Served aboard all Japanese aircraft carriers
- A key weakness: insufficient diving speed
- 108 Zeros were among 441 Japanese warplanes at Pearl Harbor

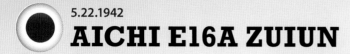

5.22.1942
AICHI E16A ZUIUN

CLUMSY IN APPEARANCE BUT A SUPERB PERFORMER

Hang on tight. The Aichi E16A *Zuiun* (Auspicious Cloud), code-named "Paul" by the Allies, was quite a ride. Despite those clunky floats seemingly adding weight beneath its fuselage, the E16A had so much power it was the only seaplane that needed dive brakes for control in near-vertical flight. Yes, it was both a scout and dive bomber, a robust, powerful craft with speed, range, and flexibility. The US Navy was so intrigued by its combination of weight and power, it brought an E16A to the United States for tests. It confirmed that despite the cumbersome seaplane configuration, the aircraft flew very well.

Engine: 1 Mitsubishi Kinsei 54 radial piston engine
Maximum speed: 274 mph
Weight: 10,000 lb. (gross)
Wingspan: 42 ft.

- First flight: May 22, 1942
- Number built: 256 in 3 models
- Some served aboard battleships
- Comparable to: Vought OS2U Kingfisher

10.1.1944
KUGISHO MXY-7 OHKA

Engines: 3 Type 4 Mark 1 Model 20 solid-fuel rocket motors (Ohka 11)

Thrust: 600 lb. each

Maximum speed: 576 mph in dive

Wingspan: 16 ft. 10 in.

- First flight: October 1, 1944
- Number built: 852
- Americans called it the *Baka* (Fool)
- A distant cousin of the Nakajima Ki-115 *Tsurugi* (Sabre)
- Required little piloting skill

"FRIGHTFUL, DESPERATE TECHNOLOGY"
—Smithsonian National Air and Space Museum

This was a flying bomb—not intended to take off or to land. Near the end of World War II, Vice Adm. Takijirō Ōnishi recommended that the Japanese navy create special squadrons to attack American warships gathering for amphibious landings in the Philippines. These *kamikaze*, or suicide, attacks, inflicted terrible damage on US military members but also claimed the lives of five thousand Japanese pilots. The *Ohka* (Cherry Blossom) 22 was designed to allow a pilot with minimal training to drop from a bomber at high altitude, and guide his aircraft with its warhead at high speed into an Allied warship. Two versions, the rocket powered Ohka 11 and jet-propelled Ohka 22 (pictured) saw limited use, although existing aircraft types flew most kamikaze missions.

NAKAJIMA KI-115 TSURUGI

3.1.1945

THIS AIRPLANE? IT'S TO DIE FOR

The Nakajima Ki-115 *Tsurugi* (Sabre) was a hastily designed and very rudimentary suicide aircraft. "Ki" comes from the Japanese word *kitai*, meaning "fuselage," and is pronounced "key" (not "kay eye"). Japan's kamikaze forces brought a swarm of devastation down on the United States and its allies—just ask any sailor aboard an American warship in 1945—but the Ki-115 was a peripheral player, intended for use in an Allied invasion of Japan that never took place. The rationale: Japan did not have enough existing aircraft to use for kamikaze attacks so huge numbers of cheap, simple suicide planes needed to be constructed quickly. The Ki-115 was simply too late, however, and is remembered today mostly as a display ornament at Yokota Air Base, Japan, during the US occupation.

Engine: 1 Nakajima Ha-35 Type 23 radial piston engine plus provision for 2 rocket boosters
Horsepower: 125
Maximum speed: 342 mph
Wingspan: 28 ft. 3 in.

- First flight: March 1, 1945
- Number built: 105
- Armament: Single 551-lb. bomb
- Had a jettisonable undercarriage (wasn't intended to land)

KAWASAKI T-4

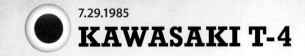

A NEAT LITTLE TRAINER WITH TWIN-JET POWER

The Kawasaki T-4 fills a niche in Japan's air arm. Hundreds of future fighter pilots have earned their wings in the roomy and sensible tandem cockpit of the T-4, practicing fighter-like maneuvers. The T-4 is both small and lightweight, being constructed mostly of aluminum alloy, but it feels like a Phantom or an Eagle when pilots fling it around. The one-piece canopy provides excellent visibility, and a recent upgrade has improved the controls and instrument layout. Instructors view the T-4 as flexible but tame, an ideal mix for its schooling duties.

Engines: 2 Ishikawajima-Harima F3-IHI-30 turbofan engines
Thrust: 3,250 lb. each
Maximum speed: 645 mph
Wingspan: 32 ft. 7 in.

- First flight: July 29, 1985
- First service: 1988
- Number built: 212
- Armament: 2 hardpoints for bombs and rockets

MITSUBISHI F-2

A BRILLIANT DESIGN
THAT BROKE THE BANK

Japan's awesome-looking Mitsubishi F-2 fighter was inspired by the F-16 Fighting Falcon but is bigger, beefier, and—alas—four times the price. It looks like a world-beater and flies like one, but the F-2 became caught up in a roiling domestic controversy because of its costs (including licensing fees to the F-16's manufacturer) and technical glitches. At the very time pilots were reporting how hot it was, the Japanese government reduced its planned purchase from 141 aircraft to 130 and then to 98, including four prototypes. The F-2 is a great ride, a thrill to handle at the outer envelope, and a fine fighter and fighter-bomber that had its production run cut sadly short.

Engine: 1 General Electric F110-GE-129 turbofan engine
Thrust: 17,000 lb.
Maximum speed: 1,630 mph (Mach 2.0)
Wingspan: 16 ft. 6 in.

- First flight: October 7, 1995
- Number built: 98
- Cost: $127 million in 2009
- Nicknamed "Viper Zero"
- Last aircraft delivered September 27, 2011

FOKKER F-27 FRIENDSHIP

A FAMOUS DUTCH NAME ON A GREAT TRANSPORT

One of the last aircraft to bear the famous Fokker name, Holland's F-27 Friendship arrived on the scene in 1955 as a potential replacement for the Douglas DC-3 with turboprop engines and a pressurized cabin for twenty-eight passengers. The F-27 eventually became not only a highly successful regional airliner but a military transport as well. Building on Dutch success with the design, Fairchild developed its F-27 and FH-227 versions in the United States. Passengers enjoy the superb view from large windows located beneath the high wing. Pilots like the Friendship's handling qualities and especially its solid performance when taxiing, taking off, and landing. It is also a good aircraft to jump out of: for decades, the US Army's Golden Knights parachute team has used one of these, called the C-31A Troopship, at air shows and other public events.

Engine:s 2 Rolls-Royce Dart turboprop engines
Horsepower: 2,250 each
Cruising speed: 286 mph
Wingspan: 95 ft. 2 in.

- First flight: November 24, 1955
- Number built: 586
- Capacity: Different versions configured for 28 to 56 passengers
- About 150 in service today worldwide
- First operator was Aer Lingus, the national airline of Ireland
- Anthony Fokker's company moved from Germany to Holland in 1919

12.11.1913

SIKORSKY ILYA MUROMETS

A PRECURSOR TO ALL THE WORLD'S HEAVY BOMBERS

This class of aircraft—large, four-engine commercial airliners and heavy military bombers used during the Great War of 1914–1918 by the Russian Empire—showcases the genius of Igor Sikorsky, the Russian who later immigrated to the United States and developed early helicopters. The airliner version offered an insulated passenger saloon, comfortable wicker chairs, a bedroom, a lounge, and even the first airborne toilet. Also included was a private cabin with a berth, small table, and cabinet. And what did pilots think of this complex flying conglomeration? No record seems to survive, but the Ilya Muromets was undoubtedly viewed as a challenge by even the most skillful cockpit practitioners.

Engines: 4 Sunbeam Crusader V-8 engines (typical)
Horsepower: 148 each
Maximum speed: 70 mph
Wingspan: 97 ft. 9 in. (top wing)

- First flight: December 11, 1913
- Number built: About 85 of all versions
- Derived from the world's first four-engined aircraft, designed by Igor Sikorsky
- Named for Ilya Muromets, a hero from Russian mythology
- Set a record by carrying 16 passengers in 1914
- 1 aircraft survives today in the Monino museum near Moscow

10.2.1939

ILYUSHIN IL-2 ŠTURMOVÍK

Engine: 1 Mikulin AM-38F liquid-cooled V-12 engine
Horsepower: 1,720
Maximum speed: 257 mph
Wingspan: 47 ft. 11 in.

- First flight: October 2, 1939
- Number built: 36,183
- Armament: Pilot had 2 forward-firing guns for strafing; carried up to 1,320 lb. of bombs

"THEY ARE AS ESSENTIAL TO THE RED ARMY AS AIR AND BREAD"
—Soviet Premier Josef Stalin

The most numerous military aircraft in history, the Ilyushin Il-2 *Šturmovík* (ground-attack aircraft) was a "flying tank" and a savior to Soviet troops who fought at Stalingrad and Kursk. It was vulnerable, though, and designers were late installing a defensive gun position behind the pilot. With its crew of two (one in early versions), the Il-2 was one of the first warplanes designed from the start for air-to-ground operations. A distinctive characteristic was the use of armor as an airframe load-bearing feature. The Il-2 did not have a comfortable cockpit and was not easy to fly, but good pilots mastered its controls and won battles.

ILYUSHIN IL-10 ŠTURMOVÍK

THE IL-2 ON STEROIDS

Under personal direction from USSR boss Joseph Stalin, the Ilyushin design bureau developed a beefed-up ground-attack aircraft derived from the better-known Il-2. The late-war Il-10, which shared the name *Šturmovík*, was actually slightly smaller than the Il-2 but heavier and roomier, with more power, fuel, and ordnance. The Il-10 had many successes in the final months of World War II, and was used effectively by North Korea's forces during the Korean War.

Engine: 1 Mikulin AM-42 liquid-cooled V-12 engine
Horsepower: 1,080
Maximum speed: 329 mph
Wingspan: 36 ft. 3 in.

- First flight: April 18, 1944
- Number built: 6,166 (4,966 Il-10, 1,200 B-33)
- Built under license in Czechoslovakia (Avia B-33)
- 2 were test-flown in the United States during the Korean War

MIKOYAN-GUREVICH MIG-15

VAUNTED AND VALIANT, BUT NOT VICTORIOUS

Shock, dread, mystery: these were some of the reactions in the Western world when the MiG-15 made its surprise debut in the Korean War. Americans knew little about the Soviet design bureau headed by Artem Mikoyan and Mikhail Gurevich, even though an earlier MiG (which means "M and G") had been part of World War II. The MiG-15, a contemporary and adversary of the F-86 Sabre, was the team's first truly successful fighter and a showcase for Soviet technology. The MiG-15 genuinely counts as one of the great fighters of all time. In Korea, the Americans defeated it because they had a comparable fighter and pilots with better training who spent more time in the combat zone. Pilots considered the MiG-15 a lightweight, nimble speedster and praised its maneuverability.

Engine: 1 RD-45F turbojet (MiG-15) or 1 Klimov VK-1 turbojet (MiG-15*bis*)
Thrust: About 6,000 lb. (VK-1)
Maximum speed: 668 mph
Wingspan: 33 ft. 1 in.

- First flight: December 30, 1947
- Number built: 16,085 in the Soviet Union, China, Czechoslovakia, and Poland
- Armament: Plenty of firepower with 2 23mm and 1 37mm cannon
- MiG-15*bis* was the improved model, MiG-15UTI the two-seat trainer version
- Shot down a US RB-45C Tornado reconnaissance bomber near Siberia in 1950
- Cockpit was considered cramped

MIKOYAN-GUREVICH MIG-17

NOT NEW, NOT FANCY, BUT RELIABLE AND LETHAL

By the time the MiG-17 "Fresco" (as NATO called it) engaged American fighters over Hanoi, it was no longer new—the more recently developed MiG-21 fought in the same war—but it remained the preferred mount of North Vietnamese air aces. They believed the MiG-17's light weight, high thrust-to-weight ratio, and outright nimbleness enabled a good pilot to fly circles around the more ponderous planes fielded by the Americans: The MiG-17 was the gnat and the F-4 Phantom II was an elephant. In reality, the MiG-17 didn't perform as well as pilots' love for it might have suggested, but though it was an aging weapon in a fast-changing era, there was never a second when it could be taken for granted.

Engine: 1 Klimov VK-1F turbojet engine with afterburner
Thrust: 7,450 lb.
Maximum speed: 715 mph
Wingspan: 31 ft. 7 in.

- First flight: January 14, 1950
- First combat: Straits of Taiwan, 1958
- Number built: About 11,060
- Ready for combat weeks too late for the Korean War
- Used by the Soviet Union and 19 other countries
- In several Cold War shootdowns of US reconnaissance aircraft

MIKOYAN-GUREVICH MIG-19

**Engines: 2 Tumansky RD-9B turbojet
engines with afterburners**

Thrust: 7,178 lb. each

Maximum speed: 909 mph

Wingspan: 29 ft. 6 in.

- First flight: September 18, 1953
- Number built: 2,172
- Considered an "interim" fighter between the MiG-17 and MiG-21

A SOLID PERFORMER, BUT NOT THE MOST MEMORABLE MIG

The MiG-19, known to Western allies by the reporting name "Farmer," was said by the Soviet media to be the world's first operational fighter capable of exceeding the speed of sound in level flight, although it first flew four months after the F-100 Super Sabre. Its designers looked ahead to an era when most fighters would have two engines, positioned side by side. It was produced in the Soviet Union, China, and Czechoslovakia in a dozen models. The MiG-19 fought in several conflicts, including a small-scale role in Vietnam, where it was credited with half a dozen victories over US aircraft. The cockpit was a little complex and the controls on the stiff side, but overall this was a superb mount for a fighter pilot.

1.17.1955

TUPOLEV TU-104

NOT PRETTY, BUT A PIONEER

The Tupolev Tu-104 was a shock to the Western world—the world's first jet airliner to provide sustained and successful service and a stunning symbol of technological achievement from the same Soviet Union that sent humankind's first satellite into space two years later. Like other aircraft that shocked the West—such as the Japanese Zero and the Soviet MiG-15—the Tu-104 seemed a sensation at first but was quickly found to have limitations, having been built under shoddy assembly-plant standards. It was never a pilot-friendly flying machine and enjoyed only a middling safety record. Still, this derivative of the Tu-16 Badger bomber paved the way for generations of jetliners that followed. Today, surviving Tu-104s are in museums.

Engines: 2 Mikulin AM-3M-500 turbojet engines
Thrust: 21,400 lb. each
Operating speed: 390 mph
Wingspan: 113 ft. 4 in.

- First flight: January 17, 1955
- Number built: 201
- Capacity: 50 to 115 passengers
- Carried 90 million passengers with the Soviet airline Aeroflot
- Known to NATO allies as "Camel"

MIKOYAN-GUREVICH MIG-21

"IT'S LITTLE, BUT IT'S MEAN"
—Robin Olds, US fighter pilot

American leaders were stunned when the Soviet MiG-21—three years older, and manufactured far more crudely—racked up a 2-to-1 kill ratio against the F-4 Phantom II over North Vietnam from 1965 to 1967. Repairs to deficient training enabled the United States to turn the tide and although American forces lost about fifty aircraft to North Vietnamese MiG-21s, the US Air Force shot down sixty-eight of them. Still, the MiG-21 (NATO reporting name "Fishbed"), a simple, bantamweight fighter devoid of bells and whistles, remained a formidable threat.

Engine: 1 Tumanski R-13-300 turbojet with afterburner (MiG-21MF)

Thrust: 14,550 lb.

Maximum speed: 1,385 mph (Mach 2.1)

Wingspan: 23 ft. 6 in.

- First flight: February 14, 1956
- First service: 1959, the year the F-4 Phantom II first flew
- Armament: First MiG series fighter with air-to-air missiles; 1 23mm cannon with 200 rounds
- Soviet pilots call it "Balalaika": it resembles the Russian stringed instrument
- "Lancer" is the name given to the upgraded MiG-21 in Romania
- In 1966, Mossad's Operation Diamond lured a MiG-21 defector to Israel

ILYUSHIN IL-18

LOVELY AND LETHAL

One of the first successful turboprop airliners, the Ilyushin Il-18 first flew six months before its US contemporary, the Lockheed L-188 Electra. To confuse matters, a one-of-a-kind aircraft a decade earlier was also named the Il-18. In Soviet service, the Il-18 "Coot" passenger version became a workhorse of the national airline, Aeroflot, while the maritime naval version was the Il-38 "May." Western observers pooh-poohed the Il-18 for being constructed on assembly lines with quality-control issues, yet many are still in service almost sixty years after this plane's maiden flight.

**Engines: 4 Ivchenko AI-20M
turboprop engines**
Horsepower: 4,200 each
Cruising speed: 388 mph
Wingspan: 37 ft. 5 in.

- First flight: July 4, 1957
- Number built: About 800
- Known to the NATO allies as the "Coot"
- So durable many have racked up 45,000 flight hours
- Built in civil and military versions

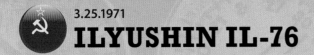

3.25.1971

ILYUSHIN IL-76

"IT'S A BIG TRUCK IN THE SKY"
—Andrey Ignatov, Russian pilot

The Ilyushin Il-76, called the "Candid" in the West, is an eminently utilitarian transport, tanker, and airborne warning and control system (AWACS) that has long been a familiar sight in the Soviet Union, present-day Russia, and allied nations. It's straightforward and functional, and it hauls a lot. On most examples, the cockpit has not been upgraded since the steam-gauge era, so pilots would welcome digital instruments on the flight deck. This is a well-regarded aircraft lacking in flair or bluster.

Engines: 4 Aviadvigatel PS-90-76 turbofan engines
Thrust: 32,000 lb.
Maximum speed: 560 mph
Wingspan: 165 ft. 8 in.

- First flight: March 25, 1971
- Number built: About 960
- Armament: Some have 2 23mm cannons in tail
- Crews use the Russian term for "fat friend" as a nickname
- Comparable to: Lockheed C-141 Starlifter (USA)

1976

YAKOVLEV YAK-52

GENTLE TO THE TOUCH, BUT FIERCE IN COMPETITION

It was a useful military trainer in the Soviet air arm, but the Yakovlev Yak-52—still in production today in Romania—is best known as the world's premier competitive aerobatic performer. Many have been brought into the United States to provide thrills and chills to air show crowds. As a challenge to a pilot, the Yak-52 doesn't amount to much because it is easy to fly, friendly in even the most dramatic maneuvers, and forgiving of most forms of clumsiness. Some pilots say the cockpit and general layout are the most sensible of any plane in any category. It's a little more difficult on the ground because of an odd air-pressure system that operates the brakes, but for most, that doesn't matter. It's fun.

Engine: 1 VMKB (Vedeneyev) M-14P 9-cylinder radial engine
Horsepower: 360
Maximum speed: 223 mph
Weight: 2,200 lb. empty
Wingspan: 30 ft. 6 in.

- First flight: 1976
- Number built: About 1,800
- A descendant of the Korean War–era Yak-18 trainer
- Considered very light and agile

10.6.1977

MIKOYAN MIG-29

TWIN ENGINES, A TWIN TAIL, AND TWICE THE SPEED OF SOUND

The MiG-29, called the "Fulcrum" in the West, was Moscow's answer to new fighters fielded by the United States in the 1970s. Sleek, fast, and formidable, the MiG-29 became a mainstay, filling out regiments in Russia and in thirty-plus nations from Nigeria to North Korea. While early versions are no longer cutting-edge, the latest MiG-29 models, especially the modernized MiG-29SMT, are considered serious existent threats in today's air-to-air arena. All versions have a roomier, more ergonomic cockpit than earlier MiG fighters. The MiG-29 is a joy to handle and a fearsome opponent.

Engines: 2 Klimov RD-33 turbofan engines with afterburners
Thrust: 18,300 lb. each
Maximum speed: 1,490 mph (Mach 2.25)
Wingspan: 37 ft. 3 in.

- First flight: October 6, 1977
- First service: Entered Soviet service in July 1983
- Armament: Seven hard points for external weapons
- Some can receive air refueling—unusual for Soviet aircraft
- Considered the Russian equivalent of the McDonnell Douglas F-15 Eagle

12.21.1988

ANTONOV AN-225 MRIYA

THIS IS WHERE YOU REALLY NEED SUPERLATIVES

The An-225 *Mriya* (Dream) is the longest and heaviest airplane ever built. The Soviet Union's Antonov design bureau, located in Ukraine, built the An-225 to carry the Buran spacecraft, which never made a manned spaceflight. After the collapse of the Soviet Union, the sole An-225 was placed in storage from 1994 to 2002, and subsequently returned to flight as a showcase for Ukraine's aircraft industry, hauling a variety of supersized cargoes. The An-225 established an absolute world record for an airlifted single item payload of 418,834 pounds. It routinely transports objects once thought impossible to move by air, such as railroad locomotives. The US and Canadian governments have chartered the An-225 to support military operations in the Middle East. With a crew of six (two pilots, two engineers, a navigator, and a radio officer) the An-225 offers a busy work environment and many challenges for those aboard.

Engines: 6 Ivchenko-Progress D-18T turbofan engines
Thrust: 51,600 lb. each
Maximum speed: 528 mph
Maximum takeoff weight: 1,410,958 lb.
Wingspan: 290 ft.

- First flight: December 21, 1988
- Number built: 1
- Began commercial freight operations January 3, 2002
- Still currently flying

61

DISCOVERY AVIATION MODEL 201

A PROMISING UTILITY AIRCRAFT TO USE IN TIGHT SPACES

The Model 201 is a business and general-aviation aircraft designed by Avia Limited of Moscow, and at first known as the Avia Accord 201. Discovery Aviation of Melbourne, Florida, brought the aircraft to the United States and now makes and markets it, emphasizing its ability to operate on unpaved runways. The Model 201 has a roomy, comfortable flight deck with superb visibility. The location of the engines well above the pilot offers great visibility below and all around the aircraft. This plane may perform utilitarian work, but piloting it is a treat.

Engines: 2 Continental IO-360ES7 piston engines
Horsepower: 210
Maximum speed: 165 mph
Wingspan: 45 ft. 1 inch

- First flight: July 17, 1997
- Capacity: 1 pilot, 7 passengers
- Displayed at the National Business Aircraft Association trade show, 2014
- Being offered for both civilian and military duties

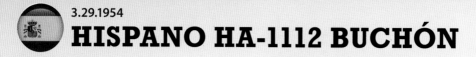

3.29.1954

HISPANO HA-1112 BUCHÓN

FAMILIAR—BUT NOT QUITE WHAT IT APPEARS

A license-built version of the Messerschmitt Bf 109 fighter of World War II that dates to 1942 in early prototype form, the HA-1112 *Buchón* (Pouter, a male dove) is best known for portraying its Teutonic cousin in films like *Battle of Britain* (1970) and *The Tuskegee Airmen* (1995). But to Spain's air arm it was a real combat plane—and one of the last propeller-driven fighters in production in the world. The *Buchón* performed only limited duty for the Spanish military, which was early to convert to jets, but it remains a favorite at air shows in the United States and Europe.

Engines: Hispano-Suiza engines on some; Rolls-Royce Merlins on others
Horsepower: 1,300 to 1,600
Maximum speed: 373 mph
Wingspan: 32 ft. 7 in.

- First flight: March 29, 1954
- Cowling shape and exhaust pipes distinguish it from Germany's Bf 109
- Preceded by the HA-1109-J1L model in 1945
- 1 each in museums in Canada, Spain, and the United States

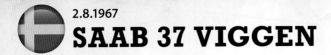

2.8.1967

SAAB 37 VIGGEN

A FIGHTER THAT LOOKED
LIKE A SPACESHIP

Not built in large numbers and never exported, the Saab J37 *Viggen* (Thunderclap) was a great fighter with outstanding performance but limited range. A double delta-wing surface made the *Viggen* so futuristic Clint Eastwood requested to use one in a film with science-fiction trappings (*Firefox*, 1982). The Swedish government said no and continued to use fighter, reconnaissance, surveillance, and trainer *Viggens* to defend its neutrality. Pilots had the special thrill of knowing they were flying a unique warplane that held worldwide respect.

Engine: 1 Volvo RM8B turbofan engine with afterburner
Thrust: 28,110 lb.
Maximum speed: 1,386 mph (Mach 2.1)
Wingspan: 34 ft. 9 in.

- First flight: February 8, 1967
- Number built: 329
- Armament: Included a 30mm cannon
- Retired from duty: November 25, 2005

SAAB 39 GRIPEN

FULL OF PEP AND PREPARED FOR THE FIGHT

Once insular in its high-tech aviation pursuits, Sweden broke into the international arena with the nimble, peppy Saab 39 *Gripen* (Griffin), considered a world-class fighter today and exported to four nations so far. Constantly being upgraded and enhanced, the *Gripen* is thought capable of taking on any fighter now in service. Pilots are pleasantly surprised after they adjust to its canard control surfaces and fly-by-wire controls, which use digital technology to maintain stability and improve maneuverability.

**Engine: 1 Volvo RM12 turbofan
    engine with afterburner**
Thrust: 18,100 lb.
Maximum speed: 1,370 mph (Mach 2.0)
Wingspan: 27 ft. 7 in.

- First flight: December 9, 1988
- Number built: About 250 as of 2014
- Cost: $69.9 million in 2006
- Armament: Includes a 27mm cannon

✚ PILATUS PC-6 PORTER

GETS YOU IN AND OUT OF TIGHT PLACES

The Pilatus PC-6 Porter is a Swiss-designed short-takeoff-and-landing (STOL) utility aircraft built in piston and turboprop versions by Pilatus in Switzerland and Fairchild in the United States, and employed widely by civilian and military users. Whether it's mountaineering by civilians or fighting by special-operations forces, the Porter operates from all types of unprepared, rough, and short airstrips, in remote areas, at high altitudes, and in all climates. The story of a military AU-23 Peacemaker (a US Air Force variant of the PC-6) landing in the courtyard of the Pentagon Building is apocryphal, but AU-23s did operate in small jungle clearings from Laos to Nicaragua. Pilatus says that Swiss workmanship results in the highest reliability and lowest maintenance possible. Although the Porter appears bulky, pilots say it handles light as a feather when getting in and out of cramped spaces. It hauls hefty cargo for its size and has the get-go that comes with plenty of power. It's also very maneuverable and can turn on a dime.

Engine: 1 Pratt & Whitney Canada PT6A-27 turboprop engine
Horsepower: 550
Maximum speed: 151 mph
Wingspan: 51 ft. 10 in.

- First flight: May 4, 1959
- Number built: 442 by Pilatus, 92 by Fairchild
- Cost: Selling for $1 million and up in 2014
- About 250 in service today
- US builder Fairchild no longer exists, but Swiss planemaker Pilatus services them worldwide
- Can use skis for landings on glaciers and snowfields

5.31.1991
PILATUS PC-12

"BUILT LIKE, AND WITH AS MANY USES, AS A SWISS ARMY KNIFE"
—Nate Wilburn, PC-12 mechanic

This hefty workhorse is in a category all its own—a robust transport capable of carrying a respectable load of passengers and cargo and able to operate anywhere, yet powered by just a single engine. Everything about the Pilatus PC-12 is unusual, including its launch customer, a group of Australian physicians. "If you've been tasked with doing more with less, the solution is simple," says planemaker Pilatus, and it is: built in several versions, some with ultra-long range, the PC-12 is uniquely versatile in both military and civilian duties. Moreover, pilots say it's a treat to fly.

Engine: 1 Pratt & Whitney Canada PT6A-67B or -67P turboprop engine
Horsepower: 1,200 shaft
Cruising speed: 313 mph
Wingspan: 53 feet ft. 3 in.

- First flight: May 31, 1991
- Cost: About $4.6 million new in 2014; used examples sell for $2.6 to $4 million
- "Essential," say the flying doctors who serve the Australian outback with 28 PC-12s
- Airline pilots express surprise when PC-12s fly at "big boy" altitudes above 20,000 ft.
- US Air Force special-operations version is the U-28A

✚ PILATUS PC-21

AN AERIAL SCHOOLHOUSE WITH STANDOUT STYLE

The Pilatus PC-21 is a military trainer and a seriously cool aircraft that is an outright pleasure to fly. Everything designers had learned over the past decades about cockpit design, instrument panel displays, and handling qualities was built from the start into this inexpensive aircraft that is clearly one of the best turboprop trainers in the world. Planemaker Pilatus is justified in claiming that the PC-21 excels in "aerodynamic performance, cockpit equipment, flexibility and ease of maintenance." Ordered by, or serving with, the air forces of Switzerland, Singapore, the United Arab Emirates, and Saudi Arabia, the PC-21 is certain to become better known and more visible on the aviation scene in years ahead.

Engine: 1 Pratt & Whitney Canada PT6A-68B turboprop engine
Horsepower: 1,600 shaft
Cruising speed: 426 mph
Wingspan: 29 ft. 11 in.

- First flight: July 1, 2002
- Cost: About $17 million in 2009
- Capacity: Pilot and instructor in tandem in zero-zero ejection seats
- Can be equipped to carry weapons
- Won an industrial design award from the Ralston Institute
- First customer: Singapore, for 19 aircraft

BRISTOL F.2B

A TWO-SEATER THAT BECAME A GREAT DOGFIGHTER

The Bristol F.2B was a British two-seat biplane fighter that initially suffered from teething troubles but matured, and it became so effective in air-to-air combat that it could often defeat single-seat fighters. Designed by an engineering team headed by Frank Barnwell, the F.2B sometimes carried a flexible machine gun in the rear position in addition to its forward-firing gun, making it a threat from all angles. It was flown in British and American versions, and with various engine types. British pilots in combat quickly learned that switching to single-seat tactics and dispensing with the cumbersome gun in the rear made the F.2B agile and effective against German fighters like the Albatros D.III.

Engine: Rolls-Royce Falcon III V-12 piston engine
Horsepower: 275
Maximum speed: 123 mph
Wingspan: 39 ft. 3 in.

- First flight: September 9, 1916
- First service: Arrived on the Western Front in April 1917
- Number built: 5,239 of all versions
- Called the "Brisfit" by pilots
- 2 real examples and numerous replicas flying today

11.22.1916
ROYAL AIRCRAFT FACTORY S.E.5

A GREAT BRITISH FIGHTER OF THE GREAT WAR

The single-seat S.E.5 ("Scout Experimental 5") biplane overcame early wing-design problems to become one of the best British fighters of the Great War. It had superb overall performance but was not as maneuverable as other fighters on both sides. It excelled in contrast to other fighters because it was strong, stable, comfortable, and easy and safe to fly, even for a novice pilot. Famous pilots of this model included Billy Bishop and Albert Ball, but many little-known and inexperienced pilots were able to transition smoothly into the S.E.5 cockpit. Pilots at all skill levels praised the S.E.5 for its roominess, rapid responses to control movements, and overall ease of handling.

Engine: 1 Hispano-Suiza 8A V-8 engine
Horsepower: 200
Maximum speed: 123 mph
Wingspan: 26 ft. 7 in.

- First flight: November 22, 1916
- Number built: 5,206 S.E.5s and S.E.5as
- Armament: Typically armed with 2 machine guns
- The S.E.5a version was renowned for its ruggedness and its dependable engine
- Many replicas are flying today

HAWKER HART

A CLASSIC OF A MEMORABLE ERA

The Hawker Hart was a two-seat British bomber and trainer designed by Sydney Camm, who was later responsible for the Hawker Hurricane fighter. In the early part of its career, the Hart was a match for contemporary fighters in speed and maneuverability. Relatively large for a two-seat, tandem military biplane, the Hart was known for its clean lines, solid construction, and reliability. It was one of the great planes of the Golden Age between wars, almost universally liked and praised by pilots. The start of World War II signaled new advances in aviation, however, and the Hart, obsolete by then, had only limited participation in the war.

Engine: 1 Rolls-Royce Kestrel 1B liquid-cooled piston engine
Horsepower: 510
Maximum speed: 185 mph
Wingspan: 37 ft. 3 in.

- First flight: June 1928
- First service: 1930
- Crew: 2, pilot and observer
- Built in numerous versions, some given the name Audax
- Swedish-built versions used radial engines

DE HAVILLAND DRAGON RAPIDE

A PRETTY SMART AIRLINER DESIGN FOR ITS ERA

The Dragon Rapide was a short-haul, biplane passenger plane eventually impressed into military service as the Dominie. As its name suggests, this was meant to be a fast airliner, and, by the standards of the mid-1930s, it was. Despite relatively primitive plywood construction, the Dragon Rapide was considered economical and durable. The pilot sat on the centerline up front, with good visibility and a well laid-out instrument array. Pilots and enthusiasts alike are extremely fond of this aircraft, and flock to see the handful performing at air shows today.

Engines: 2 de Havilland Gipsy Six liquid-cooled piston engines
Horsepower: 200 each
Maximum speed: 157 mph
Wingspan: 48 ft.

- First flight: April 17, 1934
- Number built: 731
- Capacity: 1 pilot, 8 passengers
- Famously carried Francisco Franco to Spain at the start of the Spanish Civil War

4.17.1934

FAIREY SWORDFISH

ROBUST BUT NOT ROOMY, A TORPEDO-BOMBING ACE

The Fairey Swordfish, the "Stringbag," was a biplane torpedo bomber used by Britain's Royal Navy during World War II. It also functioned as a dive-bomber and a reconnaissance craft. The Swordfish achieved a few spectacular successes, including sinking one and damaging two battleships of the Italian battle fleet in the Battle of Taranto and the famous crippling of the German battleship *Bismarck*. Although quite large for an aircraft in its class, the Swordfish could be cramped on the inside, but while pilots and crewmembers would have liked more elbowroom, they loved the plane's stable handling characteristics.

Engine: 1 Bristol Pegasus IIIM.3 radial piston engine
Horsepower: 690
Maximum speed: 139 mph
Wingspan: 45 ft. 6 in.

- First flight: April 17, 1934
- Number built: 2,391 (692 by Fairey, 1,699 by Blackburn)
- Accounted for 14 German U-boats destroyed
- "Stringbag" nickname: from a women's shopping bag that held contents of any shape
- 10 in existence today, but just 2 airworthy

GLOSTER GLADIATOR

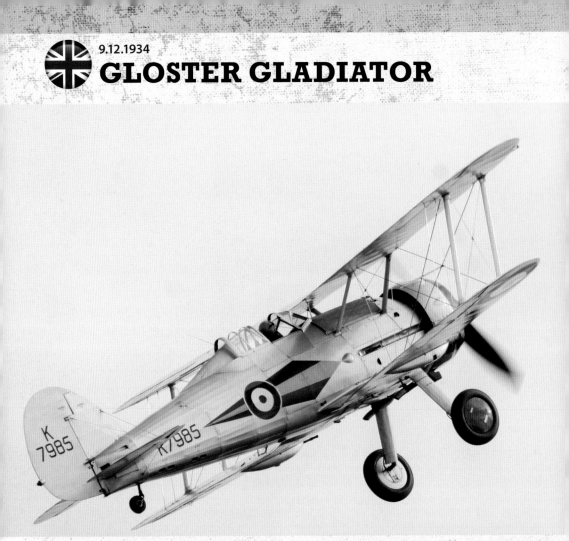

BIPLANE FIGHTER IN A MONOPLANE WAR

Designed by Henry Folland, the Gloster Gladiator was the last Royal Air Force biplane fighter. According to lore, three Gladiators named *Faith*, *Hope*, and *Charity* were pivotal in the 1940 defense of Malta. Others served the Fleet Air Arm and fought in Finland. Outgunned by monoplanes such as the Messerschmitt Bf 109, the Gladiator held its own because its pilots were superbly trained, often prevailing by leveraging agility and innovative tactics.

Engine: 1 Bristol Mercury IX radial piston engine
Horsepower: 830
Cruising speed: 210 mph
Wingspan: 32 ft. 3 in.

- First flight: September 12, 1934
- Number built: 747
- Top Gladiator ace: F. H. Maynard, 15 victories
- Just 2 in flying condition in 2014

HAWKER HURRICANE

NOT FANCY, BUT AN ALL-OUT FIGHTING MACHINE

They were called "the Few," the Royal Air Force fighter pilots who turned the tide during the 1940 Battle of Britain, but many—the largest number of them—piloted the Hawker Hurricane. If the Spitfire was the point of the spear in history's first prolonged military campaign fought entirely in the air, the more numerous Hurricane was the workhorse, a rugged and sturdy combat aircraft that never received as much recognition as its friendly rival. Sydney Camm, chief designer at Hawker Aircraft, owes no apology for a fighter that was more practical than pretty. Pilots have no quarrel with the roomy, sensible cockpit and the snappy performance of the "Hurry."

Engine: 1 Rolls-Royce Merlin XX liquid-cooled V-12 piston engine
Horsepower: 1,185
Maximum speed: 331 mph
Wingspan: 40 ft.

- First flight: November 6, 1935
- Number built: 14,533
- Served in more theaters in World War II than any other British fighter
- The Soviet Union operated 2,776 export Hurricanes
- Portugal still had operational Hurricanes in 1954
- Slower than the Spitfire and Bf 109 but able to out-turn both in a dogfight
- Several real Hurricanes and several replicas flying today

3.6.1936

SUPERMARINE SPITFIRE

"WITHOUT THEM, MOST OF US WOULDN'T BE HERE"

The quote comes from a survivor of the London Blitz who remembers the Spitfire's shining moment in the Battle of Britain. Some credit the brilliant, ballerina-like fighter from the drawing board of R. J. Mitchell with doing nothing less than saving the world. The Royal Air Force had more Hurricanes than Spitfires, but Spitfire units had a lower attrition rate and a higher victory-to-loss ratio than those flying Hurricanes. Although most versions would have benefitted from greater fuel capacity and longer range, all were fast, nimble, well-armed, and lethal. The "Spit" still performs superbly today and is always a sought-after attraction at air shows. The cockpit could be roomier and visibility at the critical six-o'clock position (the rear) could be better, but with its stable handling characteristics and great maneuverability, the Spitfire remains today a kind of hot rod of the skies—a great performer when in skilled hands.

Engine: 1 Rolls-Royce Merlin 45 Mk VB

Horsepower: 1,470

Maximum speed: 370 mph

Wingspan: 36 ft. 10 in.

- First flight: March 6, 1936
- Design work began in 1931
- Its distinctive elliptical wing, with its super-thin cross-section, increased its top speed
- The carrier-based version was dubbed the "Seafire"
- A famous German air ace asked Adolf Hitler for a squadron of Spitfires
- The only British World War II fighter with outward-folding landing gear
- About 50 are airworthy today

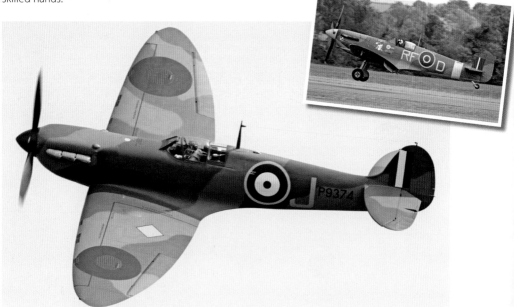

AVRO LANCASTER

THE GREATEST BRITISH BOMBER

The Lancaster was the great British bomber of World War II, overshadowing the Halifax, Stirling, and other greats, and rivaling the US B-17 Flying Fortress for a place not only in history but in lore. With a crew of seven, an unusually long bomb bay, and the economy and power of four Merlin engines, the Lancaster proved itself in the nocturnal air campaign against the Third Reich. The pilot sat side by side with the flight engineer but a few inches higher, and found the Lancaster receptive to handling cues and control inputs.

Engines: 4 Rolls-Royce Merlin XX liquid-cooled V-12 engines
Horsepower: 1,280 each
Cruising speed: 200 mph
Wingspan: 102 ft.

- First flight: January 9, 1941
- Number built: 7,377
- Flew the famous "Dambuster" raid on Germany's Ruhr Valley dams
- Operated by a single pilot
- 2 are airworthy today

ENGLISH ELECTRIC CANBERRA

REACH FOR THE HEIGHTS IN ONE OF THE GREATS

A pioneering jet bomber with extraordinary high-altitude capability, the Canberra gave Britain nuclear and conventional bombing prowess at the very dawn of the jet age. Built in several configurations for various missions, used by a dozen nations, and manufactured not just in Britain but also in the United States, the Canberra was seen as the showpiece of a new era in the early 1950s when most military aircraft were still pulled by propellers. It remains an all-time favorite of pilots and air-show audiences, with several airworthy Canberras still performing for crowds around the world.

Engines: 2 Rolls-Royce Avon RA.7 Mk 109 turbojet engines
Thrust: 7,400 lb. each
Maximum speed: 580 mph (Mach 0.88)
Wingspan: 64 ft.

- First flight: May 13, 1949
- Number built: 949
- Set an altitude record: 70,310 feet in 1957
- First combat was in the 1956 Suez crisis

DE HAVILLAND COMET

AN ADVENTUROUS LEAP FORWARD AND A SUPREME TRAGEDY

The clean, beautiful de Havilland Comet took to the air a month before Canada's Avro C-102 Jetliner and became the world's first production jet passenger aircraft. The Comet's air-conditioned, fully pressurized cabin provided passengers with a quiet, smooth ride previously unheard of in commercial aviation. Sadly, first-generation Comets suffered major losses in well-publicized accidents caused by structural issues, and the Comet design was not rendered fully reliable until the Comet 4 model introduced in 1958. Late-generation Comets achieved some success on commercial air routes and inspired the Hawker Siddeley Nimrod maritime reconnaissance aircraft. Lessons from the rigorous investigations of early Comet mishaps are credited with enabling future jets such as the Boeing 707 and Douglas DC-8 to operate safely.

Engines: 4 de Havilland Halford H.2 Ghost 50 turbojet engines (Comet 1)
Thrust: 5,000 lb. each
Maximum speed: 473 mph
Wingspan: 115 ft. (all models)

- First flight: July 27, 1949
- Capacity: 36 to 44 passengers (Comet 1); up to 81 passengers (Comet 4)
- Won several industrial design awards
- Faster than some fighters then in service

FAIREY GANNET

YOU DON'T HAVE TO BE PRETTY TO BE LOVED

The Gannet was a carrier-based anti-submarine and electronic warfare aircraft and trainer operated by Britain's Royal Navy from 1953 to 1978. Seven versions of the Gannet did their work from British ship decks, providing an effective counter to the Soviet Union's growing submarine fleet. A most unusual engine served the crew of three: the Double Mamba coupled turboprop featured two independent power sections driving separate propellers. After both were used for takeoff phase, one could be shut down to extend range and patrol time. Portly and lacking in grace, if not downright ugly, the Gannet was held in great affection by crews. The pilot sat very far forward and had superb visibility in a luxuriously expansive cockpit.

Engine: 1 Armstrong Siddeley Double Mamba ASMD 4 turboprop engine (typical)
Horsepower: 2,950
Maximum speed: 310 mph
Wingspan: 54 ft. 4 in.

- First flight: September 19, 1949
- First service: First carrier landing: June 19, 1950
- Number built: 414
- Just 1 is flying today (it's in the United States)

PERCIVAL PROVOST

A FLYING SCHOOLHOUSE THAT MADE SENSE

Whether they ultimately went into Spitfires or Javelins, a generation of British Commonwealth military pilots made their first solo flights in the Percival Provost, and the experience was memorable for all. The Provost was simple, practical, and the ideal vehicle to introduce stick, throttle, and the basics of flight. The all-metal, single-engine, tailwheel-equipped Provost was "a natural first step," said former RAF pilot Mike Dale, who today owns the only airworthy Provost in North America. It inspired a tricycle-gear, turbojet-powered Jet Provost, which retained side-by-side seating for instructor and student.

Engine: 1 Alvis Leonides Mk 25 radial piston engine
Horsepower: 550
Maximum speed: 200 mph
Wingspan: 35 ft. 2 in.

- First flight: February 24, 1950
- Number built: 461 between 1950 and 1958
- Cost: About $60,000 in 1954; roughly $2 million in restored condition today
- Hunting Group acquired planemaker Percival in 1954

AVRO VULCAN

Engines: 4 Bristol Olympus 101, 102, or 104 turbojet engines

Thrust: 11,000 lb. each

Cruising speed: 567 mph (Mach 0.86)

Wingspan: 99 ft. 5 in.

- First flight: August 30, 1952
- Number built: 136 from 1952 to 1963
- Cost: About $4.8 million in 1956
- 1 is in airworthy condition today

THE "DELTA QUEEN" OF BRITAIN'S COLD WAR BOMBER FORCE

One of the largest aircraft ever in service with a delta, or triangular, wing, the Avro Vulcan was the most elegant of Britain's "V-bombers" designed to haul nuclear bombs to the Soviet Union (the others being the Vickers Valiant and Handley Page Victor). It has now been retired so long (since 1984) that it's hard to believe the Vulcan first flew four months after the Boeing B-52 Stratofortress. While in service, Vulcan B.2 models were constantly upgraded. Although employed for so-called "Black Buck" missions in the 1982 Falklands War—at the time, history's longest-distance bombing raids—the Vulcan never fully made the transition to conventional bombing duty.

BLACKBURN BUCCANEER

DESIGNED FOR ATOMIC WAR, PROVEN IN CONVENTIONAL COMBAT

The Blackburn Buccaneer began in the 1950s as a carrier-based attack plane to sneak beneath Soviet radar coverage carrying a nuclear bomb. It served with the Royal Navy, and later the Royal Air Force, and was re-christened the Hawker Siddeley Buccaneer when Blackburn became a part of the Hawker Siddeley group. British Buccaneers carried conventional bombs in the 1991 Persian Gulf War. South African "Bucs" fought in Angola and Namibia. Early Buccaneers needed more power but the Spey engine solved that problem. Initially intended for 5,000 flight hours, some Buccaneers flew 20,000 with no structural problems. This was a robust and capable warplane, widely admired by crews. In Britain, it was replaced by the Panavia Tornado.

Engines: 2 Rolls-Royce Spey Mk 10 turbofan engines (S.2 version)
Thrust: 11,000 lb. each
Maximum speed: 667 mph
Wingspan: 44 ft.

- First flight: April 30, 1958
- Crew: 2 (pilot, radar observer)
- Only overseas user: South Africa, 1965 to 1991
- Briefly considered by the US Navy
- None airworthy today

1.17.1963

SHORT SC.7 SKYVAN

A BIG BOX WITH A MISSION

The Short Skyvan is an all-metal, high-wing transport with a very thin (high-aspect-ratio) wing. It looks like a box. And it has plenty of room inside for passengers and freight, military or civilian—one popular military use is carrying and dropping paratroops. Although eclipsed by the Northern Irish planemaker's newer Sherpa, the Skyvan shows no sign of heading for retirement. Most of those built since initial design studies began in 1958 are still flying today. Operators find the Skyvan to be cost efficient, and pilots like its old-school cockpit design and practical performance.

Engines: 2 Garrett AiResearch TPE-331-201 turboprop engines
Horsepower: 715
Maximum speed: 202 mph
Wingspan: 64 ft. 11 in.

- First flight: January 17, 1963
- Number built: 153
- Capacity: Passenger version carries 19
- Nicknamed "the shed" by pilots
- Argentina used 2 in 1982 Falklands War

12.28.1967

HAWKER SIDDELEY HARRIER

YES, IT REALLY CAN FLY BACKWARDS

The first-generation, Cold War–era Harrier "Jump Jet" ushered in a revolution: tactical aviation was no longer shackled to a fixed airfield with runways that would be vulnerable to Soviet attack. Harriers were built in single- and two-seat, land-based and shipboard (Sea Harrier) versions. Anyone who has watched a Harrier at an air show knows how rapidly it can go up, down, forward, sideways—and, yes, backwards. Now retired, the first-generation Harrier was a great air-to-ground weapon. However, pilots struggled with its unorthodox controls and often found this aircraft too hot to handle.

Engine: 1 Rolls-Royce Pegasus Mk 103 vectored-thrust turbofan engine
Thrust: 21,500 lb.
Maximum speed: 730 mph (Mach 0.96)
Weight: Some weigh up to 31,000 lb.
Wingspan: 25 ft. 3 in.

- First flight: December 28, 1967
- Number built: 278
- Exported to Spain as the AV-8S Matador
- Followed 9 developmental aircraft called Kestrels

3.21.1971
WESTLAND LYNX

IT DOESN'T GET MUCH NOTICE—BUT IT SHOULD

The Lynx rarely makes headlines, not even when fighting in the Falklands in 1982, but it's a reliable servant of men and women in uniform. The Lynx has evolved into a ubiquitous, all-purpose military and naval helicopter—although one for which its maker was unable to find civilian customers—and is flying today in more than a dozen nations. All versions have advanced digital flight controls. Some versions are armed. Built in single- and two-pilot configurations, the Lynx is a jack-of-all-trades, operating from ship decks and alongside infantry companies, and is highly regarded by both maintainers and pilots. Improved versions are expected to be on duty for decades to come.

Engines: 2 Rolls-Royce Gem 2 turboshaft engines (typical)
Horsepower: 1,120 shaft each
Cruising speed: 201 mph (planned)
Rotor diameter: 42 ft.

- First flight: March 21, 1971
- Number built: About 415
- Capacity: Typically 2 crew plus 12 passengers
- World's first fully aerobatic helicopter

8.21.1974

BAE SYSTEMS HAWK

A TRUSTED TRAINER WITH PLENTY OF POTENTIAL

The fruit of an engineering effort headed by aircraft designer Ralph Hooper, the BAE Systems Hawk is a widely respected, advanced jet trainer now producing pilots in a dozen countries. A single-seat, armed version has attracted less interest, but all versions can carry an optional centerline cannon and other ordnance. Although the world market for trainers is cluttered, BAE has high hopes that an improved variant of the Hawk can become a replacement for the T-38C Talon. This aircraft was built around the philosophy that a trainer should make flying easy, and it does. Pilots praise the Hawk for its agility, especially its ease of handing in roll and turn situations.

Engine: 1 Rolls-Royce Turbomeca Adour Mk 951 turbofan engine
Thrust: 6,500 lb.
Maximum speed: 638 mph (Mach 0.84)
Wingspan: 32 ft. 78 in.

- First flight: August 21, 1974
- Number built: More than 1,000
- Used by Red Arrows flight demonstration team
- US Navy version: T-45C Goshawk
- Replaced Folland Gnat and Hawker Hunter in 1975

SHORT C-23 SHERPA

A POPULAR AIRLIFTER PREMATURELY PUT TO PASTURE

The Short C-23 Sherpa is a small, box-shaped airlifter built by Short Brothers. Sherpas are military versions of the Short 330 (C-23A, C-23B) and the Short 360 (C-23B+, C-23C). The US Army used Sherpas in Iraq from 2003 onward for intra-theater transport of cargoes and people. The aircraft has soldiered brilliantly and is a delight to fly, but the US Army National Guard finished retiring its planes in 2014, even though a Pentagon plan to replace the Sherpa with the Alenia C-27J Spartan was abandoned as a cost-saving measure a year earlier. Ex-army Sherpas will be operated by other government agencies.

Engines: 2 Pratt & Whitney Canada PT6A-45R turboprop engines
Horsepower: 1,198 each
Maximum speed: 218 mph
Wingspan: 74 ft. 9 in.

- First flight: December 23, 1982
- 40 used by the US Army
- Unpressurized, so rarely flown above 10,000 feet
- Fondly dubbed the "box kite" by troops

WRIGHT FLYER

THE VERY FIRST

The Wright Flyer of 1903 was—as described at the National Air and Space Museum in Washington, DC, where it is displayed—"the first powered, heavier-than-air machine to achieve controlled, sustained flight with a pilot aboard." It was the first plane to master the three essential elements of flight: lift, propulsion, and in-flight control. Some detractors claim that other pioneers achieved powered, heavier-than-air flight before the Wrights—among them inventor Gustave Whitehead—but these claims are not widely accepted by scholars. Wilbur and Orville Wright—with Wilbur as the driving force but Orville as history's first pilot—pioneered the concept of flight controls in the three-axis universe (yaw, roll, and pitch) in which airplanes have operated ever since. Their work with gliders led to their construction of the Wright Flyer, which made its historic first flight amid North Carolina sand dunes with Orville prone at the controls.

Engine: Wright horizontal 4-cylinder engine
Horsepower: 12
Weight: 605 lb.
Wingspan: 40 ft. 4 in.

- First flight: December 17, 1903
- Developed from gliders tested by Wilbur and Orville Wright
- Made of "giant spruce" wood and muslin fabric
- Orville's first flight lasted 12 seconds
- Later in the day, on their fourth flight, Wilbur flew for 59 seconds
- The Wrights followed their success by sending a jubilant telegram to their father in Dayton
- Wilbur died in 1912 (age 45); Orville lived until 1948 (age 76)

CURTISS MODEL D

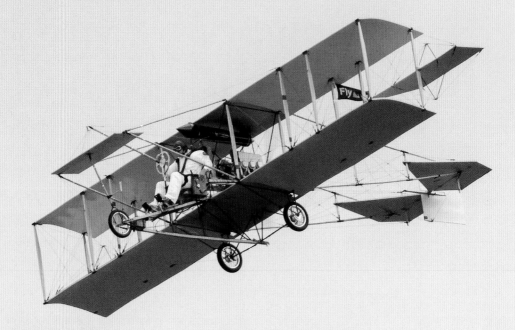

A PIONEER IN MANY WAYS

Glenn Curtiss, an aviation pioneer and a fierce competitor to the Wright Brothers, was the force behind this trailblazing aircraft design. At a time when it was an achievement for an airplane to do anything, the Curtiss Model D—or Curtiss Pusher—did almost everything. It pioneered civilian and military use of the airplane and even carried a politician, Congressman Orrin Dubbs Bleakley, on the first-ever flight by an elected official. Instrumental in naval aviation, the Curtiss Model D, piloted by Eugene Ely, became the first aircraft to operate from a ship, taking off from the USS *Birmingham* on January 18, 1911. It also introduced the tail hook, or arrestor hook, now famous on navy planes, when it landed on the USS *Pennsylvania* on October 11, 1911.

Engine: 1 Curtiss E-4 engine
Horsepower: 40
Maximum speed: 50 mph
Weight: 1,300 lb. fully loaded
Wingspan: 38 ft. 8 in.

- First flight: circa 1909
- A biplane with tricycle landing gear
- The first aircraft to be produced in numbers
- Had unique controls, including ailerons operated by the pilot's shoulder movements
- A foreplane for pitch control proved unnecessary and was dropped from late models

BALDWIN RED DEVIL

ONE OF AMERICA'S TRUE AVIATION PIONEERS

The term Baldwin Red Devil refers to a family of early pusher aircraft designed by Thomas Scott Baldwin. He is better known as a pioneer balloonist and as the first American to make a parachute jump from a balloon—not bad for someone born in 1854. The Red Devil aircraft were similar in appearance to pusher planes developed by Glenn Curtiss but used steel tubing instead of wood as the basic framework, which was then fabric-covered. Baldwin (the man) also designed dirigibles and served in the 1914–1918 war, but the Red Devil series is a spectacular achievement in an era when humankind was only beginning to stretch its wings.

Engine: 1 Hall-Scott V-8 piston engine
Horsepower: 60
Maximum speed: 40 mph
Wingspan: 42 ft.

- First flight: 1911
- Number built: Baldwin built 6 of these
- Baldwin painted struts and parts of his aircraft a crimson red
- Similar to the Curtiss Model D

5.10.1914
CURTISS JN-4D "JENNY"

BIG, CLUMSY, AND UNDERPOWERED, AND YET . . .

The J series designed by Benjamin Douglas Thomas comprised the first tractor-engine aircraft built by Glenn Curtiss, who had previously built pusher aircraft. The series evolved into one of the best known and most beloved of airplanes, the sensible Curtiss JN-4 "Jenny" biplane, which began life as a trainer and ended up doing a little of everything. This mostly-fabric-covered biplane proved adept at stunt flying and ushered in the barnstorming era of the 1920s, thrilling crowds at air shows. And, yes, the Jenny is the plane that was famously depicted upside-down in error on a US postage stamp.

Engine: 1 Curtiss OX-5/90 engine
Horsepower: 60
Maximum speed: 75 mph
Wingspan: 43 ft. 7 ⅜ in.

- First flight: May 10, 1914
- Cost: $8,160 when purchased by the US Army in 1917; $4,000 when later sold as surplus
- Used to teach thousands of Allied pilots to fly during World War I
- Early JN-3 version helped the US Army fight bandit Pancho Villa in 1916 and 1917
- 95 percent of American and Canadian pilots in the First World War trained in the Jenny
- Several replicas flying today

Library of Congress

1916
CURTISS MODEL L

IF IT HAS THREE WINGS IT MUST BE A TRIPLANE—SORT OF

Perhaps channeling its inner Cessna T-37B of the far future, this unorthodox trainer had a spacious, open cockpit that seated student and instructor side by side, prompting flyers to dub it the "Sociable Triplane." It was unusual in having its upper two wings of equal span and a shorter-span lower wing. Both the wing configuration and cockpit seating were a bit disorienting, and therefore unpopular, so the L, L-1, and L-2 models had just a brief existence.

- First flight: 1916
- Used components from a Curtiss JN-4 "Jenny"
- 3 versions, including a seaplane with floats
- 3 reached the navy; 1 went to the army

Engine: 1 Curtiss OX-2 radial piston engine
Horsepower: 60
Maximum speed: 60 mph
Wingspan: 25 ft.

1.19.1917
CURTISS-GOUPIL DUCK

IT DOESN'T LOOK LIKE A DUCK AND IT DOESN'T QUACK

It may look like an odd duck, pun intended, but the Curtiss-Goupil Duck was more conventional than it looked. Alexander Goupil built a glider version in 1883 and planned a version to be powered by a clunky steam engine. Although he never built it, Goupil called his design an "aeroplane," probably the first use of the term. In 1916, Glenn Curtiss had his Buffalo, New York, plant build the Duck to Goupil's specifications. Because it used conventional ailerons rather than the Wright Brothers' wing-warping technology, Curtiss saw the Duck as key to his marathon legal battles with the Wrights, although, in the end, it did not help his case. Curtiss conducted limited testing of the ungainly Duck at Newport News, Virginia, before parking it in a hangar. It was scrapped in 1920.

Engine: 1 Curtiss OXX-6 radial piston engine
Horsepower: 50
Maximum speed: 40 mph
Wingspan: Apparently not recorded

- First flight January 19, 1917
- Number built: 1
- Curtiss flew both sea- and landplane versions

1923
LOENING OL

A DUCK OUT OF WATER

The Loening OL amphibian looked a bit awkward taxiing on a paved runway—"a duck out of water," a coast guardsman called the first aircraft ever operated by his service (an OL-5 model in 1926). The OL-5 appeared more in its element riding the waves under the ministrations of its two-man, tandem-seated, open-cockpit crew, which is perhaps why it was also popular with army, navy, and civilian operators. It is worth remembering today that Long Island was once an aviation center of the United States, and it is here that Grover Loening built amphibians not far from the companies that became Grumman and Republic.

Engine: Pratt & Whitney R-1340-4 Wasp radial piston engine
Horsepower: 450
Maximum speed: 122 mph
Wingspan: 34 ft. 9 in.

- First flight: 1923
- Number built: 165
- Used a Duralumin hull attached to the fuselage
- 2 are in museums today

6.11.1926

FORD TRI-MOTOR

AN ICON FOR AN ERA

Other aircraft were similar in appearance, but no plane stood out like the "Tin Goose," the Ford Tri-Motor airliner designed by William Bushnell Stout and manufactured by Henry Ford. With its distinctive corrugated-metal sides and purring motor sound, the Tri-Motor was seen everywhere in America in the 1920s and 1930s, providing quality air transportation to many who had never been in a plane before. Today, the Tri-Motor is a curiosity enjoyed by audiences at air shows, but it was once a pioneer of the skies that proved commercial air travel could be both successful and comfortable.

Engines: Pratt & Whitney Wasp C radial engines
Horsepower: 420 each
Maximum speed: 150 mph
Wingspan: 77 ft. 10 in.

- First flight: June 11, 1926
- Cost: $11.8 million per plane in 1994 dollars; 1 sold for $736,000 in 2013
- Number built: 199
- 8 listed as airworthy in 2015

4.28.1927

SPIRIT OF ST. LOUIS

Engine: 1 Wright R-790 Whirlwind J-5C radial piston engine

Horsepower: 223

Maximum speed: 133 mph

Wingspan: 46 ft.

- First flight: April 28, 1927
- Number built: 1
- Cost: $10,580
- Famous flight won Lindbergh the $25,000 Orteig Prize
- Named for Lindbergh supporters in the St. Louis Raquette Club, of the pilot's hometown

LIKE A SARDINE FOR THE FIRST ATLANTIC SOLO

The Ryan NYP (for New York–Paris), better known to the world as the *Spirit of St. Louis*, was a product of the company founded by Claude T. Ryan and managed by Benjamin Mahoney. Charles Lindbergh chose the aircraft for his planned ocean-spanning record attempt after reaching the Ryan company via long-distance phone call—a bold undertaking in 1927. The aircraft derived many of its features from a proven Ryan mail plane. It was functional but not fun: Lindbergh was wedged into a cramped cockpit barely 36 inches wide, with no space to stretch his legs, and no forward vision. Crammed with fuel, loud, cold, and uncomfortable, the NYP took Lindbergh on humankind's first solo flight across the Atlantic Ocean on May 20–21, 1927, traveling from Roosevelt Field, Long Island, New York, to Le Bourget airfield, Paris, in thirty-three hours thirty minutes. The *Spirit of St. Louis* was retired in 1928 and today resides in the National Air and Space Museum, Smithsonian Institution, in Washington, DC.

1928
PIETENPOL AIR CAMPER

THIS PUTS THE FUN IN "FUN FLYING"

When Bernard H. Pietenpol designed the Pietenpol Air Camper during the Roaring Twenties, he wanted a homebuilt aircraft that would give pilots an aviation version of the era's rowdy joyousness. The parasol-wing, open-cockpit Air Camper is a straightforward, no-nonsense flying machine that's ideal for puddle jumping or even cross-country journeys. Plans for homebuilders are available today from the Pietenpol family in Cherry Grove, Minnesota, based on the original. If flying is a sport for you, this is an economical way to enjoy it.

Engine: Ford Model A (typical)
Horsepower: 65
Maximum speed: 90 mph
Wingspan: 28 ft. 2 in.

- First flight: 1928
- Cost: Selling for $11,000 used in 2014
- Won EAA trophy for best aircraft powered by a car engine
- Covered in the documentary film *Finding Flight* (2007)

3. 1929
GREAT LAKES SPORT TRAINER

AFFORDABLE AND ENJOYABLE

The Great Lakes family of Sport Trainer aircraft was in production intermittently from 1929 to 1933 and from 1972 to 1980, only to be resurrected by WACO Classic Aircraft in 2011. This peppy, maneuverable sportplane has appeared with several types of engines and periodic changes in wing design and other features, but always as an inexpensive, entry-level, open-cockpit biplane with tremendous appeal to recreational and competitive pilots alike. It is fun flying, pure and simple.

- First flight: March 1929
- Number built: About 250
- Cost: About $245,000 in 2013
- Some models constructed with Douglas fir

Engine: 1 Lycoming IO-360-B1F6 piston engine (typical)
Horsepower: 180
Maximum speed: 132 mph
Wingspan: 26 ft. 8 in.

DOUGLAS RD-2 DOLPHIN

Engines: 2 Pratt & Whitney R-1340-4 Wasp radial piston engines

Horsepower: 450 each

Maximum speed: 149 mph

Diameter 60 ft.

- First flight: July 1930 (Sinbad)
- Capacity: Typically 2 pilots and 6 passengers
- Army versions: C-21, C-26, C-29

THE "FLYING YACHT" IN COAST GUARD COLORS

Ask anybody. The Douglas Dolphin was the coolest plane ever to fly in the coast guard. The coasties bought the prototype Sinbad flying boat and thirteen of the subsequent Dolphin amphibians (of fifty-eight built), but the belle of the bunch was the sole RD-2 model, numbered 1122 and delivered in 1932 as the administrative aircraft of Secretary of the Treasury Henry Morgenthau. Teak panels, no less. The RD-2 Dolphin might have become the first Flying White House; it was offered for presidential travel, but Franklin D. Roosevelt never flew in it. Non-coast guard Dolphins served the army, navy, and marine corps and—as executive transports—the Vanderbilt family.

1932

FAIRCHILD MODEL 24

A JACK-OF-ALL-TRADES IN CHALLENGING TIMES

It came in different versions, military and civil, with different engines. It performed almost every job a working airplane could handle and stayed in production throughout the Great Depression to become an unsung contributor to Allied success in World War II. It defined the word "service" for the armed forces and epitomized style in the hands of civilians. Today, the Fairchild 24—otherwise known as the US Army C-61, Navy J2K, and Royal Air Force Argus—is in demand among private pilots as a sturdy, robust vehicle for family flying. Many consider this aircraft a true classic.

Engine: 1 Ranger L-440-5 6-cylinder inverted air-cooled engine (typical)

Horsepower: 200

Maximum speed: 124 mph

Wingspan: 44 ft. 6 in.

- First flight: 1932
- Number built: About 2,000
- Capacity: 3 to 5 passengers
- Interior by the famous industrial designer Raymond Loewy
- Stalked German U-boats with the US Civil Air Patrol

11.4.1932
BEECH MODEL 17 STAGGERWING

GIVES MEANING TO THE TERM "CLASSIC"

When you create the world's first widely used executive aircraft during the hard times of the Great Depression, you're going to be accused of making a plane for the elite. Developed by Walter Beech and by T. A. "Ted" Wells as a biplane with negative stagger (the lower wing being farther forward than the upper), the Staggerwing almost always appears on any list of the most beautiful aircraft in history. Its unique shape gave its pilot excellent all-around visibility.

Engine: 1 Pratt & Whitney R-985-AN-1 Wasp Junior (typical)
Horsepower: 450
Cruising speed: 202 mph
Wingspan: 32 ft.

- First flight: November 4, 1932
- Number built: 785
- Cost: $17,000 in 1933
- US Army version: the UC-43 Traveler
- Redesigned with lengthened fuselage in 1936
- The Netherlands' Prince Bernhard used one while in exile in England during World War II
- Many airworthy today

4.1.1933
ARUP S-2

IGNORE THAT APRIL FOOLS' DAY FIRST-FLIGHT DATE

When viewed from above, the Arup S-2 looked not so much like a flying saucer as a flying guitar pick. A "lifting body" pioneered by Arup Manufacturing Corporation, designed by Raoul Hoffman, and piloted by Glen Doolittle, the S-2 foreshadowed many future disc-like aircraft, none of which was ever built in significant numbers. Despite its unconventional appearance, it handled well, could fly at up to 35 degrees angle of attack without stalling, and could land in a parking lot. A later version was less successful than the original, but the Arup S-2 was basically a sound design that performed without a hitch.

Engine: 1 Continental A40 piston engine
Horsepower: 45
Maximum speed: 97 mph
Wingspan: 19 ft.

- First flight: April 1, 1933
- Pilot entered via a belly hatch.
- Celluloid panels on the fuselage aided pilot visibility
- Used conventional (tailwheel) landing gear

99

6.8.1934

RYAN PT-20A PRIMARY TRAINER

Engine: Kinner R-440 engine
Horsepower: 125
Maximum speed: 126 mph
Wingspan: 30 ft.

- First flight: June 8, 1934
- Number built: 1,224
- Cost: About $1,000 in 1952. About $80,000 today
- Very quiet for its size, with an engine that goes *putt-putt* rather than *varoom*
- Found at many civilian airports
- A "tail dragger," difficult to taxi with that schnoz sticking up in front
- Excellent for teaching or learning stick-and-rudder basics
- 150 flying today

TRAINING IN THE OPEN AIR

Inherent style. That's the hallmark of this family of planes built during World War II—about 150 of them airworthy today—by San Diego planemaking pioneer Claude T. Ryan, who earlier built the Ryan NYP, Charles Lindbergh's famous *Spirit of St. Louis*. PT stands for primary trainer, and for many, it's the first aircraft in a lifetime of flying. For others, now is the time for a modern-day return to aircraft like the Ryan PT-20A simply to sample the joys of basic aeronautics, stick-and-rudder technique, and open-cockpit flying. It's cold up there, but don't look for the wind to unfurl your checkered hero-pilot scarf because the oversized flat-panel, faceted windscreen prevents the slipstream from blasting you in the face. And, yes, the PT-20A looks like designer Raymond Loewy crafted it, but glamour doesn't always mean get-go. As thousands of air cadets learned, the PT-20A and other primary trainers in this family were notoriously underpowered. One veteran said that "you could watch the grass grow while making your takeoff run" in a PT-22.

CONSOLIDATED PBY CATALINA

MAYBE THE MOST FAMOUS FLYING BOAT

With distinctive bumps and bulges protruding from atop its sleek, seafaring hull, the PBY Catalina was far from beautiful—unless you happened to be stranded at sea and needed to be rescued. The Catalina is the best known and one of the most widely produced flying boats. Already obsolescent at the start of World War II, the Catalina excelled in anti-submarine patrol, communications support, and a variety of other missions. Most came from Consolidated Aircraft and were designed by Mac Laddon, but some were built in other countries, including the Soviet Union.

Engines: 2 Pratt & Whitney R-1830-92 Twin Wasp radial engines
Horsepower: 1,200 each
Maximum speed: 196 mph
Wingspan: 104 ft. 8 in.

- First flight: March 28, 1935
- Number built: 3,305
- Cost: $90,000 in 1935; 1 sold for $736,000 in 2013
- 8 listed as airworthy in 2015
- Called "Dumbo" when used for rescue

4.1.1935

NORTH AMERICAN AT-6 TEXAN

THE SCHOOL EVERYONE ATTENDED

The Texan was once the most widely used instructional aircraft in the world and today is one of the most popular warbirds. The army and air force called it the AT-6 later T-6, naval aviators called it the SNJ, and British Commonwealth operators the Harvard. It has some dubious flight characteristics and is difficult to land in a crosswind, but it trained more military pilots from more countries than any other aircraft before or since.

- First flight: April 1, 1935
- Number built: 15,495
- Cost: $25,672 in 1944
- Many portrayed Japanese Zero fighters in movies
- Popularly called "the pilot maker"

Engine: 1 Pratt & Whitney R-1340-AN-1 Wasp radial engine
Horsepower: 600
Maximum speed: 138 mph
Wingspan: 42 ft.

5.6.1935

CURTISS P-36 MOHAWK

A GOOD FIGHTER OFTEN OUTCLASSED BY BETTER FIGHTERS

The P-36 Mohawk, also called the Hawk 75, saw most of its World War II action in the hands of pilots of the French air arm during the Battle of France. This predecessor to the P-40 Warhawk, from a design team headed by engineer Don R. Berlin, performed reasonably well but was not quite a match for most of the fighters of its era. The P-36 was extremely maneuverable and easy to handle, but it was neither fast enough nor sufficiently well-armed to fill an important role in the war.

Engine: 1 Pratt & Whitney R-1830-17 Twin Wasp radial piston engine
Horsepower: 1,050
Maximum speed: 313 mph
Wingspan: 37 ft. 4 in.

- First flight: May 6, 1935
- Number built: About 1,115 (215 for US forces)
- Used by several Allied air forces
- Just 1 airworthy survivor today

BOEING B-17 FLYING FORTRESS

MOST RECOGNIZED AND MUCH LOVED

A national survey in recent years found the Boeing B-17 Flying Fortress to be the "most recognized" plane in all of aviation, ahead of the Douglas DC-3, the Supermarine Spitfire, and the Boeing 747. It says something that Korean War Air ace Dolphin Overton piloted the F-86 Sabre, but when he wanted to market a food product, he named it B-17 Steak Sauce. When the then-unnamed prototype first flew, *Seattle Times* reporter Dick Williams called it a "flying fortress" and the description stuck. Movies such as *Command Decision* (1948) and *Twelve O'Clock High* cemented its fame. The B-17 was easier to fly than the B-24 Liberator, could fly higher, and was easier to ditch, although the B-24 was faster and carried more. B-17s still draw huge crowds at air shows today and a whole new generation is now comfortable at the bomber's controls.

Engines: 4 Wright R-1820 Cyclone 9 radial engines
Horsepower: 1,200 each
Maximum speed: 287 mph
Wingspan: 103 ft. 9 in.

- First flight: July 28, 1935
- Number built: 12,731
- Cost: $204,370 in 1945; priceless today
- Carries 12,500 US gallons of high-octane fuel
- You must be skinny to use the catwalk over the bomb bay
- About a dozen flying today

8.1.1935

NAVAL AIRCRAFT FACTORY N3N

IT IMPERILED A GENERATION OF FLEDGLING FLYERS

The N3N, dubbed the "Yellow Peril" by a generation of student naval aviators, was one of the navy's primary trainers of World War II. The N3N is all-metal, constructed using bolts and rivets rather than the more common welded steel tubing. The aquatic version served at the US Naval Academy in Annapolis, Maryland, and was retired only in 1961, making it the last US biplane in military service.

- First flight: August 1, 1935
- Number built: 997
- Considered a little stiff on the controls
- Very wide, spacious cockpits

Engine: 1 Wright R-760-2 Whirlwind radial piston engine
Horsepower: 235
Cruising speed: 90 mph
Wingspan: 34 ft.

8.15.1935

SEVERSKY P-35

COMFORTABLE, BUT NOT SO COMBATIVE

Americans initially loved to fly this fighter from the company founded by Alexander Seversky, later named Republic. Their enthusiasm waned, however, when they encountered Japan's Mitsubishi A6M Zero, and many P-35As were lost during that first attack in the Philippines on December 8, 1941. A spacious, well laid-out cockpit became a Seversky, and later Republic, trademark. The P-35 was "sporty," one pilot said, "as long as no one was shooting"—but it was slower and less maneuverable than other fighters of its era.

Engine: 1 Pratt & Whitney R-1830-9 Twin Wasp radial piston engine
Horsepower 850
Maximum speed: 290 mph
Wingspan: 35 ft.

- First flight: August 15, 1935
- Cost: $22,500 in 1936
- US Army had 136 (60 P-35, 76 P-35A)
- Contemporary of: Hawker Hurricane, Messerschmitt Bf 109
- Served in Sweden as the J9

12.17.1935

DOUGLAS DC-3

METHUSELAH WITH WINGS: OLD BUT IMMORTAL

Donald Douglas's planemaking company was young when American Airlines' C. R. Smith asked to order a new transport. Now, that plane is older than most people alive today, yet five hundred of them continue to fly around the world. The Douglas DC-3 made air travel popular and airline profits possible, and it's universally regarded as one of a handful of true "greats" in aviation history. The DC-3 is renowned not merely for its performance, which was revolutionary in 1935, but for its staying power, its timeless appeal, and the many names by which it is known. It is the Dakota to the British, the R4D to the US sea services, the C-47 to the US Army and Air Force, and the "Gooney bird" to just about everybody. Yes, it was the first modern airliner, but it also hauled freight, explored the Arctic and Antarctic, and dropped paratroopers into Normandy on D-Day. It did almost everything. It still does.

Engines: 2 Wright R-1820 Cyclone radial engines
Horsepower: 1,200 each
Cruising speed: 185 mph
Wingspan: 95 ft.

- First flight: December 17, 1935
- Number built: 10,655 of all versions; hundreds still flying
- DC" stood for "Douglas Commercial"
- Manufactured in Santa Monica and Long Beach, California, and Oklahoma City, Oklahoma
- Copies manufactured in Japan and the Soviet Union
- Initially called the DST, the Douglas Sleeper Transport

1936

BOEING/STEARMAN PT-17 KAYDET

"I'M RELIVING MY YOUTH AND MY CHILDHOOD" —Tom Vogel, Stearman owner

Most call it simply the Stearman. Derived from the planemaker's earlier PT-13 (PT for "primary trainer"), it was the PT-17 in army parlance, the N2S-1 to the navy, and the Kaydet in Canada, and it was flown by thousands of trainee military pilots in World War II. Its configuration wasn't much like the warplanes to which students graduated, but the sturdy structure made it ideal for teaching aviation fundamentals.

- First flight: 1936
- Number built: 8,584 of all versions
- Cost: $10,412 in 1942

Engine: 1 Continental R-670-5 piston radial engine
Horsepower: 220
Maximum speed: 126 mph
Wingspan: 32 ft. 2 in.

3.26.1936

AUTOGIRO COMPANY OF AMERICA AC-35

A GUTSY ATTEMPT AT A FLYING CAR

The dream of an airplane that can perform double duty as an automobile refuses to die. A worthy attempt, the ambitious AC-35 was billed as an "aerial Model T" able to fly at high speed in the air and to drive at 25 miles per hour on the roadway with its rotors stowed. After tweaks that repaired early stability problems, the AC-35 worked perfectly well. Alas, its $12,500 price tag was several times the average family income in 1936.

- First flight: March 26, 1936
- Number built: 1
- A joy to fly but "painful" to drive, one expert said
- Demonstrated publicly on October 2, 1936

Engine: 1 Pobjoy Cascade air-cooled radial engine
Horsepower: 98
Maximum speed: 75 mph (air), 25 mph (road)
Rotor diameter: 36 ft. 4 in.
Fuselage length (car body): 16 ft. 3 in.

5.10.1936
MEYERS OTW

A PROMISING TRAINER
WITH AN ALUMINUM ISSUE

Meyers Aircraft Company, founded by Allen Meyers, designed the angular, lanky, two-seat OTW (Out to Win) as a primary trainer for the military at a time when many Americans anticipated a second world war. Skinny, almost spindly in appearance, the OTW was a competitor to the Stearman PT-17 Kaydet but used aluminum rather than welded tubing and stringers in its fuselage. Government officials shut off the flow of aluminum to Meyers's firm—there was a myth that strategic materials would be in short supply—so production ended sooner than planned. Some dozens of future military pilots did train on the Meyers, but tens of thousands flew the PT-17. With relatively large wings and tail, the OTW was more docile than a PT-17 and slow responding to the pilot's touch. It was built in four versions, each with a different engine.

Engine: 1 Warner Scarab radial piston engine
Horsepower: 125
Maximum speed: 120 mph
Wingspan: 26 ft.

- First flight: May 10, 1936
- Number built: 102
- Popular in postwar years as a sportplane
- About 30 are flying today

8.8.1936
SPARTAN 7W EXECUTIVE

THE ULTIMATE IN PREWAR
PERSONAL LUXURY

If you own one of these airplanes today, you own a national treasure. The Spartan 7W Executive was the private plane for the successful corporate mogul in the same way a 1936 Duesenberg Model J might have been that business bigwig's automobile. Think deep cushions, fancy ashtrays, dome lighting. William G. Skelly of Skelly Oil wanted a speedy, posh, private plane for himself for rich oil-executive colleagues and was the powerful force behind the shiny, silvery Executive. Well-known owners included Howard Hughes and J. Paul Getty. During World War II, the US Army acquired sixteen of these planes under the designation C-71 and used them for a brief period. Only a handful survive today and they are priceless.

Engine: 1 Pratt & Whitney R-985-AN3 air-cooled radial engine
Horsepower: 450 each
Cruising speed: 215 mph
Wingspan: 39 ft.

- First flight: August 8, 1936
- Number built: 34
- Cost: $23,500 in 1936
- Flew in 1939 Bendix Air Races

GRUMMAN F4F WILDCAT

A VALIANT FIGHTER IN EARLY BATTLES

The F4F Wildcat, also called the FM, was the sturdy, stubby fighter that held the line against the vastly superior Japanese Zero in early fighting in the Pacific—the only fighter available at the time. No fewer than eight Wildcat pilots were awarded the Medal of Honor, all for perilous, pointblank battles. In British service, this fighter was called the Martlet. After the F6F Hellcat took over the air-to-air mission and began pounding the crap out of the Imperial Japanese fighter force, the Wildcat continued to serve on escort carriers to confront submarine and shore threats. The Wildcat was a handful during takeoff and landing, but once in the air was a joy to fly. Several are in airworthy condition today.

Engine: 1 Pratt & Whitney R-1830-6 radial piston engine
Horsepower: 1,200
Maximum speed: 320 mph
Wingspan: 28 ft.

- First flight: September 2, 1937
- First service: 1940
- Number built: 7,885
- Cost: $67,400 per plane in 1937
- First monoplane fighter from Grumman

CURTISS XP-37

SLEEK, STREAMLINED, AND A NON-STARTER

The Curtiss XP-37 was an experiment aimed at developing a fighter with a liquid-cooled powerplant comparable to the Supermarine Spitfire or Hawker Hurricane. Unfortunately, the XP-37's engine was bulkier and more trouble-prone than the Merlin engine used on the British fighters. Moreover, with its long nose and cramped cockpit, the XP-37 had poor visibility when flying and almost none when taxiing. This turned out to be another of many promising prewar ideas that failed to gel.

Engine: 1 Allison V-1710-11 liquid-cooled radial engine with turbosupercharger
Horsepower: 1,050
Cruising speed: 340 mph
Wingspan: 37 ft. 4 in.

- First flight: April 1937
- Number built: 14 (1 XP-37, 13 YP-37)
- First XP-37 logged only 137 hours
- No survivors today

BELL YFM-1 AIRACUDA

RESEMBLING A SATURDAY-MATINEE ROCKET SHIP WITH PROPELLERS

In the late 1930s amid the Great Depression, the YFM-1 Airacuda cheered up aviation buffs who thought it was pretty funny. The Airacuda became a really neat children's toy made of die-cast metal and sold in Woolworth's Dime Stores. The real-world Airacuda was the first military aircraft from Larry Bell's company and the first to use the "Aira-" prefix later found on the P-39 Airacobra. Solidly built, deemed futuristic and evocative of spaceships in *Flash Gordon* movie serials, it was a bold design for a "bomber destroyer," with armed crewmembers in wing nacelles—in positions that were hugely uncomfortable and impossible to escape from. It was, alas, slower than molasses, unstable in some conditions, and too complicated, too heavy, and too slow. The military retired it in 1942.

Engines: 2 Allison V-1710-9 liquid-cooled radial engines
Horsepower: 1,090 each
Maximum speed: 277 mph
Wingspan: 69 ft. 10 in.

- First flight: September 1, 1937
- Number built: 13
- Cost: $219,000 per plane in 1937
- Tested from 1938 to 1942
- Set aside when the US entered World War II
- 2 crashed; no survivors today

10.1.1937

ERCO ERCOUPE

THE REALLY NEAT LITTLE SPORT FROM RIVERDALE

A recent survey in Riverdale, Maryland, found only one in ten residents knew their town was once home to Engineering Research Corporation, or Erco, which hand-built popular Ercoupe civilian sport planes. Their product included two PQ-13 target-drone versions and just one YO-55 observation ship for the US Army. Production paused during World War II and most Ercoupes were manufactured in 1946. Other planemaking companies assembled some of them. Small and light, with side-by-side seating, the Ercoupe lived up to designer Fred Weick's dream of an affordable recreational aircraft that almost anyone could operate. Purely for enjoyment, hundreds are still savoring the skies today.

Engine: 1 Continental C-75-12 piston engine
Horsepower: 75
Maximum speed: 110 mph
Wingspan: 30 ft.

- First flight October 1, 1937
- Number built: 4,400
- Cost: An affordable $2,685 in 1946
- Advertised as "The World's Safest Plane"
- At one point, Erco was building 34 per *day*

10.15.1937

BOEING XB-15

PROVING THAT BIG IS NOT ALWAYS BEAUTIFUL

The XB-15 was huge, but underpowered and delayed in development, making its maiden flight two years after Boeing's B-17 Flying Fortress. After duty as a bomber, it was fitted with a cargo hoist and door, renamed the XC-108, and used to haul cargoes and people to Albrook Field, Panama, during World War II. It transported hundreds of young women, recruited for war work, from Miami to the Canal Zone in what crews called the Georgia Peach Run. Uneconomical and difficult to operate, the sole XB-15-cum-XC-108—which would have made a great museum display—was scrapped in 1945.

Engines: 4 Pratt & Whitney R-1830-11 Twin Wasp radial engines
Horsepower: 850 each
Maximum speed: 197 mph
Wingspan: 149 ft.

- First flight: October 15, 1937
- Number built: 1
- Called the XBLR-1 while being designed
- Retired from service: December 18, 1944

CONSOLIDATED PB2Y CORONADO

A STRONG, RELIABLE FLYING BOAT

One of these transported Fleet Admiral Chester Nimitz to the surrender ceremony aboard the battleship USS *Missouri* in Tokyo Bay on September 2, 1945. Designed as a patrol bomber, it became a multi-purpose seaplane, the US Navy's largest ever to be widely used. After purchasing the sole XPB2Y-1 and six PB2Y-2s, which tested radio instruments in 1940, the navy ordered fully two hundred PB2Y-3 models. Of these, thirty-two went to the British, and thirty-one were converted into PB2Y-3R transports. The PB2Y-4 and PB2Y-6 were one-of-a-kind test models, while some Coronados were given new engines, gun turrets, and fuel tanks to become PB2Y-5s. This was a big, comfortable, friendly flying boat that served the navy well and won praise from crews.

Engines: 4 Pratt & Whitney R-1830-88 Twin Wasp radial piston engines
Horsepower: 1,200 each
Maximum speed: 194 mph
Weight: 67,500 lb. (gross)
Wingspan: 115 ft.

- First flight: December 17, 1937
- Number built: 209
- Armament: Up to 12,000 lb. of bombs or torpedoes
- Crew: 10
- 1 survives in a museum today

1938
PIPER J-3 CUB

SMALL, SIMPLE, STURDY, AND A FOND FRIEND TO THOUSANDS

It would be impossible to guess the number of civilian and military pilots who made their first-ever solo flights in the Piper J-3 Cub, but the number is indisputably in the tens of thousands. Developed by William T. Piper, the Cub was so simple and so practical that it had the makings of immortality from the beginning. While the signature J-3 model was manufactured only between 1938 and 1947, it inspired spinoffs and similar aircraft throughout both civilian and military aviation. Today, a Cub can be found at almost any grass strip in the American countryside as a new generation learns to fly in modern versions.

Engine: 1 Continental A65 engine (typically)
Horsepower: 65
Cruising speed: 75 mph
Wingspan: 35 ft. 3 in.

- First flight: 1938
- Cost: Sold for $995 in 1939; usually $100,000 today
- The first plane for thousands of new pilots
- Most did not have starters

3.1.1938
VOUGHT OS2U KINGFISHER

THE PREMIER FLOATPLANE OF THE PACIFIC WAR

The OS2U was the most numerous and famous of several World War II aircraft that were launched from a surface warship by catapult and retrieved by crane after landing. This was adventurous flying, so floatplane aviation was for volunteers only. Duties included aerial spotting for naval gunfire, a key job during the Pacific island-hopping campaign. A Kingfisher could drop bombs or depth charges but had neither the armament nor the speed to evade Japanese fighters. It was a terrific aircraft to fly when no one was shooting.

Engine: 1 Pratt & Whitney R-985-AN-2 Wasp Junior radial piston engine
Horsepower: 450
Maximum speed: 164 mph
Wingspan: 35 ft. 11 in.

- First flight: March 1, 1938
- Number built: 1,519
- Served in Australia, Britain, and the Soviet Union
- 5 in museums today, none airworthy

BELL P-39 AIRACOBRA

LITTLE LOVED, BUT LETHAL IN THE RIGHT HANDS

The P-39 Airacobra may have been the least-loved fighter ever flown by Americans. Most experienced the P-39 in training and shifted their affection to their service aircraft once they were done. Only Soviet airmen, who received half of all P-39s, praised the Airacobra to the skies, empowered by its lethal, nose-mounted 37-millimeter cannon. With its automobile-style door, the P-39 cockpit was a tight squeeze. Visibility was superb, however, and instruments were well laid out. In a close-quarters dogfight at low altitude the P-39 was as good a brawler as any of its World War II peers.

Engine: 1 Allison V-1710-85 liquid-cooled piston engine
Horsepower: 1,200
Maximum speed: 376 mph
Wingspan: 34 ft.

- First flight: April 6, 1938
- Number built: 9,588
- 4,719 went to the Soviet Union
- Australia used 23 briefly
- Postwar P-39s excelled in air races
- Just 1 airworthy today

CURTISS P-40 WARHAWK

DEPENDABLE AND USEFUL, BUT DENIED TRUE GREATNESS

It fought at Pearl Harbor and with the Flying Tigers in Burma and China, but it was obsolescent even in 1941. British Commonwealth forces flew it in the Middle East and North Africa. Designed by Don R. Berlin, the P-40 Warhawk (with variants known as the Tomahawk and the Kittyhawk) remained a stalwart throughout World War II even though it can be ranked only in the second tier of great fighters. The P-40 was tough and reliable, but limited at high altitude, and slow compared to fighters that came along only a year or two later. However, because it fought almost everywhere, it remains an icon of World War II.

Engine: 1 Allison V-1710-39 liquid-cooled V-12 engine (typical)
Horsepower: 1,150
Cruising speed: 360 mph
Wingspan: 37 ft. 4 in.

- First flight: October 14, 1938
- Number built: 13,738
- Cost: $44,892 in 1944
- 73 P-40s were among the 152 US aircraft destroyed at Pearl Harbor
- P-40 pilots shot down seven Japanese aircraft on December 7, 1941
- Several units painted a shark's mouth on the nose

1.27.39

LOCKHEED P-38 LIGHTNING

"EVERY AMERICAN YOUNGSTER WANTED TO FLY THE P-38 LIGHTNING"
—Winton "Bones" Marshall, P-38 pilot

In the Pacific, the twin-engine, twin-boom P-38 Lightning produced top American air aces Richard Bong (forty kills) and Thomas McGuire (thirty-eight). In Europe, the P-38 had a difficult fight against the Third Reich because its heater worked poorly, and pilots were all but frozen in their cockpits. No other fighter captured the imagination of young Americans the way the P-38 did, but it was a complicated aircraft that required a lot of "setting up" when beginning a fight and it lacked the range of the P-51 Mustang. Though one of the true greats of the World War II era, the P-38 nevertheless fell short of being the greatest.

Engines: 2 Allison V-1710-111/113 V-12 liquid-cooled piston engines
Horsepower: 1,600 each
Maximum speed: 414 mph
Wingspan: 52 ft.

- First flight: January 27, 1939
- Number built: 10,037
- Reconnaissance ("foto") versions: F-4, F-5
- Retired: Last flown by US forces in 1949
- About 6 are airworthy today

117

VULTEE BT-13 VALIANT

> **Engine: 1 Pratt & Whitney R-985 radial (typical)**
> **Horsepower: 450**
> **Cruising speed: 170 mph**
> **Wingspan: 42 ft.**

- First flight: March 24, 1939
- Number built: 11,538 of all versions
- Valiants made up 85 percent of the 13,626 Vultee-designed aircraft built during World War II
- The only overseas purchaser of new Valiants was Peru, which got 12
- Possibly as many as 20,000 pilots trained in the army BT-13 or navy SNV
- Many restored examples flying today

A NOISY BUT DOCILE SCHOOLHOUSE IN THE SKY

It was one of the great training planes of World War II. Pilots loved it. Pilots hated it. On paper it was the Vultee BT-13 Valiant, but a generation of airmen called it the Vultee Vibrator. The army had BT-13 and BT-15 versions, while the navy had the SNV. In the three-stage pilot program of World War II, "primary" training came first, often in the Stearman biplane; "basic" was the second stage, using the Valiant; and "advanced" training followed in the AT-6/SNJ Texan.

PIPER J-5 CUB CRUISER

A FAST-FLYING ANGEL OF MERCY FOR THE TROOPS

The Piper J-5 Cub Cruiser—the army L-14, and navy AE-1 and HE-1—was a bigger, beefed-up version of the famous J-3 Cub. It was an affordable, sensible private aircraft at a time when war had interrupted civil aviation sales. In military hands, it was the ideal ambulance, with a fairly long fuselage (22 feet 6 inches) that handled a hospital stretcher. At least some wounded US soldiers were saved because a Cub Cruiser rushed them to emergency care. There were relatively few Cub Cruisers, but they consistently drew high marks from pilots, who rated them as snappier and more agile than the familiar Cub.

> **Engine: 1 Lycoming O-145-C2 air-cooled piston engine**
> **Horsepower: 75**
> **Maximum speed: 96 mph**
> **Wingspan: 35 ft. 6 in.**

- First flight: July 1, 1939
- Cost: $1,995 in 1940
- In postwar years, it evolved into the PA-12 Super Cruiser
- A handful are flying today

9.21.1939

LOCKHEED MODEL 18 LODESTAR

VERSATILE AND CAPABLE, BUT JUST A MODEST SUCCESS

Lockheed's Model 18 Lodestar was developed in the late 1930s to improve on the planemaker's earlier Model 14 Super Electra, which did not receive a warm reception from airlines. The Lodestar was better received and operated initially with Mid-Continent Airlines of Kansas City, Missouri. In due course, a dozen airlines used the Lodestar. There were many versions, and Lockheed offered the plane with a variety of engines, but they could not fully overcome competition from the Douglas DC-3. Lockheed built the R5O version for the coast guard, as well as C-56, C-57, and C-60 versions for the US Army. The C-60 operated by the West Texas Wing of the Commemorative Air Force (pictured) represents an army version used to train paratroopers.

Engines: 2 Wright R-1820-28 radial engines (C-60A)
Horsepower: 1,200 each
Cruising speed: 232 mph
Wingspan: 65 ft. 6 in.

- First flight: September 21, 1939
- Number built: 625 of all versions
- Capacity: 15 passengers with stewardess and galley, 18 without
- Considered very pilot friendly in all phases of flight
- Some were executive transports after World War II
- Fewer than 20 are airworthy today

CONSOLIDATED B-24 LIBERATOR

BIG, BOXY, BELOVED—AND OVERLOOKED

The Consolidated B-24 Liberator is one of the great bombers all time. To B-24 veterans, it was the greatest—a plane toward which the typical crew member formed a lifelong attachment. Yet the Liberator rarely receives the accolades bestowed on the better-known B-17 Flying Fortress. Less graceful, with more sharp edges, the B-24 is jokingly criticized as "the box the B-17 came in." Yet the B-24 was built in greater numbers and was faster, carried more bombs, and traveled farther. It was also more difficult to fly, but that only gave pilots an opportunity to take special pride in mastering it. They still do, as planes like the Collings Foundation's *Witchcraft* continue the B-24 legacy at open-house events and air shows.

Engines: 4 Pratt & Whitney R-1830 radial engines
Horsepower: 1,200 each
Maximum speed: 290 mph
Wingspan: 110 ft.

- First flight: December 29, 1939
- Number built: 18,482; most numerous US military aircraft
- Cost: $297,627 in 1945; priceless today
- Actor Jimmy Stewart flew about 25 combat missions in the B-24
- Just 3 are airworthy today

4.1.1940

GRUMMAN XF5F SKYROCKET

THERE'S THAT "FIRST FLIGHT ON APRIL FOOLS' DAY" THING AGAIN

Are you kidding? You really don't remember the Blackhawk comics of the early 1940s? Okay, then, maybe you might not recall the XF5F Skyrocket, which was a cheeky attempt by an established planemaker to develop a twin-engined, carrier-based fighter. Despite engine heating problems that were resolved with tweaks, the XF5F performed well and won praise from Grumman pilot Connie Converse, who wrote that its "flying qualities . . . were good overall." Minor technical glitches were addressed with repeated changes to the sole aircraft built, and tests continued long after the US Navy decided it didn't want a fighter in this class. Finally retired in 1944, the XF5F inspired Grumman's more successful F7F Tigercat.

Engines: 2 Pratt & Whitney R-1830-40/42 radial piston engines
Horsepower: 1,200 each
Maximum speed: 383 mph
Weight: 10,138 lb.—a relative lightweight
Wingspan: 42 ft.

- First flight: April 1, 1940
- In the original version, the "nose" did not extend forward of the wing
- Propellers rotated in opposite directions, so it had no torque
- The sole XF5F-1 was scrapped

5.1.1940

DOUGLAS SBD DAUNTLESS

IT TURNED THE TIDE AT MIDWAY

The SBD Dauntless is one of the navy's best-known warplanes. Jack Northrop, who worked for Donald Douglas's southern-California aircraft company before founding a firm in his own name, designed the SBD in the 1930s. Douglas Aircraft Co. built 5,936 Dauntlesses between 1935 and 1944, even though the plane was obsolescent when the United States entered World War II. The Dauntless's shining moment came at Midway on June 4, 1942, when fifty-four of the dive-bombers attacked and destroyed the carriers *Akagi*, *Kaga*, and *Sōryū*. They also put the carrier *Hiryū* out of action. This was the Japanese carrier force that had attacked Pearl Harbor six months earlier. Some Dauntlesses were destroyed at Pearl Harbor and others participated in the flyover at the surrender ceremony at Tokyo Bay on September 2, 1945.

Engine: 1 Wright R-1820-60 radial engine
Horsepower: 1,200
Maximum speed: 255 mph
Wingspan: 41 ft. 6 in.

- First flight: May 1, 1940
- Crew: 2 (pilot in the front seat, radioman-gunner in back)
- Considered the world's best dive-bomber
- The US Army version, the A-24 Banshee, was not used successfully in combat
- Wings did not fold for aircraft-carrier stowage
- Two restored SBD Dauntlesses were airworthy in 2014

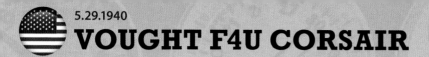

5.29.1940
VOUGHT F4U CORSAIR

AN ICON THAT SEEMED TO BE EVERYWHERE

The myth is that the F4U Corsair was a "back-up" for the F6F Hellcat. The truth: The iconic Corsair, with its unique gull-wing shape designed by Rex Beisel, although late reaching carrier decks was an outstanding warplane in World War II and Korea. It remained in production longer and later than any other propeller-driven fighter in the West (until 1953) and was built under license by Brewster (F3A) and Goodyear (FG, F2G). Although it served in Argentina, Britain, El Salvador, France, Honduras, and New Zealand, many say the Corsair was at its finest operating from land bases with the US Marine Corps. Not comfortable, not roomy, not easy to fly, the Corsair was nonetheless one of the great fighters of all time.

Engine: 1 Pratt & Whitney R-2800-18W Double Wasp radial engine
Horsepower: 2,325
Maximum speed: 453 mph
Wingspan: 41 ft.

- First flight: May 29, 1940
- Number built: 12,571
- Shot down a MiG-15 jet in Korea
- 16 production models
- An 11-to-1 kill ratio against Japan

8.19.1940

NORTH AMERICAN B-25 MITCHELL

A FAMOUS AND FORMIDABLE MEDIUM BOMBER

Named for Gen. Billy Mitchell and famous for the April 1942 Tokyo raid led by another future general, Jimmy Doolittle, the B-25 was a tough and versatile medium bomber that pulled difficult duty in all theaters of World War II (although not with US forces in England except in the Harrison Ford film *Hanover Street*.) Navy and marine corps PBJ versions bombed island bastions in the South Pacific. Even though one inadvertently flew into the Empire State Building in a 1945 aviation disaster, the B-25 was known for good performance and a fine safety record.

Engines: 2 Wright R-2600-92 Twin Cyclone radial engines
Horsepower: 1,700 each
Maximum speed: 272 mph
Wingspan: 67 ft. 7 in.

- First flight: August 19, 1940
- Number built: 9,817
- Cost: $142,194 in 1942, millions today
- About 45 are airworthy today

NORTH AMERICAN P-64

NOT THIS PLANEMAKER'S BEST FIGHTER

The little-known North American P-64 was meant as a fighter and was derived from the manufacturer's training planes, the most famous of which was the AT-6 Texan. Because it was based on a trainer, it didn't fight very well, and because it was a single seater, it wasn't much use for training. North American built seven for Peru, where the P-64 was nicknamed *Torito* (Little Bull), plus seven for Thailand that were embargoed for political reasons and diverted to the army air corps.

Engine: 1 Wright R-1820-77 radial piston engine
Horsepower: 870
Maximum speed: 270 mph
Wingspan: 27 ft.

- First flight: September 1, 1940
- Number built: 13
- Used in Ecuadorian–Peruvian war of 1941
- 2 survivors today, 1 each in museums in Peru and the United States

US Air Force

MARTIN B-26 MARAUDER

A STURDY AND POWERFUL BOMBER

When something absolutely, positively has to be blown to bits, you want a B-26 Marauder medium bomber. This burly brawler could carry 3,000 pounds of bombs or a 2,000-pound torpedo. Curiously enough, most Marauders were configured for pilot and co-pilot, but a few were set up for single-pilot operation. Oh, and they've removed all the military pyrotechnics from the only flyable B-26 in the world, owned today by a Florida museum. This plane was called the "Widowmaker" when it first entered service; a senate committee headed by Harry S. Truman (D-Mo) investigated its shortcomings, posed by high wing loading and other aeronautical issues. Redesigning and enlarging the wing solved most of the B-26's handling problems, and more thorough pilot training resolved the rest. By 1945, a report from the Pentagon credited the Marauder with having the lowest combat loss rate of any US military aircraft.

Engines: 2 Pratt & Whitney R-2800 Double Wasps
Horsepower: 1,900
Maximum speed: 287 mph
Wingspan: 71 ft.

- First flight: September 25, 1940
- First combat: Rabaul, New Britain, April 5, 1942
- Number built: 5,157
- Cost: About $102,000 in 1942
- Crew: Varied from 4 to 6
- Very effective and accurate at medium altitude

10.26.1940

NORTH AMERICAN P-51 MUSTANG

SOME CALL IT THE GREATEST

The P-51 Mustang is often called the greatest fighter of World War II, and at least one writer calls it the greatest aircraft of all time. Without the Mustang, which had the range to escort bombers all the way to Berlin, the bombing campaign might have failed—and without the bombing campaign, the Allied invasion of Western Europe might have been delayed. So the Mustang was the key. Turned loose, it could range out to attack the German air arm where it lived. In the spring and summer of 1944, a handful of Americans in P-51 cockpits defeated the German air force, one of the great victories in the history of war. It helped that the P-51 was comfortable, well heated and pressurized, and easy to fly.

Engine: 1 Packard V-1650-7 Merlin liquid-cooled, supercharged piston engine
Horsepower: 1,490
Maximum speed: 437 mph
Wingspan: 37 ft.

- First flight: October 26, 1940
- Number built: 15,500
- Cost: $50,985 in 1943
- Became F-51, fought in Korea
- A top performer in air races
- About 150 are airworthy today

CURTISS SB2C HELLDIVER

NOT EXACTLY THE DEFINITIVE DIVE-BOMBER

With its two-man crew of pilot and radioman-gunner, the SB2C Helldiver was meant to replace the Douglas SBD Dauntless, which won fame in the 1942 Battle of Midway. The Helldiver was neither as good as its designer Don Berlin hoped nor as bad as the reputation sailors gave it, calling it "the Beast" for the poor handling characteristics found in early versions. Operating from aircraft-carrier decks, Helldivers fought in the Philippines, in the last phase of the Pacific island-hopping campaign, and over the Japanese home islands. Once early technical glitches were resolved with minor design changes, the Helldiver was a success—but some Dauntlesses were still pulling duty on the final day of the war.

Engine: 1 Wright R-2600-20 Twin Cyclone radial engine
Horsepower: 1,900
Maximum speed: 295 mph
Wingspan: 49 ft. 9 in.

- First flight: December 18, 1940
- First service: December 1942
- Cost: About $48,000 in 1945
- Number built: 7,140
- France, Italy, and Thailand were among users
- Just 1 airworthy example today

REPUBLIC P-47 THUNDERBOLT

IT'S IMMORTAL—AND EVEN BETTER THAN THEY SAID

The P-47 Thunderbolt was the American fighter built in the largest numbers and one of the largest and heaviest fighters in history to be powered by a single engine. The big, tough Thunderbolt—nicknamed the "Jug" because of its portly fuselage shape—always appears on any list of the top fighters of World War II, and in recent times historians have been rating it higher than previously. From the XP-47B prototype to the clipped-wing P-47N used only in the Pacific, the Thunderbolt excelled at both air-to-air and air-to-ground fighting. Pilots loved the reliability and power of that big R-2800 engine up front, and were doubly pleased that the engine served as armor that protected them from ground fire. Despite its corpulence, the P-47 could yank and bank with the best of them.

Engine: 1 Pratt & Whitney R-2800-59 Double Wasp radial piston engine
Horsepower: 2,535
Maximum speed: 433 mph
Wingspan: 40 ft. 9 in.

- First flight: May 6, 1941
- Number built: 15,686
- Cost: About $92,000 in 1944. Want one today? Think $5 million
- Mexico and Brazil were among World War II users
- About 15 are airworthy today

STINSON L-5 SENTINEL

THE "BIG BIRD" AMONG THE L-PLANES

Among the "L-planes"—for liaison—that served the army and marine corps during World War II and Korea, none was sturdier or more versatile than the Stinson L-5 Sentinel (called the OY by marines). Whether spotting targets for artillery fire, hauling a wounded warrior out of harm's way, or enabling a general to look down at his troops, the Sentinel was a beefy, reliable warbird robust enough to be free of the weight and balance issues endemic to other aircraft in its class. In hot spots like Iwo Jima, Sentinel pilots were dodging enemy fire constantly. Today, the Sentinel is an affordable warbird that many pilots enjoy flying and displaying.

- First flight: June 28, 1941
- Number built: 3,590
- About 200 are airworthy today

Engine: 1 Lycoming O-435-11 air-cooled piston engine
Horsepower: 190
Maximum speed: 129 mph
Wingspan: 34 ft.

8.7.1941

GRUMMAN TBF AVENGER

"TOUGH AS A TIN CAN"—David Shapiro, World War II Avenger pilot

Engine: 1 Wright R-2600-20 Twin Cyclone radial engine
Horsepower: 1,900
Maximum speed: 275 mph
Wingspan: 54 ft. 2 in.

The Grumman TBF Avenger, also known as the General Motors TBM, is the iconic US torpedo-bomber that fought in every Pacific battle from Midway on and famously became the mount of George H. W. Bush, later the 41st US president. Designed by Leroy Grumman, whose company outsourced most production to GM, the Avenger used a large bomb bay that made the aircraft an outstanding ground-support bomber when carrying bombs and vice torpedoes. With its advanced radio gear, the Avenger did double duty as a reconnaissance aircraft.

- First flight: August 7, 1941
- Number built: 9,839
- Crew: 3—pilot, turret gunner, ventral gunner

1.13.1942
SIKORSKY R-4 AND HNS

THE HELICOPTER THAT CAME FIRST

The R-4 (US Army) and the identical HNS (Navy and coast guard) was the first truly practical helicopter. Britain used this aircraft and called it the Hoverfly. The R-4/HNS looked like a Jungle Jim of metal girders wrapped in fabric—it was not canvas, as widely reported, but linen—and had limited carrying capacity. It was loud, shaky, and vulnerable to weather and to hostile action. It was a pioneer and every helicopter that came after it was better.

- First flight: January 13, 1942
- Number built: 131
- Designed by Igor Sikorsky
- Army version became H-4 when designation system changed in July 1948

Engine: 1 Warner R-550 radial piston engine
Horsepower: 200
Maximum speed: 75 mph
Main rotor diameter: 38 ft.

2.14.1942
DOUGLAS DC-4 (C-54 SKYMASTER)

STYLISH PROPLINER FOR A POSTWAR WORLD

The Douglas DC-4 (C-54 or R5D Skymaster to the US military) was the first in a series of prop-driven airliners with such graceful lines they might have been designed by Raymond Loewy. Interrupted by World War II, at which point they donned military garb like everyone else—and one, called the *Sacred Cow*, served Presidents Franklin D. Roosevelt and Harry S. Truman—DC-4s fueled high hopes of postwar airline moguls. The DC-4 starred in the John Wayne movie *The High and the Mighty* (1954). Though it had respectable speed and range, the DC-4 became the forerunner of the even more capable DC-6 and DC-7. Pilots say that no flight deck was ever better designed or more comfortable.

Engines: 4 Pratt & Whitney R-2800 Double Wasp radial piston engines
Horsepower: 1,450 each
Maximum speed: 227 mph
Wingspan: 117 ft. 6 in.

- First flight: February 14, 1942
- Number built: 1,243
- Capacity: Airline version holds up to 86 passengers
- Excelled during the Berlin airlift of 1948 and 1949

NORTHROP P-61
BLACK WIDOW

DEADLY IN THE DARK

To its adversaries, it was a sinister creature of the darkness. After numerous design changes, the twin-engine, twin-boom P-61 Black Widow—named for the spider—entered service as the first US purpose-built night fighter, and the first designed from the outset to use air-to-air radar. Although it was big, burly, and slower than single-engine ships, the P-61 was a true fighter that could engage a foe from a distance but was also perfectly able to maneuver in a dogfight. Numerous changes in armament and crew composition marked the career of this gloss-black nocturnal nemesis, with the final version having cannons mounted beneath the fuselage. A recent survey of model builders showed the P-61 to be their favorite aircraft.

Engines: 2 Pratt & Whitney R-2800 Double Wasp radial piston engines
Horsepower: 2,100 each
Maximum speed: 370 mph
Wingspan: 66 ft.

- First flight: May 26, 1942
- Number built: 706
- First kill: A Japanese "Betty" (Mitsubishi GM4) bomber, July 6, 1944
- Served from 1944 to 1950
- Redesignated F-61 in 1948

6.26.1942

GRUMMAN F6F HELLCAT

"IT HAD NO FLAWS. IT WAS RIGHT FROM THE START" —Harold Andrews, US Navy aeronautical engineer

It may be the only American combat aircraft that required almost no improvements or modifications—the last was almost identical to the first. Its production run was the largest ever of a single type in a single place. The F6F Hellcat is the big brute that defeated the Japanese naval air arm in Pacific combat, shooting down 5,223 aircraft during World War II. The heavy, robust Hellcat replaced the F4F Wildcat; it was more suitable for carrier-deck operations than the F4U Corsair and was decisively superior to the Japanese Mitsubishi A6M Zero. Medal of Honor recipient and top US Navy air ace David McCampbell (thirty-four aerial victories) was only one of many aces who wrested control of Pacific skies in the cockpit of a Hellcat.

Engine: 1 Pratt & Whitney R-2800-10W Double Wasp supercharged radial piston engine
Horsepower: 2,000
Maximum speed: 380 mph
Maximum takeoff weight: 15,415 lb.
Wingspan: 42 ft. 10 in.

- First flight: June 26, 1942
- Number built: 12,275
- Cost: $35,000 in 1945
- Overseas users: Britain, Uruguay

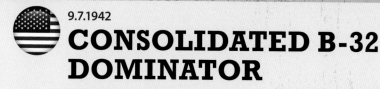

CONSOLIDATED B-32 DOMINATOR

THE LITTLE-KNOWN BOMBER THAT FLEW THE FINAL MISSION

The B-32 was fallback insurance in case the B-29 Superfortress failed, but the little-remembered Dominator had problems of its own, forcing the Army to delete its pressurization system (changing it from a high- to a medium-altitude bomber) and to redesign its tail and its defensive guns. In final form, it was an effective bomber but arrived too late to have a significant impact on World War II.

Engines: 4 Wright R-3350-23A Duplex-Cyclone radial pistol engines
Horsepower: 2,200
Maximum speed: 357 mph
Wingspan: 135 ft.

- First flight: September 7, 1942
- Number built: 118
- Crew: 10 to 12
- Twin tail on prototypes was replaced with a single fin
- Orders for 1,598 B-32s were canceled when World War II ended

VOUGHT V-173

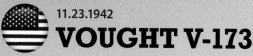

A TRUE AMERICAN FLYING SAUCER

Inspired in part by the Arup S-2, designed by Charles H. Zimmerman, and variously nicknamed the "Flying Pancake" or the "Flying Flapjack," this saucer-like, "all-wing" lifting body had no serious aerodynamic problems. Its excellent handling qualities could not compensate, however, for headaches caused by the intricate gearbox. Intended in part as a testbed for the Vought XF5U-1 fighter, which was built but never flown, the V-173 proved conclusively that an aircraft with this unorthodox shape could serve in a naval aviation unit.

- First flight: November 23, 1942
- Logged 131.5 hours in 190 flights
- Charles Lindbergh piloted the V-173 at least once
- Restored by Vought retirees at Grand Prairie, Texas

Engines: 2 Continental A60 horizontally opposed four-cylinder engines
Horsepower: 80 each
Maximum speed: 138 mph
Wingspan: 23 ft. 4 in.

BELL P-63 KINGCOBRA

A CLASSY IMPROVEMENT ON A LITTLE-LOVED FIGHTER

The P-63 Kingcobra was an effort by Bell Aircraft to improve on its somewhat pedestrian P-39 Airacobra. The P-63 exuded class and elegance in a way the P-39 did not, performed well in both air-to-air and air-to-ground action, and filled a variety of useful functions, although American pilots never flew it in combat. The Soviet Union received most P-63s, using them effectively against both Germany and Japan, and may have employed a few in Korea. Free French pilots also performed well at the controls of the Kingcobra.

Engine: 1 Allison V-1710-117 liquid-cooled piston engine
Horsepower: 1,800
Maximum speed: 410 mph
Wingspan: 38 ft. 4 in.

- First flight: December 7, 1942
- Number built: 3,303
- Cost: $65,914 in 1945
- Some, like the one pictured, were used as manned aerial targets
- 2,672 went to the Soviet Union
- Just 1 is airworthy today

1.15.1943

VULTEE XP-54

THUMBING ITS NOSE (AND TAIL) AT COMMON SENSE

The twin-boom XP-54 was the earliest (by eight months) to take to the air among three pusher-prop fighters that were tested by US pilots during World War II. The others were the Curtiss XP-55 Ascender and Northrop XP-56 Black Bullet. All of them appeared to defy conventional wisdom, and if the XP-54 seemed outwardly to be little less of an oddball than the others, its unique downward ejection seat more than compensated. The XP-55 was huge, with a fuselage longer than that of a B-25 Mitchell medium bomber. Combine its unorthodoxy with a trouble-prone engine and spare-parts problems, and the XP-54 had a very brief and unproductive life.

Engine: 1 Lycoming XH-2470-1 liquid-cooled piston engine
Horsepower: 2,275
Maximum speed: 381 mph
Wingspan: 53 ft. 10 in.

- First flight: January 15, 1943
- Number built: 2
- Nicknamed the "Swoose Goose"
- Second aircraft made only one flight

PIASECKI PV-2

FIRST OF MANY PIASECKI SUCCESSES

The PV-2 was the second successful US helicopter, after the Sikorsky R-4. Its designer, Frank Piasecki, was the first American to be granted a license to fly a helicopter without first qualifying to pilot an airplane. His PV-2 had a fabric-covered fuselage. The interior offered space for just one person, who sat in a conventional seat behind a rounded, glassed-in nose, similar to the front end of a lightplane. The PV-2 won national acclaim when it starred in a newsreel called *An Air Flivver in Every Garage*, which depicted Piasecki landing at a golf course and a gas station. Americans never got a PV-2 in every garage, but Piasecki went on to create the company that developed the HRP Rescuer, the CH-47 Chinook, and many other hugely successful helicopters.

Engine: 1 Franklin 4-cylinder air-cooled piston engine
Horsepower: 90
Maximum speed: 100 mph
Main rotor diameter: 25 ft.

- First flight: April 11, 1943
- Number built: 1
- Length: 21 ft. 6 in.
- Was easily towed on the road by an automobile
- Now on display at the Smithsonian

CURTISS XP-55 ASCENDER

WEIRD, WONDERFUL, DANGEROUS, AND UTTERLY USELESS

War is urgent. Yet amid the ghastly and pressing conflict of World War II, both sides found the luxury to evaluate unorthodox flying machines in the leisurely knowledge that they weren't needed and would have no role in the conflict. The weird Curtiss XP-55 Ascender was one of three pusher-propeller aircraft that underwent rigorous tests long after the more conventional P-51 Mustang had begun defeating the Third Reich's fighter force, the others being the Vultee XP-54 and Northrop XP-56. They were a challenge to the most resourceful test pilot—difficult to climb into, tricky to fly, and unforgiving of error. The XP-55 contributed a little to aeronautical knowledge, but by the time it was in the air it was obsolescent. It never had a chance of getting into the fight.

Engine: 1 Allison V-1710-95 liquid-cooled V-12 piston engine
Horsepower: 1,275
Maximum speed: 300 mph
Wingspan: 34 ft. 7 in.

- First flight: July 19, 1943
- Number built: 3
- Pusher propeller could be jettisoned for bailout
- 2 crashed; the survivor is in a Michigan museum

9.30.1943

NORTHROP XP-56 BLACK BULLET

THIS BULLET COULDN'T FLY STRAIGHT

The XP-56 Black Bullet was a flying wing with a vertical tail made largely of magnesium at a time when the aerodynamic properties of this volatile metal were not yet well-known. It was one of three unconventional, pusher-prop aircraft developed and tested during World War II, the others being the Vultee XP-54 "Swoose Goose" and the Curtiss XP-55 Ascender. Test pilots approached a flight in the XP-56 with great prudence, aware that it had center-of-gravity problems, and poor performance taking off and landing, as well as being generally unstable. In 1945, after one XP-56 crashed without harming its pilot—John Myers was wearing a polo helmet—the army abandoned testing, concerned the Black Bullet was unsafe.

Engine: 1 Pratt & Whitney R-2800-29 Double Wasp radial piston engine
Horsepower: 2,000
Maximum speed: 465 mph
Wingspan: 42 ft. 6 in.

- First flight: September 30, 1943
- Number built: 2
- Second aircraft made just 10 short flights
- 1 survivor, which belongs to the Smithsonian National Air and Space Museum

11.2.1943

GRUMMAN F7F TIGERCAT

A HEAVYWEIGHT WITH A STRONG NAVAL PEDIGREE

The F7F Tigercat came from Grumman, maker of so many fine naval warplanes. It was the first US Navy fighter with twin engines. Muscular and powerful, designed to fly from carrier decks, it turned out to be too heavy for service aboard ship. The Tigercat established a fine reputation with the marine corps pulling combat duty at land bases in Korea, and it excelled as both a night fighter—bagging a couple of Polikarpov Po-2 biplanes—and a fighter-bomber. It was speedy and agile with an instantaneous response to the pilot's touch and an ability to accelerate like a bat out of . . . well, you know.

Engines: 2 Pratt & Whitney R-2800-34W Double Wasp radial piston engines
Horsepower: 2,100 each
Maximum speed: 460 mph
Wingspan: 45 ft. 4 in.

- First flight: November 2, 1943
- Number built: 364
- 2 air-to-air victories in Korea
- Proposed army version, XP-65, not built
- 7 are airworthy today

11.17.1943
FISHER XP-75 EAGLE

A BIG BRUTE WITH ISSUES

The prototype XP-75 and pre-production P-75A Eagle came into existence because bigwigs in Washington wanted Fisher Body Division of General Motors to build an escort fighter. The designer was Don Berlin, who had worked for Curtiss. It was a colossal fighter but not a good one. With the engine behind the pilot and a complicated drive system connected to the propeller, the Eagle was a technical headache. It was unusually large for a fighter, but, despite major efforts to improve the design, it fell behind schedule and yielded disappointing performance. Long before delays and technical shortcomings were evident, the army ordered 2,500 P-75s but the order was soon canceled. The P-75 was shot down by the P-51 Mustang, which was escorting bombers over Berlin by the time the Eagle began flight tests.

Engine: 1 Allison V-3420-23 liquid-cooled piston engine
Horsepower: 2,885
Maximum speed: 402 mph
Wingspan: 49 ft. 4 in. (P-75A)

- First flight: November 17, 1943
- Number built: 13
- Cost: Program cost $50.12 million in 1945
- Armament: Intended to have 6 to 10 .50-caliber machine guns
- 1 survivor in a museum today

1.6.1944

MCDONNELL XP-67

A BOLD DESIGN THAT WENT UP IN SMOKE

This advanced, twin-engine fighter was the first product to be built by the planemaking dynasty founded by James S. McDonnell. Although modern-day literature calls it the Moonbat, that's a historical error: the XP-67 had no name. Intended as a long-range interceptor, the XP-67 appeared long after the need to fill that role had passed. Showing a willingness to take risk that would bring huge success to McDonnell later, the XP-67 was too complex for its era and "excruciatingly difficult to fly," according to test pilot Ed Elliott. When the only XP-67 was destroyed in a fire, the uber-costly program was abandoned while McDonnell went on to manufacture Banshees, Voodoos, and Phantoms.

Engines: 2 Continental XIV-1430-17 liquid-cooled radial engines
Horsepower: 1,350 each
Maximum speed: 405 mph
Takeoff weight: 25,400 lb.
Wingspan: 55 ft.

- First flight January 6, 1944
- Number built: 1
- Cost: $4,742,746 for the program
- A second prototype was never completed

1.8.1944

LOCKHEED F-80 SHOOTING STAR

A KEY US FIGHTER IN EARLY JET HISTORY

The F-80 Shooting Star (called the P-80 until July 1945) was the second American jet fighter after the XP-59A Airacomet, the first to become operational, and the first product of Lockheed's Burbank, California, "Skunk Works" headed by designer Clarence "Kelly" Johnson. Four Shooting Stars reached Europe before the end of World War II but did not fly combat missions. Because it had straight wings in a swept-wing age, the American F-86 Sabre and the Soviet MiG-15 outclassed the F-80 in air combat. Conceived as an air-to-air weapon, the F-80 became a valuable air-to-ground fighter-bomber during the Korean War. The F-80 was renowned as a stable platform with a mixture of aerodynamics and propulsion that made it extremely reliable in an era when most jets were not. Many US fighter pilots of the Korea and Vietnam conflicts flew the F-86 as their first fighter.

Engine: 1 Allison J33-A-35 turbojet engine
Thrust: 5,400 lb.
Maximum speed: 600 mph (Mach 0.77)
Wingspan: 38 ft. 9 in.

- First flight: January 8, 1944
- Number built: 1,715
- Lockheed built 1 F-14 "foto" reconnaissance version
- Inspired the T-33 Shooting Star trainer and F-94 interceptor
- Credited with history's first jet-versus-jet kill over a MiG-15, November 8, 1950
- 13 are in museums today; none are airworthy

REPUBLIC XP-72

"IT CLIMBED LIKE A BAT OUT OF HELL."
—Lin Hendrix, Republic test pilot

Although the Republic XP-72 made a dozen test flights, no air-to-air photo of it appears to have survived. It's possible none was taken. Intended for speed, the XP-72 was viewed in part as a remedy for Germany's high-speed V-1, the unmanned flying bomb that began raining down on England in 1944. Because the XP-72 could climb to 20,000 feet in five minutes, it was considered the ideal interceptor to cope with the robot bombs. With different propeller configurations, the two XP-72s performed superbly in tests and were easy on pilots, but by the time they appeared, the war was approaching its end and the need for an interceptor had gone away. An order for 100 production P-72s was canceled.

Engine: 1 Pratt & Whitney R-4360-13 radial engine
Horsepower: 3,500
Maximum speed: 490 mph
Weight: 17,490 lb. (maximum takeoff weight)
Wingspan: 40 ft. 11 in.

- First flight: February 2, 1944
- Armament: Intended to have 4 367mm cannons
- Range 1,200 miles

143

4.1.1944

BELL XP-77

Engine: 1 Ranger V-770-7 inverted V-12 piston engine
Horsepower: 520
Maximum speed: 330 mph
Wingspan: 27 ft. 6 in.

- First flight: April 1, 1944
- Number built: 2
- Smallest US fighter of the war
- Considered seriously underpowered
- 1 crashed, the other was scrapped

YEAH, ANOTHER ONE THAT FIRST FLEW ON APRIL FOOLS' DAY

The XP-77 was the solution to a problem that didn't exist, tailored for a mission that wasn't needed, and unable to perform as anticipated. Throughout World War II, the myth persisted that "strategic materials" such as industrial metals would be in short supply, and that alternate construction materials would be needed. Larry Bell's planemaking company fashioned a warplane constructed almost entirely of wood. This was the bantam XP-77, an exceedingly lightweight fighter at a time when US forces had no need for one. What should have been a cheap, no-frills, combat plane design was plagued with technical troubles. It might have made a great sport plane after the war, but the cockpit was cramped, the controls were difficult to handle, and visibility was poor. The XP-77 program was hastily terminated in December 1944.

4.4.1944
HILLER XH-44 HILLER-COPTER

FIRST EFFORT FROM A PIONEER DESIGNER

In 1944, at age eighteen, Stanley Hiller Jr. designed the first US helicopter with coaxial rotors. The XH-44 was the first helicopter to fly with all-metal blades and a rigid rotor. Hiller wanted the counter-rotating coaxial configuration to distinguish his efforts from the Sikorsky single main rotor designs that dominated the helicopter industry. He conducted the first tie-down tests on his parents' driveway, tested the XH-44 with amphibious floats in the family's swimming pool, and conducted the first flight at Berkeley where he was a student. This was a unique approach to helicopter flying, but it didn't sell.

- First flight: July 4, 1944
- Number built: 1
- First flight: at the University of California at Berkeley Memorial Stadium
- Now on display at the Smithsonian

Engine: 1 Lycoming piston engine
Horsepower: 125
Cruising speed: 42 mph
Main rotor diameter: 15 ft.

5.6.1944
DOUGLAS XB-42 MIXMASTER

OUTRAGEOUSLY INTERESTING— AND FILLED WITH PROMISE

The Douglas XB-42, with its "pusher" propellers, resembled Mom's kitchen-counter gadget but showed real promise during World War II. Alas, after setting a transcontinental speed record in 1945 by crossing the United States in five hours and seventeen minutes, the first XB-42 was lost in a crash. The second flew with underwing jet engines added but suffered a landing mishap and was removed from inventory in 1949. This design led to the later XB-43 jet bomber.

Engines: 2 Allison V-1710 engines (one per prop)
Horsepower: 1,325 each
Maximum speed: 445 mph
Wingspan: 70 ft. 6 in.

- First flight: May 6, 1944
- Number built: 2
- Crew: 3

LOCKHEED XP-58 CHAIN LIGHTNING

AUDACIOUS, DIFFICULT, AND A DELIGHT TO FLY

The XP-58 Chain Lightning was an outrageously big idea in a busy aircraft industry obsessed with perfecting a "convoy fighter" able to travel vast distances with heavy armament. Derived from the P-38 Lightning, the XP-58 was doomed by constant changes in its powerplant and by shifting war needs. For accountants, the XP-58 was a ledger-book nightmare, wreaking stratospheric costs. For wrench-turners, the XP-58 was a maintenance migraine. But pilots found it an easy chair in the sky, with quick and responsive controls. In some alternate universe, the XP-58 might have participated in the invasion of Japan.

Engines: 2 Allison V-3420 24-cylinder liquid-cooled radial engines
Horsepower: 3,000 each
Cruising speed: 436 mph
Wingspan: 70 ft.

- First flight: June 6, 1944
- Number built: 2 planned; just 1 built
- Cost: Total XP-58 program cost: $2,345,107
- Armament: Guns were never installed
- Made just 25 test flights

6.25.1944
RYAN FR FIREBALL

ONE TURNING, ONE BURNING . . .

The Ryan FR Fireball was a "propjet" with a piston engine in the nose and a jet in the tail, similar in concept to the Convair XP-81. This was to be the carrier-based warplane for the final fight against Japan, but although a squadron was formed, the war ended before the Fireball could see combat. Combining a propeller at one end and a hot exhaust at the other seemed a good idea, but it produced a fighter that was structurally too weak for sustained carrier-deck operations, among other problems.

- First flight: June 25, 1944
- Number built: 66
- A high-flyer with a 43,100-foot ceiling

Engines: 1 Wright R-1820-72W Cyclone piston engine plus 1 General Electric I-16 (J31-GE-3) turbojet engine

Horsepower: 1,350 (R-1820) plus 1,600 lb. thrust (J31)

Maximum speed: 404 mph

Wingspan: 50 ft. 6 in.

11.9.1944
BOEING C-97 STRATOFREIGHTER

IT TRUNDLED ALONG AND THEY LOVED IT

The big, burly C-97 Stratofreighter was a military transport derived from the B-29 Superfortress bomber and used to inspire a civilian airliner version, the 377 Stratocruiser. It was unfortunately too slow to effectively refuel fast jets, even after augmented jet power was added to KC-97L models. Those R4360 engines were never easy to maintain and the C-97 was sometimes a challenge to a busy pilot, but this aircraft won respect and affection during its long service career. The basic design inspired the unusual Guppy and Super Guppy.

- First flight: November 9, 1944
- Number built: 888 C-97s (including 811 KC-97 tankers)
- C-97s hauled cargo in the Berlin Airlift, the Korean War, and the Vietnam War
- Hawaiian musician Don Ho was a C-97 pilot

Engines: 4 Pratt & Whitney R-4360B Wasp Major radial piston engines

Horsepower: 3,500 each

Maximum speed: 375 mph

Wingspan: 141 ft. 3 in.

BOEING XF8B-1

A MUSCULAR MILITARY MACHINE

The XF8B-1 was the largest naval warplane of its era and the last fighter ever to be built entirely by Boeing. Intended to fly missions against the Japanese home islands outside the range of Japanese land-based aircraft, the XF8B-1 was designed to handle a variety of roles, including interceptor, fighter, dive-bomber, and torpedo bomber. The XF8B-1 performed brilliantly in tests, but the war ended and jet-powered aircraft came into vogue. Only a handful of pilots experienced the ease, comfort, power, and brawn of this heavyweight.

Engine: 1 Pratt & Whitney R-4360 Wasp Major radial piston engine
Horsepower: 2,500
Cruising speed: 190 mph
Wingspan: 54 ft.

- First flight: November 27, 1944
- Number built: 3
- Navy plane, but the army tested it, too
- Heavy and nimble at the same time
- No survivors today

1945

VOUGHT XF5U-1

WHEN PILING ON ISN'T THE SOLUTION

Developed from the Vought V-173, distantly related to the Arup S-2, and designed by Charles H. Zimmerman, the pancake-shaped XF5U-1 was intended to be the US Navy's next great carrier-based fighter. Instead, it appears in retrospect to have been way too much of a good idea. If the V-173 was light and agile, the XF5U-1 weighed in like an anvil. In fact, it was so solidly built that when its end came, it had to be scrapped using a wrecking ball. Overbuilding, technical delays, changes in navy needs, the end of World War II, and a persistent gearbox problem prevented the heavy XF5U-1 from ever taking to the air. Shortsightedness prevented it from being saved for a museum.

Engines: 2 Pratt & Whitney R-2000 radial engines
Horsepower: 1,350 each
Maximum speed: 475 mph (maybe)
Wingspan: 32 ft. 6 in.

- First flight: Planned for 1945, but didn't happen
- Number built: 2 (1 completed)
- Underwent several ground taxi tests
- Canceled by the navy March 17, 1947

2.11.1945
CONVAIR XP-81

WELL, IT SEEMED LIKE AN IDEA . . .

The idea: a propeller turning in front and a jet blowing out the back. The Convair XP-81 was one of two "propjet" fighters developed for World War II, the other being the Ryan FR Fireball. The XP-81 was explicitly meant to be a long-range escort fighter for those arduous, over-water missions to Japan. Nothing was wrong with the "propjet" concept, but development of the TG-100 turboprop engine (later called the XT31) was delayed and the XP-81 flew initially with a Merlin piston engine, subsequently becoming the first US turboprop fighter to fly on December 21, 1945. With a commodious perch for the pilot, the XP-81 performed brilliantly—but only after the war was over and the pure-jet age was dawning.

Engines: 1 General Electric TG-100 (XT31) turboprop engine plus 1 General Electric J33-GE-5 turbojet engine

Horsepower: 2,300 (XT31) plus 3,750 lb. thrust (J33)

Maximum speed: 507 mph

Wingspan: 50 ft. 6 in.

- First flight: February 11, 1945
- Number built: 2
- Cost: $6 million for the program in 1945
- An order for 13 YP-81 models was canceled
- Both XP-81s are in museum storage today

2.25.1945

BELL XP-83

A JET FIGHTER THAT WASN'T QUITE GOOD ENOUGH

The XP-83 was portly—and big—for a reason: the brass in the newly built Pentagon Building wanted greater range and endurance than offered by other first-generation jets. But the XP-83 was underpowered and unstable, and a redesign of its tail surfaces helped only a little. Inferior to the P-80 Shooting Star (or F-80), the XP-83 became a powerplant test bed. The first aircraft was lost in a non-fatal mishap, and the second flew only briefly, before officials concluded that this aircraft offered no significant advantage over others then being developed.

Engines: 2 General Electric J33-GE-5 turbojet engines
Thrust: 4,000 lb. each
Maximum speed: 522 mph
Weight: 26,024 lb. (gross)
Wingspan: 53 ft.

- First flight: February 25, 1945
- Number built: 2
- Had no speed brakes, which meant a rapid approach speed
- Considered sluggish on takeoff and climbout
- No survivors today

3.1945

PIASECKI HRP RESCUER

A FRUITFUL SHAPE, FUN, BUT A LITTLE LIMP

This is the original "Flying Banana," the evocative term coined by designer Frank Piasecki for the tandem, twin-rotor configuration pioneered with his HRP Rescuer. It really did look like a banana: to make certain the rotors did not hit each other, the rear of the fuselage curved upward so the rear rotor was higher than the forward rotor, based on a design by Drago "Gish" Jovanovich, who worked for Piasecki. The mostly fabric-covered HRP was sorely underpowered but was a joy to fly nonetheless. When the Piasecki firm became Vertol and, later, Boeing, this twin-tandem design influenced helicopters such as the H-21 Shawnee and CH-47 Chinook.

Engine: 1 Pratt & Whitney R-1840-AN-1 radial engine, driving twin rotors
Horsepower: 600
Maximum speed: 105 mph
Diameter of both main rotors: 41 ft.

- First flight: March 1, 1946
- Number built: 28 (3 for the coast guard)
- Cost: $256,912 each in 1948
- Capacity: 2 crewmen plus 8 to 10 passengers

3.18.1945

DOUGLAS A-1 SKYRAIDER

THE AIRPLANE THAT DID EVERYTHING

The Douglas A-1 Skyraider, initially named the Dauntless II and known as the AD until 1962, was big, tough, noisy, and much beloved. Pilots joked that the enemy couldn't kill you in it, but you might perish slipping on the quantities of oil its engine famously leaked. A workhorse of the US Navy and Marine Corps in the Korean War and thereafter, the Skyraider belatedly joined the US Air Force, which used single-seat (A-1H, A-1J) and multi-place (A-1E, A-1G) models in Vietnam. Two pilots of the "Spad"—the Skyraider's Vietnam-era nickname, a throwback to the French SPADs of World War I—were awarded the Medal of Honor for valor in combat. Although these were propeller-driven warplanes and the other side had jets, two Skyraiders shot down MiGs in Vietnam. Many are on the air show circuit today.

Engine: 1 Wright R-33560-26WA Duplex-Cyclone radial piston engine
Horsepower: 2,700
Maximum speed: 322 mph
Wingspan: 50 ft.

- First flight: March 18, 1945
- Number built: 3,180
- Served from 1946 to 1970

NORTH AMERICAN F-82 TWIN MUSTANG

EVEN IF IT DOESN'T LOOK RIGHT, IT IS—REALLY

If you take two P-51 Mustang fuselages and attach them, it'll be twice as good, right? Well, not exactly, but the F-82 Twin Mustang (P-82 until July 1948), which looked like an oddball, was a practical long-range escort fighter. Hey, it was even a little faster than a P-51. Among its milestones, it was the last piston-engined fighter ordered into production in the United States, and it scored the first air-to-air victory in the Korean War, downing a North Korean Yakovlev. With a pilot on the left and a navigator on the right, the Twin Mustang was not the cobbled-together menagerie it appeared to be but, rather, an integrated design that handled and maneuvered with the best of them.

Engines: 2 Allison V-1710-143/145 liquid-cooled piston engines
Horsepower: 1,380 each
Maximum speed: 482 mph
Wingspan: 51 ft. 3 in.

- First flight: June 15, 1945
- Number built: 272
- Cost: $215,154 in 1946
- Crew: 2 (pilot, navigator)
- 5 survive today in museums

NORTHROP F-15 REPORTER

A FOUR-LETTER WORD BEGINNING WITH "F"

Today, the "F-15" is a jet fighter. During the 1940s, "F-planes" were camera-equipped reconnaissance—or "foto"—aircraft. The F-15 Reporter was derived from the P-61 Black Widow with changes that optimized it for high-speed photo taking. The changes introduced a more streamlined fuselage and a tandem cockpit. The Reporter arrived too late for World War II but was on duty at a US base in Japan as late as 1949, and F-15 aerial photographs of the Korean Peninsula proved vital in 1950, when North Korea invaded the south. The National Advisory Committee on Aeronautics—predecessor of NASA—used an F-15 for drop tests of scale models of experimental aircraft.

Engines: 2 Pratt & Whitney R-2800-73 Double Wasp supercharged radial piston engines
Horsepower: 2,285 each
Maximum speed: 440 mph
Wingspan: 66 ft.

- First flight: July 3, 1945
- Number built: 36
- Crew: 2—pilot, camera operator
- Served from 1945 to 1949
- Redesignated RF-61D in 1948

NORTHROP XP-79B

A TRAGIC IDEA BUILT ON GOOD INTENTIONS

Here's an idea. How about a flying-wing battering ram to destroy enemy planes by slicing through them like a butter knife? Oh, and let's put the pilot in the prone position, flying it using a tiller bar. Sadly, the XP-79B flew only once, with fatal results—the only aircraft ever to be terminated on the day of its maiden flight. The prone-pilot thing was a bummer and the rocket-powered XP-79A version was never built. On the only flight of the jet-powered XP-79B, much-loved test pilot Harry Crosby went into a stall and a nose-down spin. Crosby escaped but was struck by a portion of the plane and his parachute never opened. The program was abandoned. The flying wing idea lives on in today's B-2 Spirit stealth bomber, but no operational aircraft has ever carried a pilot lying on his stomach.

Engines: 2 Westinghouse 19B turbojet engines
Thrust: 1,150 lb.
Maximum speed: 547 mph
Wingspan: 38 ft.

- First flight: September 12, 1945
- Number built: 2 ordered but only 1 built
- An adventurous idea that turned deadly
- Designed as a rocket, flew as a jet

12.8.1945
BELL 47

THAT MEDEVAC HELO IN *M*A*S*H* AND MUCH MORE

Larry Bell and his chief designer Arthur M. Young were only a couple of years behind Igor Sikorsky in pioneering the helicopter in America. Bell's two-blade, single-engine Model 47 (the US Army H-13 Sioux) was a spectacular success in military and civilian attire. US Navy versions trained pilots and explored the Antarctic. Early models had an open cockpit, but the bubble canopy that adorned most of these helicopters is a distinguishing feature familiar to pilots, air show crowds, and Robert Altman fans.

Engine: 1 Lycoming TVO-435-F1A six-cylinder piston engine (47G-3B)
Horsepower: 280
Maximum speed: 105 mph
Rotor diameter: 37 ft. 2 in.

- First flight: December 8, 1945
- Number built: About 5,600
- US military versions: R-13, H-13, HTL, HUL
- Manufactured under license in Britain, Italy, and Japan
- Set an altitude record of 18,550 ft. on May 13, 1949

12.19.1945
GRUMMAN AF GUARDIAN

THE ANSWER TO LURKING SOVIET SUBMARINES

An unsung hero of the Cold War and almost unremembered as a participant in Korea, the Grumman AF Guardian was the largest single-engine warplane to operate from US aircraft carriers. After the navy rejected torpedo-bomber versions called the XTB3F (later the AF-1), it deployed Guardians in two-plane, hunter-killer teams using the AF-2W (the hunter, with radar in a "guppy" bulge under its belly) and AF-2S (the killer, carrying munitions). A final version, the AF-3S, combined both missions in one airframe. The Guardian was unpopular with pilots for being heavy on the controls and underpowered. It remained on duty only from 1952 to 1957.

Engine: 1 Pratt & Whitney R-2800-48W Double Wasp radial engine
Horsepower: 2,400
Operating speed: 253 mph
Wingspan: 60 ft. 8 in.

- First flight: December 19, 1945
- Number built: 389
- Armament: AF-2S carried 4,000 lb. of bombs and depth charges
- Replaced by Grumman S2F Tracker

12.22.1945
BEECH BONANZA

LIFE'S A BEECH

Kansas air pioneers Walter and Olive Beech gave us the first all-metal postwar private plane that could be afforded by, well, a physician. It's a four- to six-seat general-aviation aircraft often called the "doctor killer" not because there's anything wrong with the design—there isn't—but because your friendly cardiologist doesn't spend enough hours in the cockpit to stay current. Even the safest aircraft can crash, and Bonanza crashes have claimed the lives of Buddy Holly and company (1959), Jim Reeves (1964), and game show host Peter Tomarken (2006). But this model is believed to have made more than ten million successful flights for weekend fun and utility business travel. From A to V, or ailerons to V-tail—(found on most versions)—it's all in the details. Others have tried to compete, but the Bonanza is still coming off assembly lines today. Okay, so newer versions have a standard tail with rudder and elevators, but who's perfect? The Wichita Wonder proves the old adage that if it looks right, it will fly right. Much of the credit belongs to Ralph Harmon, unsung head of the Beech design team.

Engine: Continental IO-520-B engine
Horsepower: 260
Cruising speed: 203 mph
Wingspan: 27 ft. 6 in.

- First flight: December 22, 1945
- Number built: 17,000
- Cost: About $1,800 in 1957; about $800,000 in 2014
- Most had really cool V-tail with an elevator-rudder called a "ruddervator"
- In production longer than any other aircraft

1946
BELL H-12

COULDA, SHOULDA, WOULDA—AND DIDN'T

This was a military-only helicopter, the Model 48 in Bell corporate jargon, whose moment never quite arrived. The joint army–air force H-12 (R-12 before July 1948) was bashed in a Pentagon report that said the rotorcraft would "require considerable development and time delay before it was a successful ship." It was early days for helicopters and the H-12's main rotor system was problem-plagued. H-12s flew in exercises, but with better helicopters available, they were hastily consigned to the scrap heap—despite their potential value to museums.

Engine: 1 Pratt & Whitney R-1340-55 Wasp piston engine (H-12B)
Horsepower: 600
Cruising speed: 90 mph
Main rotor diameter: 47 ft. 6 in.

- First flight: 1946
- Number built: 13 in 3 versions
- Cost: Just $175,00 in 1946
- Among criticisms was that it was loud for military use

1.19.1946

BELL X-1

BULLET-SHAPED EXPLORER OF THE UNKNOWN

The Bell XS-1 (for "experimental, supersonic") achieved humankind's first flight faster than sound on October 14, 1947, piloted by Capt. Charles E. Yeager, and was redesignated the X-1 months later. (There have been claims that other aircraft achieved this feat earlier, but experts have refuted this.) The small rocket research plane resembled the spaceships seen in *Flash Gordon* movie serials of the 1930s. The XS-1 was the progenitor of four improved models, including the X-1A, which had more fuel (and more rocket burn time) and reached a speed of 1,650 miles per hour and an altitude of 90,000 feet. The X-1E model took pilots to the edge of space. These aircraft set the stage for advanced research by "X-Planes" in the 1950s and 1960s.

Engine: 1 Reaction Motors XLR-11-RM3 liquid fuel rocket engine
Thrust: 6,000 lb.
Maximum speed: 957 mph
Wingspan: 28 ft.

- First flight: January 19, 1946
- Carried aloft by a B-29 "mother ship"
- Landed in the desert at Muroc, California
- 3 X-1 variants are in museums today

REPUBLIC XF-12 RAINBOW

2.4.1946

SHAPED LIKE A BULLET AND FLEW LIKE ONE

Among the few who know about the XF-12 Rainbow at all, some have called it the most beautiful airplane ever built. One of the "F-planes," or "foto" reconnaissance aircraft, designed during World War II, the XF-12—which was redesignated XR-12 in July 1948—looks like the work of industrial design artists rather than aeronautical engineers. Its sleek, pointy shape makes it appear to be flying even faster than it really is—and it was a very fast propeller-driven aircraft. Sadly, the end of World War II ended the need for the XF-12, and neither of those built has survived today.

Engines: 4 Pratt & Whitney R-4360-31 Wasp Major radial engines
Horsepower: 3,250 each
Maximum speed: 480 mph
Wingspan: 129 ft.1 in.

- First flight: February 4, 1946
- Number built: 2
- Cost: $1.25 million in 1946
- Proposed airliner version was never built

2.15.1946
DOUGLAS DC-6

AN ELEGANT AND MUCH-ADMIRED POSTWAR PROPLINER

The Douglas DC-6 was a classy, pressurized, propeller-driven airliner designed for the military (and used as the air force C-118 and navy R6D Liftmaster) but grabbed up by civilian airlines in the postwar years. It filled a gap between the DC-4 and DC-7 in the family of propliners from Donald Douglas's fabled planemaking company. Passengers rode the DC-6 in cushioned seats with plenty of elbowroom (and lots of cigarette smoke) while pilots marveled at the spaciousness of its flight deck. One DC-6, the *Independence*, became a flying White House for President Harry S. Truman.

Engines: 4 Pratt & Whitney R-2800 Double Wasp piston engines
Horsepower: 1,800 each
Cruising speed: 311 mph
Wingspan: 117 ft. 6 in.

- First flight: February 15, 1946
- Capacity: 48 to 68 passengers
- First deliveries to: American Airlines and United Airlines
- Won a Ralston Foundation design award in 1949

2.28.1946

REPUBLIC F-84 THUNDERJET

VERY BUSY DURING KOREA AND THE COLD WAR

The F-84 Thunderjet (called the P-84 until July 1948) was a jet fighter that became an air-to-ground workhorse in the Korean War and a bulwark of NATO defenses. The straight-wing Thunderjets were F-84A to E and F-84G models (the latter the first fighter built from the start to receive air-to-air refueling), and should not be confused with the swept-wing F-84F Thunderstreak or XF-84H Thunderscreech. Many F-84s participated in tests, including tests of a zero-length launcher that dispensed with the need for a runway for takeoff (pictured). Like most Republic products, the Thunderjet gave its pilot a roomy, comfortable cockpit and plenty of power.

Engine: 1 Allison J35-A-29 turbojet engine
Thrust: 5,560 lb.
Cruising speed: 622 mph (Mach 0.81)
Wingspan: 36 ft. 5 in.

- First flight: February 28, 1946
- Cost: $237,247 in 1950
- Flew 86,408 missions in Korea
- Credited with 8 aerial victories over the MiG-15
- Stood alert in Europe with nuclear weapons
- Served in 14 air forces

HUGHES XF-11

BEAUTIFUL AND PROMISING BUT DELAYED AND DIFFICULT

Howard Hughes was a genius, among many attributes, but a couple of his grandest ideas were tailored for World War II and were delayed too long to be part of that conflict. The XF-11, one of the "F-planes" of the war era was beautiful to see but difficult to fly and pricey to maintain. Hughes mishandled the maiden flight and crashed in Culver City, California, narrowly surviving the destruction of the first XF-11. The prototype's contra-rotating propellers were replaced with conventional props on the second ship, which Hughes also piloted, but the XF-11 was simply too complex, too costly—and too late.

Engines: 2 Pratt & Whitney R-4360-31 radial piston engines
Horsepower: 3,000 each
Maximum speed: 450 mph
Wingspan: 101 ft. 4 in.

- First flight: July 7, 1946
- Number built: 2
- Crew: 2—pilot and photographer
- 1 crashed
- Piloted by Leonardo DiCaprio in *The Aviator* (2004)

CONSOLIDATED B-36 PEACEMAKER

"MORE COMPLICATED THAN A MARCHING BAND" —B-36 pilot Col. James Murphy

The B-36 was big, complicated, loud, and solid as a brick, and for a decade it was the principal US strategic bomber, ready on minutes' notice for a nuclear strike on the Soviet Union. It was the largest propeller-driven aircraft ever to serve operationally. Most were boosted by four jet engines added to the initial powerplant of six props. The long pan of a B-36 takeoff in the James Stewart movie *Strategic Air Command* (1955) was one of the most dramatic moments in film. Some B-36s were equipped to carry F-84 parasite fighters while others carried cameras on reconnaissance missions. Costly to maintain and fly, the B-36 is remembered today for its comfort, size, and strength.

Engines: 6 Pratt & Whitney R-4360-53 Wasp Major radial engines plus 4 General Electric J47 turbojet engines

Horsepower: 3,800 per R-4360

Thrust: 5,200 lb. per J47

Maximum speed: 418 mph

Wingspan: 230 ft.

- First flight: August 8, 1946
- Number built: 384
- Crew: Flight crew of 13
- Armament: Able to carry 73,000 lb. of bombs
- 5 are in museums today

9.11.1946
NORTH AMERICAN FJ-1 FURY

COMFORTABLE, RELIABLE— BUT WITH STRAIGHT WINGS

Among the first generation of US Navy carrier-based jet fighters, the FJ-1 Fury was almost alone in actually reaching squadron service. The Fury had a unique feature that enabled it to "kneel," nose-down, for ease of maintenance, but because of its high-set fuselage, it remained a difficult aircraft to maintain. The feature the Fury needed most and lacked was swept wings. When those were added to a revised version of the basic design, this aircraft evolved into the FJ-2 Fury and the F-86 Sabre.

Engine: 1 Chevrolet/Allison TG-180 (J35-GE-2) turbojet engine
Thrust: 3,820 lb.
Maximum speed: 489 mph
Wingspan: 38 ft. 1 inch

- First flight: September 11, 1946
- Number built: 33 (3 XFJ-1, 30 FJ-1)
- Began as a jet-powered P-51 Mustang
- 2 are in museums today; neither is airworthy

10.2.1946
VOUGHT F6U PIRATE

ONE OF THE FIRST NAVAL JET FIGHTERS

The F6U Pirate came from the same planemaking company that gave the world the F4U Corsair, but Vought's little-known first jet was in some ways inferior to its immortal prop-driven fighter. It was a pioneer in jet propulsion and the first naval fighter with an afterburner, but it was sluggish and slow, in part because of the disappointing performance of early turbojet engines. Development and production were disrupted by Vought's 1948 move from Stratford, Connecticut, to Dallas, Texas. In an age when not having a propeller out front was a new experience, pilots reveled in the great ride the Pirate provided, but the aircraft was canceled without ever reaching a squadron.

Engine: 1 Westinghouse J34-WE-30A turbojet engine with afterburner
Thrust: 3,150 lb.
Maximum speed: 596 mph
Wingspan: 37 ft. 7 in.

- First flight: October 2, 1946
- Number built: 33
- 1 became the F6U-1P reconnaissance version
- 1 survives today in a museum

RYAN XF2R DARK SHARK

IT HAD EVERYTHING, INCLUDING GOOD LOOKS

In a postwar age of experimentation, the XF2R Dark Shark combined a turboprop engine in the nose with a jet in the tail, features it shared with the Convair XP-81. The navy loved it as a potential carrier-based fighter but was too heavily invested in pure jet aircraft to spend on a turboprop-jet combo. The air force, which was flying the XP-81, liked it a lot, and evaluated a version with a different jet engine, the Westinghouse J34, in the tail. In the hands of civilian, navy, and air force pilots the XF2R-1 with the original powerplant, and the XF2R-2—the same airframe with the J34— proved to be a trouble-free, responsive, highly maneuverable fighter—but was not, alas, as fast as a pure jet. Pilots loved it and fighter experts wanted it, but in the end only one Dark Shark was built—and nobody bothered to save it.

Engine: 1 General Electric T31-GE-1 turboprop engine plus 1 General Electric J31-GE-3 turbojet engine
Horsepower: 1,750 shaft (T31) plus 1,600 lb. thrust (J31)
Maximum speed: 497 mph
Weight: 11,000 lb. (a lightweight)
Wingspan: 42 ft.

- First flight: November 1, 1946
- Number built: 1
- Armament: 4 .50-caliber Browning M2 machine guns
- The last manned aircraft built by Ryan, builder of Lindbergh's *Spirit of St. Louis*
- The sole aircraft was scrapped

LOCKHEED R6O-1 CONSTITUTION

THE NAVY'S TRANSPORT BEHEMOTH

The looming, double-deck R6O-1 Constitution was meant to improve on the transport capabilities of US Navy flying boats. Designed by a team led by Willis Hawkins, the R6O-1 (re-named the R6V-1 in 1951) was the largest landplane ever operated by the navy and had enormous capacity to move people and equipment overseas. It was a terrific symbol of American might in the Cold War 1950s and a huge hit at air shows. This was a friendly giant, popular with crews and passengers, but it was too big for routine duties and it amounted to navy encroachment on an air force mission. The two Constitutions served operationally for several years before being retired and later scrapped.

Engines: 4 Pratt & Whitney R-4360 radial piston engines
Horsepower: 3,000 each
Maximum speed: 303 mph
Wingspan: 189 ft. 1 inch

- First flight: November 9, 1946
- Number built: 2
- Capacity: Crew of 12, capacity for 168 passengers
- Man-sized tunnels within the wings permitted engine access
- Neither survives today

BOWLUS-NELSON BB-1 DRAGONFLY

A GREAT-LOOKING MOTOR GLIDER THAT NEEDED A LITTLE MORE OOOMPH

This aircraft had every prospect of being perfect for the adventurer—a two-seat, strut-braced, high-wing motor glider intended for fun flying with all the elements out there right around the pilot. The designer was Hawley Bowlus, a trailblazing engineer in sport glider design. The impetus for this aircraft came from engine maker and sailplane pilot Ted Nelson, whose motor, unfortunately, turned out to offer insufficient power. The Dragonfly looks great, and the cockpit feels comfortable, but it turned out to have a disappointing climb rate and glide ratio. Nelson eventually decided not to continue his partnership with Bowlus, so production of the Dragonfly came to an end.

Engine: 1 Nelson H-44 four-cylinder, two-stroke engine
Horsepower: 16
Maximum speed: 38 mph
Wingspan: 47 ft. 4 in.

- First flight: 1947
- Number built: 7
- Two-bladed, 3-ft.-6-in. wooden propeller

MCDONNELL F2H BANSHEE

COMFY, CARRIER-BASED FIGHTER

The F2H Banshee bombed North Korea in real life and in James Michener's novel *The Bridges at Toko-Ri*—but not in the William Holden movie, which used the F9F Panther instead. The Banshee was one of the primary US fighters of the Korean War, although it never claimed an air-to-air victory and was always somewhat overshadowed by the Panther. The Banshee was bigger, substantially heavier, and more comfortable; pilots who flew both gave the Banshee higher marks for instrument layout and control responsiveness.

- First flight: January 11, 1947
- Number built: 895
- Royal Canadian Navy used 39 Banshees on its aircraft carrier *Bonaventure*
- A dozen are in museums today; none is flyable

Engines: 2 Westinghouse J34-WE-34 turbojet engines
Thrust: 3,250 lb. each
Maximum speed: 580 mph
Wingspan: 41 ft. 9 in.

3.16.1947
CONVAIR LINERS

FOR PILOTS AND PASSENGERS, POSTWAR PROMISE

The Convair 240, 340, and 440—collectively dubbed the Convair Liners—were the closest thing to a successful post–World War II attempt to replace the aging Douglas DC-3. To a new pilot entering civilian flying after the war, a Convair Liner offered a roomy flight deck, easy handling, responsive controls, and plenty of power. To passengers, many experiencing airline travel for the first time aboard a Convair Liner, roominess meant comfort, and these aircraft offered plenty of both.

Engines: 2 Pratt & Whitney R-2800 Double Wasp radial engines
Horsepower: 2,400 each
Maximum speed: 337 mph
Wingspan: 105 ft. 4 in.

- First flight: March 16, 1947
- Cost: $316,000 in 1947; about $3 million today
- Crew: Pilot, co-pilot, engineer and 2 stewardesses (typically)
- Convair was an abbreviated version of the name Consolidated Vultee Aircraft

3.17.1947
NORTH AMERICAN B-45 TORNADO

Engines: 4 General Electric J46-GE-13 turbojet engines
Thrust: 5,200 lb. each
Maximum speed: 569 mph
Wingspan: 89 ft. 1 in.

JET-POWERED BOMB HAULER

The B-45 was the first operational American jet bomber and part of the US nuclear deterrent. It became the RB-45 reconnaissance aircraft, flying clandestine missions near and over Soviet territory in the hands of American and British pilots. In 1950, one became the first aircraft of any type to be shot down by a Soviet MiG-15 fighter. It was maintenance intensive and difficult to fly, but when all was going well, it out-performed every warplane in its class.

- First flight: March 17, 1947
- Number built: 143
- Cost: About $1 million in 1949
- Armament: 2 machine guns in tail; bombload 22,000 lb.

CONVAIR XB-46

SPECTACULARLY BEAUTIFUL BUT NOT VERY GOOD

The Convair XB-46 bomber would have made the front row in any beauty contest with its elegant shape and sleek lines. However, it was long delayed in development, and suffered glitches with its engine de-icing, cabin air system, and vertical oscillations that were caused by harmonic resonance between the wing and flight surfaces. It would have been nearly impossible for the three-man crew to take to their parachutes, since the pneumatic system was needed to hold the egress hatch open against the airstream. Beautiful but high maintenance, the XB-46 was cancelled in the year of its first flight.

Engines: 4 Allison J35-A-3 turbojets
Thrust: 4,000 lb. each
Maximum speed: 545 mph
Wingspan: 113 ft.

- First flight: April 2, 1947
- Number built: 1
- Crew: 3
- Made 64 flights totaling 127 hours

5.21.1947
FULTON AIRPHIBIAN

THE MOST VISIBLE OF THE FLYING CAR DESIGNS

Robert E. Fulton Jr. designed the best-known flying car. His Airphibian shed its wings, tail, and three-bladed propeller when it made the transition from sky to road. Normal turning of the steering wheel provided steering on the highway while a rudder pedal served as the brake. The Airphibian worked just fine, thank you, but America wasn't ready for a flying car—and still isn't.

Engine: 1 Franklin 6A4-165-B3 piston engine
Horsepower: 165
Cruising speed in flight: 143 mph
Highway speed: 55 mph
Wingspan: 36 ft. 5 in.

- First flight: May 21, 1947
- Number built: 4
- Prototypes drove 200,000 miles and made 6,000 car/plane conversions
- 1 of only 2 roadable aircraft types ever certified by the feds
- The Smithsonian displays 1

8.29.1947
MCDONNELL XH-20 LITTLE HENRY

IN THIS HELICOPTER, YOU'RE AN OUTDOORSMAN, SO TO SPEAK

It was an idea worth trying, even if it exposed the pilot to all the elements and was definitely not for those afraid of heights. The XH-20 Little Henry, named for a cartoon character, was a research helicopter consisting of welded tubes carried on three vertical legs ending in free-castoring wheels, coupled with ramjet-powered rotors. The XH-20 turned out to be unbearably loud, and plans for an enlarged version, the XH-29, were cancelled.

Engines: 2 McDonnell ram jet engines, 1 mounted at each rotor tip
Rotor tip speed: 410 mph
Maximum forward speed: 50 mph
Weight: 290 lb. empty
Rotor diameter: 20 ft.

- First flight: August 29, 1947
- Number built: 2
- 1 is in a museum today

CHASE C-122 AVITRUC

TRUCKING ALONG IN SMALL NUMBERS FOR A SHORT TIME

The C-122 Avitruc ("Aviation Truck") was a military transport designed by Michael Stroukoff's Chase Aircraft Company and produced in uneconomically small numbers in the late 1940s, first as a glider (XCG-18A), but definitively in powered form. The C-122 first flew on the day the US Air Force became an independent service branch. Chase later became embroiled in a corporate scandal after Henry J. Kaiser bought it—with consequences for the subsequent C-123 aircraft—but nothing was wrong with the C-122, which was built in versions designated YC-122 (one), YC-122A (two), YC-122B (a conversion), and YC-122C (nine built). C-122s served dutifully with a troop carrier squadron at Ardmore Air Force Base, Oklahoma, but it was costly to keep such a small fleet in operation. After the type was retired in 1957, a C-122 fuselage was used as the basis for the Hiller X-18.

Engines: 2 Wright R-1820-101 radial piston engines
Horsepower: 1,425 each
Maximum speed: 240 mph
Wingspan: 95 ft. 8 in.

- First flight: September 18, 1947
- Number built: 12 C-122s, following 6 XG-18A gliders
- Capacity: Carried 30 troops or 24 litter patients
- 1 pilot, Capt. Phillip C. Gromley, logged 1,000 hours in the C-122

10.1.1947

NORTH AMERICAN F-86 SABRE

LOVELY AND LETHAL

Beautiful and capable, the F-86 Sabre prevailed over the Soviet MiG-15 in Korea, made the swept wing a routine feature, and served widely around the world. It was the West's most numerous fighter of its era. Developed by a North American Aviation Inc. design team that had access to World War II German sweptwing technology, the F-86 began as an air-to-air fighter but ultimately served as an all-weather interceptor and, in most recent times, as a warbird—a restored military aircraft that thrills crowds at air shows. One pilot called the day-fighter version "the sports car of the skies." Another called the Sabre "a real pedigree."

Engine: 1 General Electric J47-GE-27 turbojet engine (F-86F)
Thrust: 7,200 lb.
Maximum speed: 688 mph
Wingspan: 39 ft. 1 in.

- First flight: October 1, 1947
- Number built: 6,297 in the United States, 2,448 elsewhere
- Some argue it flew faster than sound before Chuck Yeager's XS-1 on October 14, 1947
- Inspired the navy's FJ-2 and FJ-3 Fury
- Began life as the XP-86 "experimental pursuit" aircraft

10.24.1947
GRUMMAN SA-16 ALBATROSS

THE LAST US MILITARY FLYING BOAT

This amphibious flying boat was a Good Samaritan in peacetime and a combat-rescue angel in Korea and Vietnam. Most were used by the air force, where the Albatross earned a reputation for ruggedness and seaworthiness. Its deep-V hull cross-section and substantial length enabled it to land and take off on the open sea. The HU-16B model, with a widened wing, remained in US service into the 1970s, and some were painted black and given special-operations duties. Fondly called the "Goat" in the coast guard, which was the last service branch to operate the aircraft, the Albatross was the last seaplane in US military service.

Engines: 2 Wright R-1820-76 Cyclone radial piston engines
Horsepower: 1,425 each
Maximum speed: 236 mph
Wingspan: 96 ft. 8 in.

- First flight: October 24, 1947
- First service: Entered US service in 1949
- Number built: 466

11.2.1947
HUGHES H-4 HERCULES

HOWARD HUGHES' REALLY BIG MASTERPIECE

The one-of-a-kind, 400,000-pound H-4 Hercules is the largest flying boat ever built and has the greatest wingspan and height of any aircraft in history. Initially planned by Henry Kaiser and called the HK-1, the re-named H-4 became reclusive millionaire entrepreneur Howard Hughes's showpiece response to a US government request in 1942 for a transport that would not be vulnerable to German submarines, and not use critical wartime materials, substituting wood for aluminum in its construction. It's nicknamed the "Spruce Goose" even though it's 95 percent birch. It flew just once, at a spectacular press event choreographed by Hughes and witnessed by half a million people. Today, it's a museum property in Oregon.

Engines: 8 (count 'em, 8) Pratt & Whitney R-4360 Wasp Major radial engines
Horsepower: 3,000 each
Planned cruising speed: 230 mph
Wingspan: 321 ft. 11 in.

- First and only flight: November 2, 1947
- A mechanic could walk inside the wing and service the engines in flight
- Height: 79 ft. 4 in.

CONSOLIDATED XC-99

BIG AND NOT ALWAYS BELIEVABLE

Designed in 1942 and based on the B-36 bomber, the XC-99 had a spacious, double-deck interior designed to carry 400 combat troops or 101,000 pounds of cargo. It was the largest landplane in the world in the 1950s and remains the largest propeller-driven aircraft ever built. It served in the US Air Force from 1949 to 1957, operating from Kelly Air Force Base, Texas. At one public event attended by the XC-99 while it was still very much an operational part of the air force, a woman asked pilot Capt. Jim C. Douglas, "How will you move this thing from here?" Douglas replied, "We fly it, lady." The woman quickly retorted, "Young man, what kind of a fool do you take me for?" The XC-99 soldiered on until retirement and, today, awaits restoration.

Engines: 6 Pratt & Whitney R-4360-41 Wasp Major pusher engines
Horsepower: 3,500 each
Maximum speed: 310 mph
Wingspan: 230 ft.

- First flight: November 23, 1947
- Cost: $4.3 million in 1947; priceless today
- Crew: 5, plus a relief crew of 5 more on long flights
- In 1952, carried 7 million lb. of equipment to support the Korean War
- Used a double-deck fuselage interior
- Not equipped to receive air-to-air refueling
- The National Museum of the US Air Force hopes to restore the XC-99 at a future date

BOEING B-47 STRATOJET

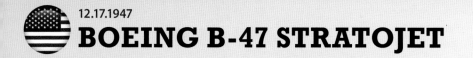

"IT'S A BIG BOMBER THAT THINKS IT'S A FIGHTER" —Col. Walter J. Boyne, B-47 pilot

The Boeing B-47 Stratojet was the United States' first sweptwing, multi-engine bomber, a true milestone in aviation history and a revolution in aircraft design. Every large jet aircraft today is a descendant of the B-47. At the height of the Cold War, the nuclear-armed B-47 was the most numerous bomber in the Strategic Air Command and was on constant alert, if called upon, to carry out a difficult doomsday mission. Despite its newness and complexity, it was an easy aircraft to fly. "It took no unusual ability or education," said test pilot Robert Robbins. "You can maneuver it all over the place and not break it. The B-47 handles like a baby."

Engines: 6 General Electric J47-GE-25 turbojet engines
Thrust: 7,200 lb. each
Maximum speed: 607 mph
Wingspan: 116 ft.

- First flight: December 17, 1947
- Number built: 2,032
- Crew: 3
- Built in 17 bomber and reconnaissance versions
- In 1959, the United States had 1,854 nuclear bombers (1,366 B-47s, 488 B-52s)

LONG MIDGET MUSTANG

AN INSPIRED AIR RACER THAT BECAME A UNIVERSAL HOMEBUILT

An air racer that didn't win any races became progenitor of the most admired and enduring homebuilt aircraft ever. Dave Long, chief engineer at Piper Aircraft, designed the Long Midget Mustang—its name inspired by the P-51 Mustang fighter—and flew it from 1948 until his untimely death during a test flight in 1950. The design was acquired by others, and in its modern-day incarnation is known as the Mustang Aeronautics Midget Mustang, or MM-1. The modern version is little changed from the prototype, except that it has a bubble canopy so that it more closely resembles the fighter for which it's named. One pilot calls the Midget Mustang's flight controls "well balanced, not twitchy," and points out that it has a small cockpit and high landing speed.

Engine: 1 Continental piston engine (prototype)
Horsepower: 85
Maximum speed: 288 mph
Ceiling: 9,400 ft.
Wingspan: 18 ft.

- First flight: 1948
- Cost: Currently $70,000 according to an owner
- Homebuilders have made 400 all over the world

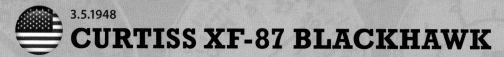

CURTISS XF-87 BLACKHAWK

"THE MOST BEAUTIFUL AIRPLANE EVER BUILT"

—Charles Vasiliadis, air force fighter pilot

The XF-87 Blackhawk (called the XP-87 until July 1948) was the last aircraft from Curtiss and contributed to the company's demise as a planemaker. It was a spectacularly appealing design that didn't fly as well as it looked and failed to win a production contract. Begun on the drawing boards as an attack plane initially dubbed XA-43, the Blackhawk evolved into a night fighter with a side-by-side crew of pilot and radio operator. Super-heavy at 49,900 pounds, it lacked sufficient power with its four J34s (even though the 26,850-pound F3D Skyknight performed well using two). Ironically, the crew compartment was spacious, well laid out, and offered superb visibility, but the two XF-87s made only a few flights, and only a handful of pilots enjoyed the experience of handling the controls.

Engines: 4 Westinghouse XJ34-WE-7 turbojet engines
Thrust: 3,000 lb. each
Maximum speed: 600 mph (Mach 0.77)
Wingspan: 60 ft.

- First flight: March 5, 1948
- Number built: 2
- Cost: Program cost $11.3 million in 1948
- Armament: Plans for a powered nose turret with four guns did not materialize
- Program was canceled October 10, 1948, and both prototypes were scrapped

3.19.1948
PIASECKI HUP RETRIEVER

A WORKHORSE—OR, MAYBE, A MULE — WITHOUT MUCH HORSEPOWER

The US Navy's HUP Retriever, known to soldiers as the H-25 Army Mule, was one of the first successful helicopters built around the tandem, twin-rotor configuration that later became familiar with the CH-47 Chinook. The HUP—pronounced as an acronym, "Hupp!"—was a clever, workmanlike helicopter design that offered good visibility and a user-friendly cockpit. A handful saw action in the Korean War. The HUP was underpowered, however, and limited in its capacity to carry and lift people and things.

- First flight: March 19, 1948
- Number built: 339; 70 for the army
- Served in French and Canadian navies

Engine: 1 Continental R-975-46A radial piston engine
Horsepower: 550
Maximum speed: 105 mph
Rotor diameter: 35 ft.

3.23.1948
DOUGLAS F3D SKYKNIGHT

BIG, FAT, BELOVED NIGHT FIGHTER

The F3D Skyknight was planned as a carrier-based aircraft but never operated routinely from carrier decks. It was a successful night fighter in Korea—the only really adequate response to the nocturnal MiG threat—and a useful intelligence gatherer in Vietnam. Marines called it the "Drut," which has meaning only when spelled backward, but it was a term of endearment for a robust, roomy, lethal warplane that served valiantly even though its J34 engines barely provided adequate power. Efforts to restore an example to flying condition in the 1980s never reached fruition.

Engines: 2 Westinghouse J34-WE-38 turbojet engines
Thrust: 3,600 lb. each
Maximum speed: 495 mph
Width: 50 ft.

- First flight: March 23, 1948
- Number built: 265
- Side-by-side cockpit seating
- Flew 4,447 missions in Vietnam
- None flying today

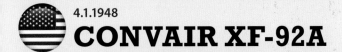

CONVAIR XF-92A

REAL EXPERIMENTS AND MOTION-PICTURE MAGIC

The XF-92A never had a name, but it paved the way for the F-102 Delta Dagger by conducting prolonged research into delta-winged aeronautics. The XF-92A (called the XP-92A until July 1948) acted out the part of a notional Soviet "MiG-23" in the Howard Hughes movie *Jet Pilot* (1950), but its cameo role ended up on the cutting room floor. It appeared in *Toward the Unknown* (1957) as an experimental plane piloted by William Holden. The delta, or triangle, wing was a new idea in the late 1940s, and to wring it out, the XF-92A pilot was provided with ample space in the cockpit and flight controls that, while a little stiff, were very responsive in the right hands—one pilot who flew it being Charles E. "Chuck" Yeager. Yes, this is another aircraft that completed its maiden flight on April Fools' Day, but nothing was foolish about the XF-92A. It was a comfortable, pilot-friendly research ship that advanced aviation knowledge and offered a little excitement to those who observed it in action.

Engine: 1 Allison J33-A-29 turbojet engine
Thrust: 7,500 lb.
Maximum speed: 718 mph
Wingspan: 31 ft. 4 in.

- First flight: April 1, 1948
- Number built: 1
- Program cost $6.1 million from 1948 to 1953
- Delta-wing design was derived in part from wartime German research
- Ejection seat and canopy were borrowed from the cancelled Convair XP-81
- World's first flying delta-wing aircraft
- In a museum today

6.1.1948
CESSNA 170

A GREAT TAIL DRAGGER FOR GENERAL-AVIATION PILOTS

The 170 began life in post–World War II years as an enlarged, four-seat version of the two-seat, tailwheel-equipped Cessna 140. It won universal approval, eventually being built in half a dozen versions, and can be found today at general-aviation airfields all over the world. Whether the purpose was a family vacation, a business trip, or a jaunt to the backwoods, the Cessna 170 was ideal—affordable, simple, and reliable. It was a huge success but might have won even more laurels if tricycle landing gear had not come along. It inspired the nosewheel-equipped Cessna 172, which was even more widely used.

Engine: 1 Continental C-145-2 air-cooled radial engine
Horsepower: 145
Maximum speed: 140 mph
Wingspan: 36 ft.

- First flight: June 1, 1948
- Number built: 5,174
- Cost: $7,245 in 1952; typically about $50,000 today

7.3.1948
NORTH AMERICAN AJ SAVAGE

THE NAVY'S FIRST CARRIER-BASED MEDIUM BOMBER

The AJ Savage resulted from the US Navy's unsuccessful effort in the 1950s to nail down a strategic nuclear role for carrier-based aircraft. The Savage was customized to carry the Mk 4 nuclear bomb, the postwar equivalent of the "Fat Man" plutonium weapon dropped on Nagasaki. It was a "propjet," with two piston engines on the wing and a jet engine in the tail, and was built in XAJ-1, AJ-1, and AJ-2 bomber versions, and the AJ-2P photo-reconnaissance model. The Savage was not popular aboard ship where it was difficult to maintain and cumbersome to move around. It had reliability issues but when working properly was considered a dream to fly, with performance much like a fighter.

Engines: 2 Pratt & Whitney R-2800-44W radial engines plus 1 Allison J33-A-10 turbojet engir
Horsepower: 2,400 each (R-2800s) plus 4,600 lb thrust (J33)
Maximum speed: 471 mph
Wingspan: 71 ft. 5 in.

- First flight: July 3, 1948 (XAJ-1); August 14, 1950 (AJ-2)
- Number built: 143
- Crew: 3

8.8.1948
MERCURY AIR SHOESTRING

ONE OF THE WINNINGEST CONTENDERS IN AIR RACING

Shoestring—designed by Rodney Kreimendahl and also called the Mercury Air Special—was a midget-class (Formula One) racer. It captured the imagination of 1940s modelers because of its brilliant yellow and orange colors. Kreimendahl and a few friends built Shoestring at home; Kreimendahl's wife Elizabeth named the aircraft after the group's budget. Pilot Bob Downey provided the engine and raced the aircraft from 1949 to 1952. Kreimendahl died in the crash of an air force transport in 1955 and Shoestring was placed in storage. Pilot Ray Cote purchased it in 1965, changed its paint scheme and flew it for sixteen years, winning an unprecedented forty-one races. Shoestring was retired to California's Planes of Fame Museum in 1981.

Engine: 1 Continental C85 piston engine
Horsepower: 65
Maximum speed: 198 mph
Wingspan: estimated 17 ft. 6 in.

- First flight: August 8, 1948
- First big win: 1951 Continental Trophy
- Number built: 1

8.16.1948
NORTHROP F-89 SCORPION

NOT COMFORTABLE, NOT PRETTY BUT FUNCTIONAL AND FORMIDABLE

The F-89 Scorpion (called the P-89 until July 1948) was the odd, corpulent interceptor that defended North American skies for a decade and was armed primarily with missiles, including one type with an atomic warhead. The US Air Force preferred it to the Curtiss XF-87 Blackhawk and fielded it in squadrons all over the United States. Front-seat pilots and back-seat radar operators had a businesslike attitude toward the Scorpion, never really learning to love it, but finding it more than adequate for the intended job of protecting against Soviet bombers. It was rated difficult to fly in tests but chosen because it met performance goals. The Scorpion was somewhat unusual in that it was used by only one US military service branch and no overseas air forces. A swept-wing version was proposed but never built.

Engines: 2 Allison J35-A-35 turbojet
**   engines with afterburners**
Thrust: 5,440 lb. each
Maximum speed: 635 mph (Mach 0.81)
Wingspan: 59 ft. 9 in.

- First flight: August 16, 1948
- Number built: 1,052
- Only fighter to fire a live nuclear missile, detonated in a Nevada test

MCDONNELL XF-85 GOBLIN

IT SHOOK AND RATTLED BUT COULDN'T FIGHT

The idea: a "parasite fighter," a small, bug-shaped warplane departing and returning to a mother-ship bomber in mid-air over the target, where it would battle enemy jets. The McDonnell XF-85 Goblin, or "Wobblin' Goblin," was tailored for its unorthodox assignment with an egg-shaped fuselage and forked tail that snuggled inside a bomb bay. The air force intended to put the XF-85 aboard the giant B-36 Peacemaker, but, instead, tested it by attaching to a trapeze (or "skyhook") extended by a B-29 Superfortress. Ed Shoch, the only pilot to fly the XF-85 flights, said that when running all-out at maximum speed, it flew "half as fast as a MiG-15," the Soviet fighter. The XF-85 was unreliable and unstable and would have been useless in combat, but it left a legacy—a strong influence on the later FICON (fighter conveyor) project, in which a "parasite" F-84 was carried along by a B-36 bomber.

Engine: 1 Westinghouse J34-WE-22 turbojet engine
Thrust: 3,000 lb.
Maximum speed: 314 mph
Wingspan: 21 ft. 1 inch

- First flight: August 23, 1948
- Number built: 2
- Spent more time aloft in cargo planes (being transported) than flying
- First ship made 1 flight; second XF-85 made 6
- A McDonnell engineer called the concept "scary"
- Both in museums today

NORTHROP X-4 BANTAM

AN X-PLANE THAT PROVED SOMETHING, SORT OF

The Northrop X-4, unofficially called the Bantam, is a near-flying-wing distant cousin to today's B-2 Spirit stealth bomber. It was not quite a flying wing, but almost: it had no horizontal tail. This was an aircraft intended purely for research, and after exhaustive tests it proved a negative—that technology was not yet ready for this type of almost-tailless design, although it's demonstrably ready today. The X-4 looks like fun but was exceedingly unstable and considered dangerous to fly.

Engines: 2 Westinghouse J30-WE-79 turbojet engines
Thrust: 1,600 lb. each
Maximum speed: 625 mph
Wingspan: 26 ft. 10 in.

- First flight: December 15, 1948
- Number built: 2
- Tested from 1950 to 1953
- Ship no. 1 was grounded after 10 flights
- Both are in museums

4.16.1949

LOCKHEED F-94 STARFIRE

STOOD ALERT AT HOME AND WENT TO WAR OVERSEAS

The F-94 entered service without a name, and gun-armed F-94A and F-94B models fought in night skies of Korea without one. The name Starfire was introduced with the rocket-armed F-94C model and is often mistakenly applied to all F-94s. A distant relative of the F-80 Shooting Star, the F-94 was an all-weather interceptor that guarded North America against Soviet bombers, operating alongside the Northrop F-89 Scorpion. F-94s scored some of the first nocturnal air-to-air kills in Korea, remained on air defense duty for a decade, and served with air national guard units. Once a bigger engine with afterburner (J48) was introduced on the F-94C model, this fighter had enough power although it could have used a faster rate of climb than 7,980 feet per minute. Cockpit accommodation was a little squeezed but smartly arranged, so the F-94 was popular with crews.

Engine: 1 Pratt & Whitney J48-P-5 turbojet engine with afterburner (F-94C)
Thrust: 6,350 lb.
Maximum speed: 640 mph
Wingspan: 42 ft. 5 in.

- First flight: April 16, 1949
- First service: May 1950
- Number built: 855
- Cost: $534,073 per plane (F-94C)
- Crew: 2 (pilot, radar observer)
- Retired: 1959

5.9.1949

REPUBLIC XF-91

"THE GREATEST DEVELOPMENT IN AVIATION" —Mundy Peale

The XF-91 came at a crossroads. Many experts believed aviation would quickly transition from jet to rocket power. Because it employed both, the XF-91 (called the XP-81 until July 1948) was seen as paving the way for future rocket-propelled warplanes; using both power sources, it became the first US warplane to fly faster than sound in level flight. In addition, it tested "inverse taper" wings—wider at the wingtip than at the wing root—to explore improved performance in pitch. The XF-91 offered a comfortable cockpit and stellar performance but did not carry sufficient fuel for a flight of longer than twenty-five minutes and lacked an up-to-date fire control system. Much loved, but ultimately deemed a dead-end design, the XF-91 was put to pasture. One survives.

Engine: 1 General Electric J47-GE-17 turbojet engine plus 4 Reaction Motors XLR11-RM-9 rocket motors
Thrust: 5,200 lb. (jet) plus 1,500 lb. each (rockets)
Maximum speed: 984 mph (Mach 1.21)
Wingspan: 31 ft. 3 in.

- First flight: May 9, 1949
- Number built: 2
- Armament: 4 20mm cannons planned

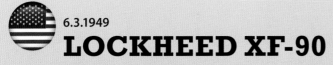

6.3.1949

LOCKHEED XF-90

A POINTY NOSE, GOOD LOOKS, AND NO PRODUCTION CONTRACT

The XF-90 was not given a name and was operational only in the *Blackhawk* comic books, where it was a late-generation successor to the Grumman XF5F Skyrocket. The first American jet with an afterburner, the XF-90 was designed by Willis Hawkins and was a product of the Clarence "Kelly" Johnson's Lockheed Skunk Works. Together with another fighter of its era, the Curtiss XF-87, the XF-90 is rated as one of the most beautiful airplanes ever built. However, it was woefully underpowered. The XF-90 participated in a US Air Force contract for a "penetration fighter" that would be able to evade the Soviet Union's air defenses. When the program was ended without any aircraft being chosen for production, the two flying XF-90s were retired.

Engines: 2 Westinghouse J34-WE-15 turbojet engines with (retrofitted) afterburners
Thrust: 4,100 lb. each
Maximum speed: 665 mph (Mach 0.85)
Wingspan: 40 ft.

- First flight: June 3, 1949
- Number built: 2
- Cost: $5.1 million for the program

10.14.1949
FAIRCHILD C-123B PROVIDER

A PROLIFIC AERIAL WORKHORSE

From the Arctic to the tropics, the C-123 Provider went beyond its seminal mission of tactical airlift to serve in duties from reconnaissance (air force) to facilities inspection (coast guard). The C-123 arguably had more talent than any other participant in the Nicholas Cage movie *Con Air* (1997). Yet to millions the C-123 will be remembered solely for spraying Agent Orange in Vietnam. Although it did many jobs well, it was demanding on pilots, especially in versions that used jet engines to augment its twin props.

- First flight: October 14, 1949
- Number built: 307
- Crew: 4 (2 pilots, navigator, loadmaster)

Engines: 2 Pratt & Whitney R-1800-99W Double Wasp radial piston engines plus (on UC-1123K) 2 General Electric J86-GE-17 turbojet engines

Horsepower: 2,500 (plus 2,850 lb. more on the UC-1123K)

Maximum speed: 228 mph

Wingspan: 110 ft.

10.28.1949
MARTIN XB-51

UNCONVENTIONAL AND UNDERUSED

The XB-51 was an extremely promising early jet bomber from Martin featuring a unique three-jet configuration with two of the engines in pods at its forward fuselage. It outperformed everything around it in tests, including fighters that were unable to keep up, and would have made a superb weapons platform in the Vietnam War. In months of exhaustive testing, the XB-51 exhibited no flaws; while both examples crashed, neither loss was due to any fault of the design. For purely political reasons, the US Air Force chose instead to purchase a US version of the British Canberra—assembled in the United States by Martin.

- First flight: October 28, 1949
- Number built: 2
- Crew: 2 (pilot, navigator)
- Initially designated XA-45
- Was the "XF-120" in the William Holden movie *Toward the Unknown* (1956)
- Both aircraft lost in crashes

Engines: 3 General Electric J47-GE-13 turbojet engines

Thrust: 5,200 lb. each

Maximum speed: 540 mph

Wingspan: 53 ft. 1 in.

NORTHROP YC-125 RAIDER

IT WAS PRETTY UGLY, BUT IT WORKED PRETTY WELL

Is it possible to be both ugly and cool? The Northrop YC-125 Raider, a military craft derived from a civilian design, was the last major propeller-driven trimotor in the United States. Not exactly a candidate in a beauty contest, it was a friendly and utilitarian transport and rescue plane. And if you wanted a real kick, the YC-125 could use jet-assisted takeoff, or JATO—clusters of small rocket bottles—to blast itself aloft in fewer than 500 feet. The air force used this not-so-gorgeous but very pleasant aircraft for half a dozen years, found the planes difficult to maintain, and retired the fleet.

Engines: 3 Wright R-1820-00 Cyclone radial piston engines
Horsepower: 1,200 each
Maximum speed: 207 mph
Wingspan: 86 ft. 6 in.

- First flight: November 14, 1949
- Number built: 23
- Capacity: 13 YC-125As seated 30 troops
- 13 YC-125As seated 30 troops
- 10 YC-125Bs, with skis for Arctic rescue
- 2 in museums today

DOUGLAS XA2D-1 SKYSHARK

A BRAVE IDEA WITH DISAPPOINTING RESULTS

A March 23, 1953, press release by Douglas Aircraft credited the innovative, turboprop-powered XA2D-1 Skyshark carrier-based attack plane with "the latest design innovations." It would "outstrip all its predecessors in performance." Conceived as a derivative of, and intended to share common features with, the piston-powered AD Skyraider, the XA2D-1 evolved into a wholly new plane. It was costly, complicated, and almost immediately caught up in a fatal crash. Problems persisted with its engine, gearbox, and propellers, and performance was disappointing. Harold Andrews, a Navy engineer who worked on the program, said: "It was a dog." The program was canceled in 1954. No turboprop-powered warplane ever flew in combat from a US Navy carrier deck.

Engine: 1 Allison XT40-A-2 turboprop engine
Horsepower: 5,100 shaft
Maximum speed: 435 mph
Wingspan: 50 ft.

- First flight: March 23, 1950
- Number built: 12
- 4 never flew
- Never landed on a carrier
- A lone survivor is displayed in a museum today

6.3.1950

REPUBLIC F-84F THUNDERSTREAK

A BULWARK OF TACTICAL AVIATION DURING THE COLD WAR

The F-84F Thunderstreak was billed as a sweptwing version of the straight-wing F-84 Thunderjet. In fact, it was about 85 percent a totally new aircraft. It became a workhorse of US tactical aviation and in friendly air forces around the world, especially among the North Atlantic Treaty Organization allies. The F-84F overcame early engine problems and a shortage of production facilities—in addition to Republic, some were built in Kansas City by General Motors. Pilots liked its brute strength and reliability. In part because of the shape of its snout, they affectionately called it the "Hog."

Engine: 1 Wright J65-W-3 (Sapphire) turbojet engine
Thrust: 7,220 lb.
Maximum speed: 695 mph (Mach 0.91)
Wingspan: 33 ft. 8 in.

- First flight: June 3, 1950
- Maiden flight of first production version: November 22, 1952
- Number built: 2,711 (1,301 to NATO)
- Armament: Many were poised to use tactical nuclear weapons
- Remembered especially for duty with NATO allies

8.11.1950

FAIRCHILD XC-120 PACK PLANE

"THE MOST SIGNIFICANT DEVELOPMENT EVER PRODUCED BY THE AMERICAN AIRCRAFT INDUSTRY"
—US Army Gen. James M. Gavin, August 31, 1950

Engines: 2 Pratt & Whitney R-4360 Wasp Major radial engines
Horsepower: 3,250 each
Cruising speed: 165 mph
Wingspan: 106 ft. 6 in.

- First flight: August 11, 1950
- Number built: 1
- Cost: About $1 million for the program
- Production version (unbuilt) would have been XC-128
- It doesn't survive today

Okay, so maybe Jumpin' Jim wasn't right every time. Or maybe the army saw something the air force didn't. The idea behind the XC-120 Pack Plane was obvious. A cargo plane lands. Its cargo becomes a trailer, to be towed on the highway. Specifications called for the trailer to be towed in either direction from the aircraft when it was parked. In flight tests with and without the trailer, or "pack," attached, and with the pack both empty and full, the XC-120 performed well and met all test objectives. The aircraft had no flaws but was considered unduly complicated, so flights were ended in November 1952 and the sole XC-120 was scrapped. No aircraft using this concept has ever become operational.

PROJECT TIP-TOW

HALF-BAKED HOOK-UP:
AN IDEA THAT DIDN'T WORK

In Project Tip-Tow, alias the MX-1016 Program, F-84 Thunderjets were towed through the sky coupled to the wingtips of a B-29 Superfortress. Tip-Tow was an interim stage in the "parasite fighter" experiments of the Cold War 1950s that included the McDonnell XF-85 Goblin and the FICON (fighter conveyor) effort. The purpose was to extend fighters' range so they could accompany bombers into enemy territory. But attaching an F-84 to a B-29 produced unexpected aerodynamic effects and, ultimately, disaster: during an April 24, 1953, hook-up, an F-84 and B-29 collided, and all on both planes were lost. A subsequent wing-coupling effort dubbed Project Tom-Tom used a B-36 and was also unsuccessful. In the end, the "parasite fighter" concept was rendered unnecessary by the advent of air-to-air refueling.

Longest hook-up: three hours, in October 1950
B-29 speed, while towing F-84: 295 mph
Combined weight of B-29, F-84: 133,000 lb.
B-36 fuselage length: 99 ft.

- First air-to-air hookup: September 15, 1950
- The pilot maintained manual control of the F-84 during couplings
- A key test pilot: air ace Clarence "Bud" Anderson
- Vortex from the wings of the "mother" B-29 made docking difficult
- F-84 engine was shut down during B-29 tow

10.21.1950
MARTIN 4-0-4

A MAJESTIC JOURNEY FROM POINT A TO POINT B

In the heyday of air travel, the Martin 4-0-4 was a luxury liner in the sky, although a loud one. The proud Glenn L. Martin Company in Baltimore built aircraft that were straightforward, tough, and reliable. After missteps with earlier designs, the 4-0-4 got it right and drew a large following, especially among pilots who liked its stability and comfort. By the time it appeared, however, propliners were becoming the wave of the past, so the 4-0-4 had a brief service life.

Engines: 2 Pratt & Whitney R-2800-C816 Double Wasp 18-cylinder radial engines
Horsepower: 2,400 each
Cruising speed: 312 mph
Wingspan: 93 ft. 3 in.

- First flight: October 21, 1950
- Number built: 103
- Capacity: Typically 40 passengers
- The US Coast Guard used 2

1.23.1951
DOUGLAS F4D SKYRAY

THEY LOVED THIS FAST AND PILOT-FRIENDLY INTERCEPTOR

It was a short, sweet career for the F4D Skyray (called the F-6 after October 1962). The last fighter built by Douglas was a delta-winged interceptor that earned a special place in the hearts of navy and marine pilots for its ability to fly faster than sound in level flight and for being an all-around superb fighter (after the original J40 engine was replaced by the J57). An important quality was its extreme rate of climb, enabling it to join a battle at 40,000 feet within two minutes. Like the McDonnell F3H Demon, the Skyray was developed to fight MiGs in Korea but entered service too late to ever encounter a foe in the air. The Skyray inspired the less successful F5D Skylancer and spent its brief career defending the United States.

Engine: 1 Pratt & Whitney J57-P-6/8A/8B turbojet engine with afterburner
Thrust: 10,200 lb.
Maximum speed: 763 mph (Mach 1.1 at 38,000 ft.)
Wingspan: 33 ft. 6 in.

- First flight: January 23, 1951
- Number built: 422
- Called "the Ford" (for F4D) by pilots

4.1.1951

KAMAN HH-43 HUSKIE

OFTEN ON THE SIDELINES

The HH-43 Huskie was a utility craft for the sea services and firefighting vehicle for the air force. In practice, it performed other duties, including behind-the-lines rescue sorties in Vietnam. Early versions used a radial engine and wooden rotors, while late models employed a gas turbine and metal rotors. This aircraft far exceeded its design goals, sustained battle damage without going down, and established a brilliant service record.

- First flight: April 1, 1951 (HTK-1)
- Crew: 3 (2 pilots, 1 pararescue jumper)
- 2 became navy QH-43G target drones for weapons practice
- Set several time-to-climb speed records

Engine: 1 Lycoming T53-L-1B or T53-L-11A gas turbine engine
Horsepower: 825 shaft
Maximum speed: 110 mph
Main rotor diameter 47 ft.

4.21.1951

CHASE XC-123A AVITRUC

QUICK, CAN YOU NAME THE FIRST US JET TRANSPORT?

The one-of-a-kind XC-123A came from Michael Stroukoff's Chase Aircraft Company and was based on the planemaker's earlier gliders and transports aircraft, but with a twist. The XC-123A had podded jet engines hanging under its wings, something never before attempted with an airlifter. Chase named it the Avitruc, the name also applied to the C-122 aircraft. In tests, the XC-123A proved that it could land on rough surfaces near the front lines to deliver supplies and ammunition to embattled ground troops—at the time, a new concept—and pilots found that the aircraft handled exceedingly well. Unfortunately, the jet engines required so much fuel for a flight of any reasonable distance that the XC-123A's cargo-carrying capacity was compromised. The US Air Force ultimately invested instead in the Fairchild C-123 Provider and Lockheed C-130 Hercules.

Engines: 4 General Electric J47-GE-11 turbojet engine
Thrust: 5,200 lb.
Maximum speed: 500 mph
Wingspan: 110 ft.

- First flight: April 21, 1951
- Crew: 3—2 pilots, loadmaster
- Engine pods identical to those on B-47 Stratojet bomber
- Because wings were thin, fuel was positioned under the fuselage floorboards

6.20.1951

BELL X-5

A NOVEL IDEA, A NEAT AIRPLANE, BUT A FLAWED DESIGN

The X-5 was a jet research ship to explore variable-sweep wings of the kind that appeared in later years on the F-111 Aardvark, F-14 Tomcat, and B-1B Lancer. It was the first aircraft capable of changing its wings in flight (at 20, 40, or 60 degrees) and was derived from the unfinished Messerschmitt P.1101 of World War II. Although it offered the pilot an unusually spacious and well-designed cockpit, the X-5 suffered vicious spin characteristics arising from a flawed aerodynamic layout, including a poor tail design. A deadly spin caused the crash of an X-5 at Edwards Air Force Base, California, on October 14, 1953, killing Capt. Ray Popson. The second aircraft is displayed at the National Museum of the United States Air Force in Dayton, Ohio.

Engine: 1 Allison J35-A-17 turbojet engine
Thrust: 4,900 lb.
Maximum speed: 716 mph
Weight: 9,980 lb. fully loaded
Wingspan: 32 ft. 9 in. wings extended; 22 ft. 8 in. wings swept

- First flight: June 20, 1951
- First flight of the second X-5: December 10, 1951
- Number built: 2

MCDONNELL F3H DEMON

THE GOOD, THE BAD, AND THE NOT SO UGLY

This is a turnaround story. The Demon evolved from a dismal failure to a modest success. The first fifty-eight Demons (F3H-1N) were so pitifully underpowered and trouble-plagued that most never flew but were shipped by barge from the St. Louis, Missouri, factory to a Memphis, Tennessee, naval station where they were used as ground trainers. After the original J40 engine was replaced with the J71, the remaining Demons (239 F3H-2N, 80 F3H-2M, 239 F3H-2) performed reasonably well and had a brief but successful career on carrier decks. Built to confront the Soviet MiG-15 in Korea, the Demon never saw an enemy aircraft during that conflict, but it intercepted Soviet reconnaissance aircraft during the Cold War and guarded the navy's carrier battle groups.

Engine: 1 Allison J71-A-2E turbojet engine with afterburner
Thrust: 14,750 lb.
Maximum speed: 716 mph
Wingspan: 35 ft. 4 in.

- First flight: August 7, 1951
- Number built: 519
- Used only by the US Navy
- Supersonic only in a dive
- 4 Demons survive today in US museums

FICON

THE STRANGE AND INTRIGUING FINALE TO THE "PARASITE FIGHTER" SAGA

In the FICON (fighter conveyor) Project, several models of the F-84 were carried aloft by a B-36, and traveled to and from the bomber in mid-air. FICON capped off the "parasite fighter" experiments of the 1950s that began with the McDonnell XF-85 Goblin and included the wing-coupling experiment Project Tip-Tow. The goal was to extend the range of fighters to enable them to accompany bombers into enemy territory. The mission changed from fighter-escort to reconnaissance when F-84E and F-84F models were replaced with the RF-84K Thunderflash: now, the B-36 would carry a photo plane deep into enemy territory for high-speed reconnaissance runs. The US Air Force invested heavily in FICON, modifying 10 B-36s and 25 RF-84Ks and operating a squadron within the Strategic Air Command. However, the project was short-lived and air-to-air refueling proved a better solution.

Combined weight (B-36, RF-84K): 455,000 lb.
B-36 speed, while carrying fighter: 366 mph
B-36 service ceiling: 43,600 ft.
B-36 fuselage length: 152 ft. 1 in.

- First air-to-air hookup: January 9, 1952
- Early on, an F-84E made 170 launches and retrievals
- B-36, RF-84K stationed at Fairchild Air Force Base, Washington
- Early tests at Eglin Air Force Base, Florida

REPUBLIC RF-84F THUNDERFLASH

A STRONG, VERSATILE, AND LITTLE-RECOGNIZED PICTURE TAKER

The RF-84F was a sweptwing reconnaissance aircraft derived from the straight-wing F-84 Thunderjet and developed simultaneously with the sweptwing F-84F Thunderstreak fighter. The RF-84F was in most respects a new aircraft. It became the photo-taking flagship for the Western allies during the Cold War. It was the first reconnaissance fighter to have a camera control system and a viewfinder for the pilot, who was also the cameraman. A handful were modified to RF-84K standards to be carried aloft by, and operate from, B-36 Peacemaker bombers following tests in the FICON (fighter conveyor) program. The "parasite" aircraft concept proved impractical, however, and was soon dropped. Pilots found the RF-84F to be powerful and bullish and just hard enough to handle to be a bit of a challenge.

Engine: 1 Wright J65-W-7 (Sapphire) turbojet engine
Thrust: 7,800 lb.
Maximum speed: 629 mph
Wingspan: 33 ft. 7 in.

- First flight: February 1, 1952
- Number built: 715
- Cost: $890,000 in 1952
- Armament: 4 .50-cal. guns
- A camera plane
- 25 were rebuilt as RF-84K models

4.15.1952

BOEING B-52 STRATOFORTRESS

OLD, UGLY, BIG, BAD, AND GOING STRONG

It's the graybeard of them all, the oldest and longest-serving warplane in US inventory—indeed, in US history—and still combat ready, every day. They designed the B-52 Stratofortress to haul hydrogen bombs to the Soviet Union. They gave it a new job plastering Viet Cong guerrillas in Southeast Asia. It fought in both Persian Gulf conflicts. During Operation Desert Storm, B-52s struck wide-area troop concentrations, installations, and bunkers, and decimated Iraq's Republican Guard. The Gulf War involved the longest strike mission in history at the time when B-52s took off from Barksdale Air Force Base, Louisiana, launched cruise missiles, and returned to Barksdale—a thirty-five-hour, non-stop combat mission. Today, this long-range heavy bomber is assigned to both conventional and nuclear bombing duties, and conducts anti-ship and mine-laying operations.

Engines: 8 Pratt & Whitney TF33-P-3/103 turbofan engines (B-52H)
Thrust: 17,000 lb. each
Maximum speed: 650 mph (Mach 0.89)
Wingspan: 185 ft.

- First flight: April 15, 1952
- Number built: 744
- 76 in inventory in 2014
- Nickname: the BUF (Big Ugly Fellow)
- Last one (a B-52H) delivered in October 1962

4.18.1952

CONVAIR YB-60

THE BIG BOMBER THAT COULDN'T

The eight-jet YB-60 was the big bomber that wasn't a B-52. It had 72 percent commonality in parts, and shared a fuselage, with Convair's earlier B-36—in fact, it was initially called the B-36G. The YB-60 made its first flight only three days after the B-52 Stratofortress, but was seen from the beginning as a distant second candidate to become the Strategic Air Command's next nuclear workhorse. The YB-60 was fully 100 miles per hour slower than the B-52, and pilots such as Convair's Beryl Erickson found it tricky and difficult to handle. The $14.3 million YB-60 program contributed a little to general aeronautical knowledge but was canceled only a year after the experimental bomber's debut.

Engines: 8 Pratt & Whitney J57-P-3 turbojet engines
Thrust: 8,700 lb. each
Maximum speed: 507 mph
Wingspan: 206 ft.

- First flight: April 18, 1952
- Number built: 1
- Crew: 5
- Logged just 66 flight hours
- Second aircraft never completed

DOUGLAS X-3 STILETTO

FUTURISTIC BUT FLAWED, WITHOUT ENOUGH OOMPH

The Douglas X-3 Stiletto was designed and shaped for research at extremely high speed—around twice the speed of sound—but because of inadequate power it never approached this goal. With its unusually rakish fuselage and tiny, trapezoidal wings, the X-3 contributed to aeronautical knowledge in other ways and strongly influenced the design of future fighters like the Lockheed F-104 Starfighter. Seriously underpowered, cramped and uncomfortable, and extremely difficult to control, the X-3 had an abbreviated flight career before becoming a museum artifact.

Engines: 2 Westinghouse J34 turbojet engines with afterburners
Thrust: 3,370 lb. each
Maximum speed: 690 mph
Wingspan: 22 ft. 8 in.

- First flight: October 15, 1952
- Number built: 1
- Final flight: May 23, 1956

HUGHES XH-17

DIFFERENT, BUT NOT THE ODDBALL IT SEEMED

Howard Hughes is remembered for many reasons yet often overlooked as a right-stuff aviation pioneer. Hughes willingly took risks with aircraft designs. None was more outlandish—seemingly—than the XH-17 helicopter, which makes everyone's list of weird aircraft, but which was a smart idea for a freight hauler. Building upon a Kellett design and borrowing the shape of a freight vehicle used in logging, Hughes built the XH-17 in part from components of other aircraft and was on the scene for its early flight tests. The XH-17 displayed no technical problem that couldn't be overcome, but a production order never came.

Engines: 2 General Electric J35 turbojet engines feeding exhaust to hollow rotor tips

Thrust: 3,000 lb. (each rotor)

Maximum speed: 90 mph

Rotor diameter: 129 ft. 11 in.

- First flight: October 23, 1952
- Number built: 1
- Proposed XH-28 derivative wasn't built
- Plagued by high fuel consumption
- Still on record as having the world's largest rotor system

10.28.1952
DOUGLAS A3D SKYWARRIOR

THIS DOOMSDAY BOMBER TOOK ON MANY DUTIES

The A3D Skywarrior (redesignated A-3 in October 1962) was the replacement for the AJ Savage carrier-based bomber. The Skywarrior was the heaviest operational aircraft to operate from US carriers, one of the longest serving, and unquestionably one of the best loved. Its role as a nuclear bomber did not last long, nor did its duty as a conventional bomber in Vietnam, but the Skywarrior proved adaptable as a tanker, trainer, transport, and electronic warfare platform. Its close cousin was the air force B-66 Destroyer. The Skywarrior was retired from service in 1991. Despite its size, it was easy to handle and amenable during carrier landings.

- **Engines: 2 Pratt & Whitney J57-P-10 turbojet engines with water injection**
- **Maximum speed: 610 mph**
- **Thrust: 10,500 lb. each**
- **Wingspan: 72 ft. 6 in.**

- First flight: October 28, 1952
- Number built: 282

1.14.1953
CONVAIR F2Y SEA DART

SEAPLANE FIGHTER THAT ALMOST WAS

The F2Y Sea Dart was the US Navy's only seaplane fighter. An advertising poster in the 1950s showed a squadron of Sea Darts rising from the Tidal Basin in Washington to defend the US capital against Soviet bombers. Trouble plagued the seaplane hull, which lifted from the water via a hydro-ski, and the Sea Dart program took a tragic turn November 4, 1954, when Charles E. "Chuck" Richbourg was killed in the no. 2 aircraft as it disintegrated during a low-level, high-speed flypast in San Diego. The program lasted until 1955 but the production F2Y-2 version was never built.

- First flight: January 14, 1953
- Number built: 5
- Tested from 1953 to 1965

Engines: 2 Westinghouse J46-WE-2 turbojet engines

Thrust: 4,600 lb. each

Maximum speed: 695 mph

Width: 34 ft. 8 in.

5.18.1953

DOUGLAS DC-7

THE LAST WORD IN "DOUGLAS COMMERCIAL" PROPLINERS

The Douglas DC-7 was the last great propeller-driven airliner from its famous maker, and the only plane in the series not to have a military version—although the civilian freighter model was terrifically successful. Faster than most World War II fighters but with a history of occasional minor engine troubles, the DC-7 offered stability and comfort, and in 1956 the DC-7C (Seven Seas), with more fuel and extended range, became the ultimate Douglas piston-engined airliner.

Engines: 4 Wright R-3350-30W Duplex-Cyclone turbo compound piston engines
Horsepower: 3,250 each
Maximum speed: 405 mph
Wingspan: 117 ft. 6 in.

- First flight: May 18, 1953
- Number built: 343
- Cost: About $500,000 for the DC-7C "Speedfreighter" cargo version
- Same wing as the DC-4, 3 ft. longer than the DC-6

NORTH AMERICAN F-100 SUPER SABRE

A DOGFIGHTER AND GROUND POUNDER WITH SPEED AND PROWESS

The F-100 Super Sabre was introduced with much fanfare as the first in the "century series" of new fighters in the 1950s. It was widely billed as the first fighter able to exceed the speed of sound in level flight, although the Soviet MiG-19 was only four months behind it. Widely seen as a post-Korea, air-to-air MiG killer, the Super Sabre surprised everyone by becoming a potent air-to-ground weapon in Vietnam, where it flew more combat sorties than any other fighter. It was long the flagship of the Thunderbirds flight demonstration team. Pilots, who liked its spacious cockpit but grumbled about its slow responses on the controls, were being affectionate when they dubbed the F-100 "the Hun."

Engine: 1 Pratt & Whitney J57-P-21/21A turbojet engine with afterburner
Thrust: 10,200 lb.
Maximum speed: 864 mph (Mach 1.1)
Wingspan: 38 ft. 9 in.

- First flight: May 25, 1953
- Number built: 2,294
- Cost: $697,029 in 1953
- Armament: Some stood alert with nuclear weapons
- Overcame early problems with fin design
- In US service from 1954 to 1979

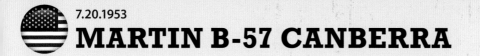

MARTIN B-57 CANBERRA

THE LAST LIGHT JET BOMBER IN US SERVICE

It performed engine starts with noisy belches of smoke that distracted onlookers. It dropped bombs in Vietnam and flew reconnaissance in the Cold War. It became a weather scout and an engine testbed. The Martin B-57 Canberra, Baltimore-built cousin of Britain's first jet bomber, won friends and influenced enemies during three decades of US service, including yeoman duty with air national guard units. It looked a little different from other jets, and to many that meant it had style. After heavy-duty strike fighters got into inventory, a twin-engined bomber no longer had a job to perform. Still, the B-57 lives in the hearts of veterans who saw something classy about this broad-winged, muscular warplane.

Engines: 2 Wright J65-W-5 turbojet engines
Thrust: 7,200 lb. each
Maximum speed: 600 mph (Mach 0.89)
Wingspan: 64 ft.

- First flight July 20, 1953
- Number built: 403 in the United States
- Crew: 2 (pilot, navigator-bombardier)
- 2 squadrons served in Vietnam, 1965 to 1969

10.24.1953
CONVAIR F-102 DELTA DAGGER

THE AIR DEFENSE ICON OF THE 1950S

Part of the celebrated century series, the F-102 was a delta-winged, radar-equipped interceptor designed to guard North America against Soviet bombers. It acquired an excellent reputation as a defender but was less successful during brief tours in Vietnam, where one was shot down by a MiG-21 while no F-102 ever shot down a MiG. Air national guard service rounded off the F-102's long career and 146 became pilotless target drones.

Engine: 1 Pratt & Whitney J57-P-23 turbojet engine with afterburner
Thrust: 11,720 lb.
Maximum speed: 825 mph (Mach 1.09)
Wingspan: 38 ft. 1 in.

- First flight: October 24, 1953
- Number built: 1,000
- Cost: $1.1 million in 1959
- Extensively redesigned after prototype tests
- Introduced area rule, or "wasp waist," fuselage for easy supersonic flight
- In US service from 1954 to 1979

12.15.1953
LOCKHEED T2V-1 SEASTAR

A CARRIER-CAPABLE T-BIRD ON STEROIDS

The T2V-1 SeaStar, called the T-1A after October 1962, was a new US Navy jet trainer derived from the successful T-33 Shooting Star, or T-Bird. With a new, greatly strengthened wing, it was tailored for the one job the T-Bird didn't do well—training student pilots to land and take off from aircraft carriers. Several thousand naval aviators had their first carrier experience in this eminently sound and reliable trainer. The raised rear position for the instructor made it easy to offer tutoring in this aerial schoolhouse. Well liked but expensive to operate, the T2V-1 had a relatively short life training naval aviators.

Engine: 1 Allison J33-A-24/24A turbojet engine
Thrust: 6,100 lb.
Maximum speed: 580 mph
Wingspan: 42 ft. 10 in.

- First flight: December 15, 1953
- Number built: 150
- Served from 1956 to 1970

CONVAIR R3Y TRADEWIND

2.22.1954

UNDERPOWERED SEA MONSTER

The Convair R3Y Tradewind tanker-transport, along with the closely related XP5Y-1 patrol boat, had the potential to give strategic reach to the post-Korea US Navy of the 1950s but was stymied by the unreliable engines. The R3Y-2 version was intended as a flying LST, or landing ship tank, but using it to put vehicles and troops ashore on a beach proved impractical. Modified for tanker duties, the R3Y-2 could refuel four navy jets at once—often, Grumman F9F Cougars—but first it had to get there. Plagued by powerplant failures, the R3Y program was abandoned in 1958.

Engines: 4 Allison T40-A-10 turboprop engines
Horsepower: 5,100 each
Maximum speed: 403 mph
Wingspan: 145 ft. 9 in.

- First flight: February 22, 1954
- Number built: 13 (2 were XP5Y-1s, 5 were R3Y-1s, and 6 were R3Y-2s)
- In 1954, set a seaplane speed record: 403 mph
- R3Y-2 model introduced a hinged, clamshell nose loading door

LOCKHEED F-104 STARFIGHTER

3.4.1954

"I CONSIDERED IT A HOT ROD OF THE SKIES"
—Vietnam-era F-104 pilot Al Bache

The "missile with the man in it" was the 1950s advert for the F-104 Starfighter, a futuristic fighter from Lockheed's famous Skunk Works that looked great but appeared only briefly in Vietnam, and racked up a poor safety record in German service. The unique spurs that fitted onto the F-104's ejection seat and clanked when pilots strutted around the O Club fostered the notion that the "Zipper"—a not-very-friendly nickname—was mostly for show. The F-104 spent most of its career overcoming its good looks and bad reputation.

Engine: 1 General Electric J79-GE-11A turbojet engine with afterburner
Thrust: 10,000 lb.
Maximum speed: 1,328 mph (Mach 2.01)
Wingspan: 21 ft. 9 in.

- First flight: March 4, 1954
- Number built: 2,578, most in Europe
- Cost: $1.7 million in 1954

3.8.1954

SIKORSKY H-34 CHOCTAW

"THE CADILLAC OF PISTON ENGINED HELICOPTERS"
—US Coast Guard Cmdr. Frank Shelley

The medium-lift H-34 had many names and missions—the Seabat as a US Navy anti-submarine craft, the Seahorse as a marine corps transport, and the Choctaw as an army cargo hauler. Nearly all helicopters in this enduring family rolled out of the factory doors powered by piston engine power, but a few were built or modified with gas turbines. Sikorsky built most in Connecticut, but Sud-Aviation in France manufactured 177. Remembered for so many deeds in so many places, the H-34 stands out for introducing modern helicopter mobility to the earliest marines in Vietnam, beginning in 1962. In recent years, two restored marine H-34s have made regular appearances at air shows.

> **Engine:** 1 Wright R-1820-84 radial piston engine
> **Horsepower:** 1,515
> **Maximum speed:** 123 mph
> **Main rotor diameter:** 56 ft.

- First flight: March 8, 1954
- Number built: 2,108
- Produced between 1953 and 1970
- Some were used for astronaut recovery

4.19.1954

CONVAIR XFY-1

IT GOES UP, IT GOES DOWN, BUT . . .

Seeking to dispense with runways and carrier decks, the US Navy in the 1950s tested two "tail-sitter" fighters, designed to take off and land vertically from a jungle clearing or the aft deck of a destroyer. The Convair XFY-1, or "Pogo," did more flying than the Lockheed XFV-1. Landing was especially difficult because the pilot had to look back over his shoulder while doing it to stabilize the aircraft. The navy concluded that only the most experienced pilots would be able to fly a tail-sitter and abandoned the concept. No one has ever fielded an operational tail-sitter.

Engine: 1 Allison YT40-A-16 turboprop engine
Horsepower: 5,500
Maximum speed: 610 mph
Weight: 16,250 lb. fully loaded
Wingspan: 27 ft. 8 in.

- First tethered flight: April 19, 1954
- First free flight: August 1, 1954
- Number built: 3
- 1 flew; it now belongs to Smithsonian Museum (not on display)

6.16.1954

LOCKHEED XFV-1

AN IDEA WHOSE TIME HADN'T COME, AND STILL HASN'T

The Lockheed XFV-1, initially designated XFO-1 and sometimes called the Salmon, was one of two tail-sitter fighters tested by the US Navy in the 1950s, along with the Convair XFY-1. Tests of the XFV-1 went poorly despite brave ministrations by test pilot Herman "Fish" Salmon. The XFV-1 made only one vertical takeoff and never landed vertically. Other flights were made traditionally and horizontally. The tail-sitter concept was an intriguing idea but was abandoned as impractical.

- First flight: June 16, 1954
- Number built: 2
- 1 flew
- Made 32 conventional flights
- Both are in private museums today

Engine: 1 Allison YT40-A-14 turboprop engine
Horsepower: 5,332 mph
Maximum speed: 580 mph (never attained)
Wingspan: 30 ft. 22 in.

209

6.22.1954

DOUGLAS A-4 SKYHAWK

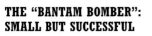

THE "BANTAM BOMBER": SMALL BUT SUCCESSFUL

The A-4 Skyhawk (A4D until 1962) was a product of Ed Heinemann's design team at Douglas Aircraft and was conceived as a purposely very small, carrier-based warplane able to carry an atomic bomb under its belly. Plans for a carrier-based nuclear strike force never materialized, but the miniscule A-4—called a "hot rod," by pilots—proved itself as a conventional bomber in Vietnam. Although not meant as a fighter, one scored an air-to-air victory using Zuni rockets. Sure, you have to be shoehorned into the cramped cockpit, but the A-4 pilot revels in an ability to fling this aircraft all over the sky while keeping it under total control.

Engine: 1 Pratt & Whitney J52-P-8 turbojet engine
9,100 lb. thrust
Maximum speed: 673 mph
Weight: 24,500 lb. (a real lightweight)
Wingspan: 26 ft. 6 in.

- First flight: June 22, 1954
- Number built: 2,960
- Cost: $860,000 in 1955, millions today
- Important to Israel in the 1973 Yom Kippur War
- Used by Argentina in the 1982 Falklands War

DOUGLAS B-66 DESTROYER

BOMBING AND RECONNAISSANCE IN PEACE AND WAR

The B-66 Destroyer was the last light bomber developed for the US Air Force, which no longer uses warplanes in this category. It was developed from its close cousin, the navy A3D Skywarrior. Like the Skywarrior, the Destroyer began as a bomber with both nuclear and conventional capability, but evolved into a series of weather, photo, and electronics intelligence aircraft with the designations RB-66B, RB-66C, EB-66C, WB-66D, and EB-66E. The R- and E-prefix intelligence-gathering aircraft served valiantly in Southeast Asia, including combat over North Vietnam. The B-66 was a bit of a gas-guzzler and demanded much of its single pilot. The last serving example was retired in 1975.

Engines: 2 Allison J71-A-11/13 turbojet engines
Thrust: 10,200 lb. each
Maximum speed: 631 mph
Wingspan: 75 ft. 2 in.

- First flight June 28, 1954
- Number built: 294
- Cost: $2.55 million each (RB-66B)
- Crew: 3 (typical)
- Called "the Bomb" by airmen

7.15.1954
BOEING 707

THE JETLINER THAT STARTED IT ALL

The "Seven Oh Seven" was one of the first practical jet-powered airliners. By overshadowing the contemporary Douglas DC-8, this long-range, four-engine, narrow-body classic is also responsible for the glamour, pampering, and "jet set" elitism associated with so much early jet travel. Military versions include the E-3 Sentry Airborne Warning and Control System (AWACS), a kind of flying radar station, and, of course, President Dwight D. Eisenhower's VC-137A, the first plane to use the call sign "Air Force One."

- First flight: July 15, 1954
- First service: October 26, 1958
- Number built: Almost 2,000 of all versions

Engines: 4 Pratt & Whitney JT3C-6 turbojet engines (typical)
Thrust: 11,200 lb.
Cruising speed: 570 mph
Wingspan: 130 ft. 10 in.

8.23.1954
LOCKHEED C-130 HERCULES

A "TRUCK OF ALL TRADES"

Originally, a response to a Korean War need for a transport to land and take off on unpaved surfaces the C-130 became a front-line supply truck and much more. It's a tactical airlifter, a gunship, a spyplane, a weather scout, and more. Willis Hawkins and his design team at Lockheed (later Lockheed Martin) came up with a design so simple, so straightforward, and so utterly practical that the C-130 Hercules, all these years later, just keeps going and going. It now handles forty distinct missions, and has evolved into the latter-day C-130J Super Hercules model (separate entry).

- First flight: August 23, 1954
- First service: 1956
- Capacity: 92 passengers or 64 airborne troops
- Can transport most military armored vehicles and helicopters
- In production longer than any other US military aircraft (since 1954)

Engines: 4 Allison T56-A-9 turboprop engines
Horsepower: 4,590 shaft (C-130H)
Maximum speed: 366 mph
Wingspan: 132 ft. 7 in.

9.29.1954
MCDONNELL F-101 VOODOO

FAST AND FURIOUS ON OFFENSE AND DEFENSE

The F-101 Voodoo was second in the "century series" of new jet fighters in the 1950s. Single-seat RF-101 reconnaissance versions flew the fastest combat missions ever undertaken in modern warfare, snapping pictures over North Vietnam. In the hands of US and Canadian crews, two-seat F-101B/F interceptor versions—with their phenomenal rate of climb of almost 50,000 feet per minute, and with a radar operator out back—guarded North America from Soviet bomber attack.

Engines: 2 Pratt & Whitney J57-P-55 turbojet engines with afterburners

Thrust: 11,990 lb. each

Maximum speed: 1,134 mph (Mach 1.72)

Wingspan: 39 ft. 8 in.

- First flight: September 29, 1954
- Number built: 807
- Cost: $1.24 million in 1956 (RF-101C)
- Flew supersonic on its maiden flight
- Hughes MG-1B fire control system (F-101B)

10.12.1954
CESSNA T-37

NOISY, HOT, UNCOMFORTABLE, INEFFICIENT, AND FONDLY REMEMBERED

Possibly the loudest small jet ever built, the T-37 was dubbed the "Tweet" or the "5,000-Pound Dog Whistle" by pilots because of the decibels (though its true weight was 6,600 pounds). This was the primary jet trainer for all US Air Force pilots from the 1950s until 2005 and has trained pilots in sixteen countries. As the author of this book can testify after an orientation flight, it truly is loud and hot, but it's a great ride and a good way to be introduced to the fundamentals of flight.

Engines: 2 Continental J69-T-25 turbojet engines

Thrust: 1,025 lb. each

Maximum speed: 445 mph

Wingspan: 38 ft. 10 in.

- First flight: October 12, 1954
- 9,000 airmen served as T-37 instructors
- First T-37 pilot class convened January 21, 1958
- Side-by-side seating: student (left) and instructor
- US Army tested three T-37s

213

11.22.1954

DE LACKNER HZ-1 AEROCYCLE

"FIGHTING SOLDIERS FROM THE SKY . . ."
—Staff Sgt. Barry Sadler, "Ballad of the Green Berets"

Afraid of heights? Imagine looking down to see rotor blades thrashing around beneath your feet—while you're trying to aim your rifle at that bad guy on the next hill. One of many outlandish schemes pursued by the US Army during an intense period of experimentation in the 1950s, the HZ-4 Aerocycle was meant to be a one-man "personal helicopter" to be used by an everyday soldier on the front lines. The Cold War was at its height and the army wanted to move dogfaces around on an atomic battlefield. The soldier-pilot would control the craft through "kinesthetics," meaning body movements. This plan for aerial eyes and ears for ground troops was more ambitious than anything that could be supported by technology, soldier training, or any realistic need. The UH-1 Huey helicopter proved a better solution for the army.

Engine: 1 Mercury Marine 20H outboard motor
Horsepower: 40
Maximum speed: 75 mph
Rotor diameter: two rotors, 5 ft. each

- First flight November 22, 1954
- Number built: 12
- Logged 15 flight hours during 160 flights
- Proved difficult to control in flight
- Test pilot Selmer Sundby was awarded the Distinguished Flying Cross

3.29.1955
VOUGHT F8U CRUSADER

DIFFICULT, DEMANDING, AND SUPER-HOT

In combat over North Vietnam, Crusaders shot down 19 MiGs with just three losses. The F8U Crusader (F-8 from October 1962) was a contemporary of the F-100 Super Sabre and the first US Navy fighter with reliable, supersonic performance. The F8U-1P photo version completed the first supersonic transcontinental flight July 16, 1957, in the hands of future astronaut John Glenn. This was a heavily armed, hot warplane that could outfight any fighter of its era but was difficult to fly and exceedingly difficult to land—some dubbed it the "ensign killer."

- First flight March 29, 1955
- Number built: 1,219
- Just one two-seater, nicknamed the "Twosader"

Engine: 1 Pratt & Whitney J57-P-20A turbojet engine with afterburner
Thrust: 10,700 lb.
Maximum speed: 1,225 mph (Mach 1.86)
Wingspan: 35 ft. 8 in.

6.12.1955
CESSNA 172 SKYHAWK

FUNCTIONAL AND FUN: THE UNIVERSAL FOUR-SEATER

It's a super ship to fly. It's that simple. The Cessna 172 started life as a tricycle-landing-gear variant of the tail-dragger Cessna 170 but from the mid-1950s onward outpaced the 170 in sales and popularity. It's comfortable, pilot friendly, and suitable for everyone from the beginning student to the high-hour pro. Instructors like the 172 because its roomy, sensible cockpit was designed in part to be amenable to training. Executives like this aircraft because it has access to more airports than any other really comfortable business aircraft.

Engine: 1 Lycoming IO-360-L2A four-cylinder engine
Horsepower: 160
Cruising speed: 140 mph
Wingspan: 36 ft. 1 in.

- First flight: June 12, 1955
- Number built: About 60,000, more than any other aircraft; 1,400 were built in 1956, the first year of sales
- Cost: $350,000 to $400,000 today
- More than a dozen versions, including diesel
- Late versions have a sweptback tail and an aft window

215

REPUBLIC XF-84H "THUNDERSCREECH"

AN IDEA WHOSE TIME NEVER CAME

What if they made a plane so loud its noise was painful to maintainers working around it? That was one of the technical challenges the unorthodox XF-84H, known as the Thunderscreech, was unable to overcome. Derived from the more conventional F-84F Thunderstreak, the XF-84H was one of the last-ever attempts to combine a turboprop engine with a jet-style warplane design. It was so loud that engine run-ups on the ground could be heard 25 miles away. In the air, it was unstable and dangerous to fly although it ranks today as one of the fastest propeller planes ever built.

Engine: 1 Allison XT40-A-1 turboprop engine
Horsepower: 5,850
Maximum speed: 520 mph
Wingspan: 33 ft. 5 in.

- First flight: July 22, 1955
- Number built: 2
- Logged only 6 hours 40 minutes flight time
- Vibrations inflicted illness on maintenance crews

8.1.1955

LOCKHEED U-2 DRAGON LADY

THE WORLD'S BEST-KNOWN SECRET

The U-2 is one of the most recognized aircraft in aviation. First-generation U-2s flew reconnaissance at the height of Cold War tensions; one was shot down over the Soviet Union, another over Cuba. Later models, introduced in the 1980s, have pulled spyplane duty in every recent crisis. Plans to replace the U-2 are on hold. Pilots revel in flying high enough to witness the curvature of the earth, but it's not a joy-ride: a specialized pressure suit is required, physiological preparations for a flight to the edge of space take hours, and the cockpit is extremely cramped.

Engine: 1 General Electric F118-GE-101 turbofan engine (U-2S)
Thrust: 19,000 lb.
Maximum speed: 580 mph
Wingspan: 103 ft.

- First flight: August 1, 1955
- Number built: 86
- Flies routinely at 70,000 ft.
- 33 in inventory in 2014
- A mission lasts up to 14 hours
- Packed with cameras and electronic gear

10.22.1955

REPUBLIC F-105 THUNDERCHIEF

TOUGH AND DURABLE AGAINST FORMIDABLE ANTI-AIRCRAFT FIRE

The F-105 Thunderchief is the iconic Mach 2 warplane of the Vietnam war that went against the world's most heavily defended targets, scored numerous successes, and ultimately was withdrawn from battle due to its high loss rate. The Thunderchief—forever the "Thud" to airmen—was built to carry a nuclear weapon in its fuselage bay, but will always be remembered for conventional combat around Hanoi, where pilots named one mountain range "Thud Ridge." Two F-105 missions resulted in Medal of Honor awards. This was a sturdy, robust, roomy flying machine with a cadre of pilots who loved it unstintingly, and mechanics who wished it had been made a little easier to keep in the air.

Engine: 1 Pratt & Whitney J75-P-19W turbojet with afterburner
Thrust: 24,500 lb.
Maximum speed: 1,372 mph (Mach 2.08)
Wingspan: 34 ft. 11 in.

- First flight: October 22, 1955
- Number built: 833
- Cost: $2.14 million in 1960
- Last flown in reserve and air guard squadrons
- Retired: February 25, 1984

11.18.1955

BELL X-2

TRIUMPH AND TRAGEDY AT THE EDGE OF THE ENVELOPE

The Bell X-2 rocket research aircraft explored the outer extremes of speed and altitude in the 1950s, investigating flight characteristics at Mach 2 to 3 at a time when no one had been there. In the hands of Korean War air ace Capt. Iven C. Kincheloe, the X-2 became the first aircraft to reach 100,000 feet. Sadly, both X-2s were lost in mishaps after only ten powered flights, one of which claimed the life of Capt. Mel Apt. Despite tragedy, the X-2 was the fastest, highest-flying aircraft of its era and paved the way for many advances in aeronautical design.

Engine: 1 Curtiss-Wright XLR25 rocket engine
Thrust: 15,000 lb.
Maximum speed: 2,094 mph (Mach 3.0)
Wingspan: 32 ft. 3 in.

- First flight: November 18, 1955
- Appears on a Guyana postage stamp
- First US aircraft with a throttleable rocket motor
- Carried aloft by a B-50 Superfortress bomber

12.10.1955
RYAN X-13 VERTIJET

A JET TAIL SITTER—
AND IT ACTUALLY WORKED

The US Air Force's X-13 Vertijet was a vertical takeoff and landing research aircraft of the 1950s. Its purpose was to demonstrate the ability of a pure jet to vertically take off, hover, transition to horizontal flight, and vertically land. This gave it much in common with the US Navy's Convair XFY-1 and Lockheed XFV-1 turboprop tail sitters. The two X-13s performed better than the navy tail sitters, and in July 1957 one demonstrated its capabilities by landing at the Pentagon Building. Even though the X-13s were able to make fully transitional flights, the jet tail-sitter concept was deemed impractical and was not adopted on any operational aircraft, then or later.

Engine: 1 Rolls-Royce Avon RA.28 turbojet engine
Thrust: 10,000 lb.
Maximum speed: 350 mph
Wingspan: 21 ft.

- First flight: December 10, 1955
- Number built: 2
- Ended tests September 30, 1957
- Flown by Ryan company test pilots
- Both in museums today

2.13.1956

GOODYEAR INFLATOPLANE

AFTER YOU GET BLOWN UP,
YOU ESCAPE BY BLOWING IT UP

In the post-Korea 1950s, US Army aviation had the luxury of testing dozens of outlandish flying concepts, some of which appeared contrary to common sense. The queer and somewhat quirky Goodyear Inflatoplane was a bizarre concept for rescuing soldiers trapped behind the lines. A larger aircraft would airdrop the Inflatoplane inside a hardened container. Stranded soldiers would blow it up using a bicycle pump and would fly to safety. The Inflatoplane performed exactly as the army requested, despite a fatal crash during tests, but the service decided not to proceed with it because the brass considered it too vulnerable to small-arms fire.

Engine: 1 McCulloch 4318 air-cooled radial engine
Horsepower: 60
Maximum speed: 70 mph
Rotor diameter: 28 ft.

- First flight February 13, 1956
- Number built: 12 (single- and two-seaters)
- Required less air pressure than a car tire
- 2 are in museums today

4.21.1956
DOUGLAS F5D SKYLANCER

LEFT AT THE STARTING GATE

The Douglas F5D Skylancer would have whacked any MiG in the world had it fulfilled its mid-1950s promise to be the US Navy's next carrier-based fighter. In test situations, it was a joy to fly and unbeatable in a fight. Many believe that politics, which favored Vought over Douglas, contributed to the F8U Crusader becoming the navy's choice instead. Future moonwalker Neil Armstrong also piloted the F5D. The survivor among four planes built is displayed at the Neil Armstrong Air and Space Museum in Ohio.

- First flight: April 21, 1956
- Number built: 4
- Test flown by future astronaut Alan B. Shepard Jr.

Engine: 1 Pratt & Whitney J57-P-8 turbojet engi
   with afterburner
Thrust: 10,200 lb.
Maximum speed: 990 mph (Mach 1.48)
Wingspan: 33 ft. 6 in.

8.23.1956
DOUGLAS C-133 CARGOMASTER

LARGE, LONG-RANGED, AND VERY USEFUL, BUT NOT QUITE LOVABLE

The C-133 Cargomaster was the US Air Force's only turboprop-powered strategic airlifter, following the C-130 Hercules, which had tactical duties and was replaced by the jet-powered C-5 Galaxy, which also had ocean-spanning strategic reach. This was a very useful, heavy-hauling transport that appeared in two similar models (C-133A, C-133B), offering a cargo compartment that was pressurized, heated, and ventilated. Although it set some cargo-carrying records and served far beyond its intended fatigue life, the C-133 was never well liked by pilots, crew, or passengers and had the poorest safety record of any aircraft of its era, thanks to poor stall characteristics. The C-133 was retired in 1971 and no airworthy examples exist today.

Engines: 4 Pratt & Whitney TF34-P-9W
   turboprop engines
Horsepower: 7,500 shaft each
Maximum speed: 359 mph
Wingspan: 179 ft. 8 in.

- First flight: August 23, 1956
- Number built: 50 (32 C-133A, 18 C-133B)
- 9 were lost in crashes
- Some transported Titan and Minuteman missiles

BOEING KC-135 STRATOTANKER

THE DEPENDABLE TANKER THAT SEEMS TO BE EVERYWHERE

The Boeing KC-135 Stratotanker was designed to be a filling station in the sky and to refuel other aircraft at jet speed. It performed other missions, including VIP transport and airborne command post duty. One served NASA as an in-flight weightlessness laboratory, dubbed the "Vomit Comet." But the KC-135 remains the first purpose-built tanker, and the first able to keep pace with the jet fighters and bombers that were in inventory by the late 1950s. Today's re-engined KC-135R model, operating worldwide, can refuel any US or friendly-nation combat aircraft. Eventually, the Boeing KC-46A Pegasus will replace some KC-135s.

Engines: 4 CFM International F108-CF0-100 (CFM56) turbofan engines (KC-135R)
Thrust: 21,650 lb. each
Maximum speed: 580 mph
Wingspan: 130 ft. 10 in.

- First flight: August 31, 1956
- Number built: 820
- Last one delivered in October 1965
- 414 in inventory in 2014
- 200,000 sorties during the Vietnam war

BELL UH-1 "HUEY"

THE HELICOPTER EVERYONE KNOWS

It was called the XH-40 and the HU-1—source of its "Huey" nickname—but for most of its career the iconic helicopter of the Vietnam era was dubbed the UH-1. The single-engine Bell UH-1 Iroquois, or Huey, was everywhere in Vietnam with the air force (UH-1F), army (UH-1A, B, C, D, H), marine corps (UH-1E), and navy (UH-1B) all the time; the distinctive sound of its two-blade, 48-foot rotor became inseparable from images and memories of the Southeast Asia conflict. Hueys also served in two dozen countries around the world in every mission from medical evacuation to troop transport. Pilots felt exposed in the glass nose but praised the Huey's responsiveness and overall performance.

Engine: 1 Lycoming T53-L-13 gas turbine engine (UH-1H)
Horsepower: 1,400 shaft
Maximum speed: 135 mph
Main rotor diameter: 48 ft.

- First flight: October 20, 1956
- Number built: More than 16,000
- Most famous action: Ia Drang November 14–18, 1965 (seen in the 2002 film *We Were Soldiers*)
- 7,000 saw action in Vietnam
- 8 Huey pilots received the Medal of Honor for Vietnam actions

12.26.1956
CONVAIR F-106 DELTA DART

"THE 'CADILLAC OF THE SKIES' OF OUR ERA" —Bud Tauscher, F-106 pilot

It started out as the ultimate interceptors of the Cold War, tasked with defending North America in a Doomsday War. It flew in active-duty air force and air national guard squadrons, although none was ever exported. It ended up as a pilotless drone, swatted out of the sky as a target for other defensive systems. There were many of them—only 277 single-seat F-106As and 63 two-seat F-106Bs were built—but the F-106 Delta Dart may have been the most beloved of the "century series" fighters and one of the most beautiful aircraft ever built. The pointy-nosed, delta-winged "Six," as pilots called it, performed spectacularly and gave pilots a comfortable and trouble-free ride.

Engine: 1 Pratt & Whitney J75-P-17 turbojet engine with afterburner
Thrust: 24,500 lb.
Maximum speed: 1,525 mph (Mach 2.3)
Wingspan: 38 ft. 4 in.

- First flight: December 26, 1956
- Number built: 340
- Cost: $4.7 million in 1960

9.12.1957
CESSNA 150

A FAMILIAR FRIEND AT AIRPORTS EVERYWHERE

It's possible that more student pilots—the author of this book among them—made their first solo flight in the Cessna 150 than in any other aircraft. The fifth most numerous civilian aircraft in history with 23,949 built, the high-wing, side-by-side Cessna 150, together with its derivative Cessna 152, sets the standard for a straightforward and sensible general-aviation airplane for flight training, touring, and personal recreation. It's affordable, easy to fly, and forgiving. Even pilots of high-performance jets often come back to the 150 for a ride they can really savor.

Engine: 1 Continental O-200-A flat-4 engine
Horsepower: 100
Cruising speed: 123 mph
Wingspan: 33 ft. 34 in.

- First flight: September 12, 1957
- Cost: $12,000 to $25,000 used in 2014
- US Air Force version: the T-51A

1.31.1958
NORTH AMERICAN T-2 BUCKEYE

BIG, BURLY, AND BETTER THAN IT LOOKS

Face it: it's tubby. But the North American T-2 Buckeye (known as the T2J until 1962) performed far more energetically than its portly shape suggests. Designed as a single-engine aircraft, it became operational and spent most of its life with twin engines. At least ten thousand naval aviators and naval flight officers underwent training in this fat flying machine before pinning on pilot wings. One describes the Buckeye as a "gentle giant," burly in appearance but quick on the controls.

- First flight: January 31, 1958
- Number built: 529, all in Columbus
- Pulled navy training duty from 1959 to 2004

Engines: 2 General Electric J85-GE-4 turbojet engines (T-2C)
Thrust: 2,950 lb. each
Maximum speed: 522 mph
Wingspan: 38 ft. 1½ in.

5.22.1958
SIKORSKY HH-52 SEAGUARD

UNIQUE TO THE COAST GUARD AND MUCH ADMIRED

The HH-52 Seaguard, called the HU2S-1G until October 1962, is often billed as the only aircraft ever manufactured solely for the US Coast Guard although it was derived from a design used by intra-city helicopter airlines in the 1960s. It was the first helicopter with a flying boat-type hull. Coast guardsmen flew the Seaguard from ships' decks and from shore installations. They found it resilient, adaptable, and almost invulnerable to salt-water corrosion. Whether on ice patrol or carrying out a search and rescue mission, the Seaguard was for almost thirty years a real workhorse, and was immensely popular with pilots and crews. A handful survive today, including one that went secondhand to the Icelandic Coast Guard, and at least two are airworthy.

Engine: 1 General Electric T58-GE-8B gas turbine engine
Horsepower: 700 shaft
Maximum speed: 109 mph
Main rotor diameter: 53 ft.

- First flight: May 22, 1958
- Number built: 99
- Capacity: Pilot, co-pilot, and 11 passengers

MCDONNELL F-4 PHANTOM II

"FOR A GENERATION, PHANTOMS ROSE FROM LAND AND SEA TO TAKE COMMAND OF THE AIR" —McDonnell, 1988

In the late years of the Cold War and in battle-ravaged skies over North Vietnam, the F-4 Phantom II was the premier fighter of its time. The twin-engine, two-crew Phantom II had been designed as an interceptor—until 1962, the navy version was called the F4H-1, the air force model, the F-110—but proved itself in both air-to-air and air-to-ground combat. Fighter pilots, being fighter pilots, resisted having a weapons officer in the back seat until they discovered that an extra pair of eyes and a second opinion were invaluable in combat. The F-4 was famous for the expansive comfort of its cockpit, speed, maneuverability, and the enormous power in its twin engines. This was the most important fighter in the West during its era, but, to a pilot who mastered its quirks and complexities, it was a fun aircraft, a sheer joy to fly.

Engines: 2 General Electric J79-GE-17A turbojet engines with afterburners
Thrust: 11,905 lb.
Maximum speed: 1,471 mph (Mach 2.23)
Wingspan: 38 ft. 5 in.

- First flight: May 27, 1958
- Number built: 5,174
- Armament: Initially built without a gun; late models had an internal 20mm cannon
- Used by 13 countries
- Set numerous speed and altitude records

8.18.1958
GRUMMAN GULFSTREAM I

A TURBOPROP WITH NUMEROUS DUTIES

Before Gulfstream became the name of a planemaker (founded in 1978 after Grumman sold its Savannah, Georgia, factory), the name referred to a smart, turboprop executive transport designed and developed by Grumman. Trim and economical, the Gulfstream I made the mistake of entering the upscale travel market in an era when pure jets were taking over from turboprops. But pilots loved its intelligent layout and many preferred it to the jets that followed.

- First flight: August 18, 1958
- Number built: 200
- Capacity: Typically seats 12 passengers
- About 30 in corporate service today

Engines: 2 Rolls-Royce Dart Mk 529 turboprop engines
Horsepower: 2,210 each
Maximum speed: 357 mph
Wingspan: 78 ft. 4 in.

8.31.1958
NORTH AMERICAN A-5 VIGILANTE

"THIS AIRPLANE WAS A REAL BADASS"
—Rear Adm. Jerome Brand, RA-5C pilot

The A-5 Vigilante (called the A3J until October 1962) was designed as a high-performance, carrier-based nuclear bomber to replace the Douglas A3D Skywarrior. Initially, it was thought the aircraft would carry a nuclear bomb in its fuselage between its twin engines but that aspect of the design was dropped. The Vigilante was a unique design in other respects. Its swept wing incorporated no ailerons: the pilot achieved roll control by using spoilers in conjunction with differential use of an all-flying tailplane on each side of the fuselage. It was the first US production aircraft with variable-geometry air intakes, later found on many advanced warplanes. After it switched jobs and became a reconnaissance plane, the Vigilante was crucial in Vietnam. None are airworthy today.

Engines: 2 General Electric J79-GE-8 turbojet engines with afterburners
Thrust: 10,900 lb. each
Maximum speed: 1,320 mph (Mach 2.0)
Wingspan: 53 ft.

- First flight: August 31, 1958
- Number built: 156
- Crew: 2
- 140 served as RA-5C reconnaissance ships

NORTH AMERICAN SABRELINER

A TRANSPORT AND A TRAINER, IN UNIFORM AND IN MUFTI

It was meant to be a business jet, but most became military trainers. The North American Sabreliner (military T-39) drew many of its design features from the F-86 Sabre. In many ways it not only looked, but also acted, a lot like the famous fighter. It was one of the fastest executive transports when introduced. It later became so valuable to the US Air Force, Marine Corps, and Navy for navigator training that a second generation of Sabreliners, dubbed T-39Ns, were refurbished and reintroduced to service in the 1980s. They're still at it today.

Engines: 2 Pratt & Whitney J60-P-3 turbojet engines
Thrust: 3,000 lb. each
Cruising speed: 500 mph
Wingspan: 44 ft. 6 in.

- First flight: September 16, 1958
- Number built: About 800
- Capacity: 7 to 10 passengers
- Monsanto was the first company to operate a corporate jet, a Sabreliner

PIASECKI VZ-8 SKY-CAR

"PRETTY GOOD PLATFORM, BUT COULD BE SCARY TO SOME"—Test pilot Tommy Atkins

The VZ-8 Sky-Car, also called the Airgeep, was one of many outlandish ideas pursued by US Army aviation in the mid-1950s, in this case for the purpose of developing a Flying Jeep. It used two tandem, three-bladed ducted motors to provide lift and carried a crew of two. Tested with no fewer than five different engines employed on two airframes during development, the VZ-8 is a contemporary of the de Lackner HZ-1 Aerocycle and was similarly intended to be used by everyday soldiers with little specialized training. After the VZ-8 went through several modifications and performed reasonably well, the army decided it did not need a Flying Jeep after all and wisely shifted its funding to the UH-1 Huey.

Engines: Turbomeca Artouste IIC turboshaft engines (typical)
Horsepower: 550 each
Maximum speed: 85 mph
Width: 9 ft. 3 in.

- First flight: September 22, 1958
- Number built: 2, repeatedly modified during tests from 1958 to 1963
- Intended to be smaller and easier to fly than a helicopter
- 1 survives in a museum today

12.22.1958
VOLMER SPORTSMAN

ON LAND AND SEA, A NEAT PLANE FOR THE OUTDOOR TYPE

Volmer Jenson, a sailplane designer, was the genius behind this family of small, amphibious aircraft for recreational use in the civilian world. A typical Volmer Sportsman is a side-by-side, two-seat, high-wing, single-engine aircraft that operates on both land and sea. Jenson had hoped to manufacture these aircraft but ended up selling plans to homebuilders instead of fabricating planes. The Sportsman is a lightweight with limited range and carrying capacity. It's great for fun flying, and ideal for a fishing trip.

- First flight: December 22, 1958
- 889 plans sold
- Plans selling for $250 in 2014

Engine: 1 Continental C85 air-cooled radial piston engine (typical)
Horsepower: 90
Cruising speed: 92 mph
Weight: 1,600 lb. (typical gross)
Wingspan: 35 ft. 5 in.

1.27.1959
CONVAIR 880

STYLE AND CLASS

The Convair 880 was a better looking, faster, more comfortable contemporary of the Boeing 707 and Douglas DC-8, but it failed competing for airline purchases. Its J79 engines gave extra speed but made it costly to operate. One, the *Flying Mandarin Palace* of Taiwan's Civil Air Transport, was perhaps the most luxurious jetliner ever serving regular commercial routes. Another, the *Lisa Marie*, became Elvis Presley's aircraft, named for the singer's daughter. The US Navy dubbed the sole military example the UC-880.

- First flight: January 27, 1959
- Number built: 65
- Convair's name, "Golden Arrow," never caught on

Engines: 4 General Electric J79 (CJ805-3B) turbojet engines
Thrust: 11,650 lb. each
Cruising speed: 610 mph
Wingspan: 120 ft.

4.10.1959

NORTHROP T-38 TALON

THE FASTEST SCHOOLHOUSE IN THE SKY

Designed by a Northrop engineering team headed by Lee Begin, the T-38 Talon filled a unique role for four decades—the only supersonic trainer that *all* would-be pilots flew. Even if you were going to spend your career in a big, slow tanker or transport, you had to start out in the T-38, and for many US Air Force pilots who put the Talon through its paces before pinning on their wings, it was the fastest plane they ever flew. This "universal" scheme ended in the 1990s when the air force limited T-38 training to those student pilots with fast-jet assignments. That was about the time the Talon acquired a gray-green camouflage, but until then it had been gloss white and everybody called it the "white rocket."

Engines: 2 afterburning General Electric J85-GE-5A turbojets
Thrust: 3,850 lb. each
Top speed: 812 mph (Mach 1.08)
Wingspan: 25 ft. 3 in.

- First flight: April 10, 1959
- Cost: $756,000 in 1961
- Number built: 1,187 through January 31, 1972
- Delivered to its first squadron March 17, 1961
- By 2010, all T-38A models had been upgraded to T-38Cs with digital cockpits
- "Climbs like you've lit a fire under it," said Lt. Gen. James E. Briggs

GRUMMAN OV-1 MOHAWK

AN ARMED AIRPLANE IN, OF ALL PLACES, THE ARMY

The US Army is not supposed to operate armed, fixed-wing aircraft. That job belongs to the air force, which opposed development of the twin-turboprop OV-1 Mohawk every step of the way. The OV-1 (called the AO-1 until October 1, 1962) was so useful and so effective that, despite opposition, the army operated five companies of Mohawks in Vietnam. Advanced models of the Mohawk did reconnaissance and electronic warfare work in the 1991 Persian Gulf war. With its prominent bubble top and broad cockpit, the OV-1 won affection easily from soldiers, and the army retired the aircraft only reluctantly.

Engines: 2 Lycoming T53-L-701 turboprop engines
Horsepower: 1,400 shaft each
Maximum speed: 305 mph
Wingspan: 48 ft.

- First flight: April 14, 1959
- Number built: About 380 of all versions
- 2 are flying today
- A dozen are displayed in museums

NORTH AMERICAN X-15

FASTER AND HIGHER

Forty-five years after it was retired never to fly again, X-15 holds the official record for the highest speed ever attained by a manned aircraft, 4,520 miles per hour. The X-15 was a rocket-powered research ship that set epoch-making speed and altitude records, soared to the very edge of space, and contributed enormously to knowledge that went into future aircraft and spacecraft. Everything about it was superlative, including the mind-boggling complexity of its cockpit instrument array, and its sometimes lagging responses to the pilot's controls.

Engine: 1 Thiokol XLR99-RM-2 liquid-fuel rocket engine
Thrust: 70,400 lb.; 5,200 lb. thrust per J47
Maximum speed: 4,520 mph
Wingspan: 22 ft. 4 in.

- First flight: September 17, 1959
- Number built: 3
- Carried aloft by a B-52 Stratofortress
- X-15s made 155 powered flights
- Future moonwalker Neil Armstrong flew the X-15
- 1 fatal crash; 2 in museums

11.24.1959

HILLER X-18

A CONGLOMERATION OF STUFF THAT CONTRIBUTED TO AVIATION KNOWLEDGE

The X-18 looked as if Stanley Hiller went to a junkyard, gathered bits and pieces from different piles, and fastened them together almost willy-nilly. In fact, the X-18 was the culmination of aviation pioneer Hiller's lifelong pursuit of vertical flight, but it contained hardly a single new part, wasn't smooth, wasn't pretty, and wasn't built to last. The hope was that it would teach a new government agency, NASA (founded in 1958), something about the behavior of large airframes in vertical flight. Hiller created the X-18 by cobbling building parts from several discarded airplanes around the fuselage of a Chase C-122, which made the X-18 fully the size of a tactical transport. This aircraft did a creditable job of demonstrating capabilities, with its unique method of propulsion that comprised two turboprop engines plus a turbojet, added not for power, but to assure stability. The X-18 test program was brief, but paved the way for further tests by the LTV XC-142.

Engines: 2 Allison T40-A-14 turboprop engines (salvaged from Lockheed XFV-1s) plus 1 Westinghouse J34 turbojet engine

Horsepower: 6,000 shaft each (T40); 3,000 lb. thrust (J34)

Maximum speed: 253 mph

Wingspan: 47 ft. 11 in.

- First flight: November 24, 1959
- Number built: 1
- Cost: Program cost $3.7 million in 1960
- Made 20 flights between 1959 and 1961
- Scrapped in 1964

CONVAIR 990 CORONADO

IT WAS PRETTY AND COSTLY AND DIDN'T LAST LONG

The Convair 990 Coronado (together with the upgraded 990A model) was a "stretched" version of the planemaker's 880, with a longer, sleeker shape and distinctive anti-shock fairings on the upper trailing edge of the wing to increase the critical Mach and reduce drag. It was the fastest airliner that was not supersonic. It was developed explicitly for American Airlines, which called it the Astrojet, but it carried fewer passengers and had greater operating cost than the contemporaneous Boeing 707 and Douglas DC-8. NASA used one for space research, and others used it for charter flights, but the 990 was simply too expensive to be an enduring success with the airlines.

Engines: 4 General Electric J79 (CJ805-23B) turbojet engines
Thrust: 16,050 lb. each
Maximum speed: 621 mph (Mach 0.91)
Wingspan: 120 ft.

- First flight: January 24, 1961
- Number built: 37
- Capacity: 96 to 121 passengers
- Critics of operating costs called it the "Convair Calamity"
- Named for being able to fly at 990 ft. per second

MERCURY SPACE CAPSULE

THE FIRST AMERICAN SPACECRAFT

Because primates flew as test subjects before humans went into space, pilot Chuck Yeager derided the Mercury space capsule—which had no wings or powerplant—as "a Spam can with a seat covered in monkey shit." Still, the iconic Mercury vehicle made six manned flights, advancing the United States in its space rivalry with the Soviet Union. The Mercury spacecraft was cone shaped, with a neck at the narrow end and a convex base where the heat shield for re-entry was located. The capsule was boosted aloft by a booster rocket and descended to Earth via parachute, coming down at sea where the astronaut-pilot was recovered by helicopter.

Engines: 3 small rocket engines used for mid-course adjustment (not for power)
Length: 10 ft. 10 in.
Width: 6 ft.
Controls: 55 electrical switches, 30 fuses, 35 mechanical levers

- First American space flight: *Freedom 7* (Alan Shepard) May 5, 1961, suborbital
- Second flight: *Liberty Bell 7* (Gus Grissom), July 21, 1961, suborbital
- First American in orbit: *Friendship 7* (John Glenn), February 20, 1962
- Others: *Aurora 7* (Scott Carpenter), May 24, 1962; *Sigma 7* (Wally Schirra) October 3, 1962
- Final solo spaceflight: *Faith 7* (Gordon Cooper), May 15, 1963

9.21.1961

BOEING CH-47 CHINOOK

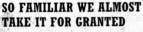

SO FAMILIAR WE ALMOST TAKE IT FOR GRANTED

The long-lived, twin-tandem CH-47 Chinook is the ultimate redemption of trailblazing efforts by designer-pilot Frank Piasecki. His company evolved into present-day Boeing Rotorcraft Systems, and his twin-tandem concept, seen early in the HRP Rescuer, reached real maturity when the Chinook led the way in every conflict from Vietnam to the present. Whether it was hauling howitzers from one artillery site to another, or functioning as a gunship, an infantry transport, or a special-operations bird, the Chinook has been everywhere soldiers go, and has done just about everything. Still on the assembly line in 2014, it's one of the longest-serving military aircraft in history, along with the B-52 Stratofortress and the C-130 Hercules.

Engines: 2 Lycoming T55-GA-714A turboshaft engines
Horsepower: 4,733 each
Maximum speed: 198 mph
Main rotor diameter: 60 ft.

- First flight: September 21, 1961
- Number built: About 1,200
- Cost: About $38 million (CH-47F, 2014)
- Operated by 16 nations

7.7.1962

LOCKHEED XV-4 HUMMINGBIRD

IT WAS COMPLICATED, BUT IT SHOWED PROMISE

The US Army was high in the 1950s and 1960s on aircraft that took off and landed vertically. Poorly prepared to use helicopters in Korea, the army exploited the period immediately following that war to study new concepts, which they implemented in Vietnam. One was the odd but graceful XV-4 Hummingbird. The XV-4 achieved vertical flight by directing jet efflux through a diverter valve in each exhaust. Gases were ejected at high speed into a mixing chamber by twenty ducts, creating a low-pressure area, and drawing stream air through doors atop the fuselage. Once speed reached 90 miles per hour, the diverter valve of one engine was switched to provide normal thrust. The second engine was similarly switched on when speed reached 145 miles per hour. The XV-4 subsequently returned from horizontal to vertical flight by reducing speed progressively and reversing the process. The XV-4 achieved most goals, but a fatal crash cut the program short.

Engines: 2 Pratt & Whitney JT12 turbojet engines on the fuselage sides (XV-4A); 4 General Electric J85-GE-19 turbojet engines (XV-4B)

Thrust: 3,000 lb. thrust each (XV-4A) 3,015 lb. thrust each (XV-4B)

Maximum speed: 510 mph

Wingspan: 25 ft. 8 in. (XV-4A)

- First flight: July 7, 1962
- Number built: 2 (XV-4A and XV-4B)
- US Army's first jet-powered aircraft

AERO SPACELINES PREGNANT GUPPY

AN ORIGINAL IDEA FOR A USEFUL PURPOSE

The Pregnant Guppy was former air force fighter pilot Jack Conroy's concept for a colossal cargo hauler for outsized items like NASA's components of the Apollo moon program. After mortgaging his house to invest in converting a Boeing 377 Stratocruiser (the military C-97) into a gigantic transport, Conroy won the job of transporting S-IV Saturn rocket stages in hours by air, rather than weeks by land, at a cost of just $16.00 per mile. The Pregnant Guppy featured a rear section, tail included, that could be removed for loading and unloading. The sole Pregnant Guppy airlifted heavy items from 1962 to 1979, its potential limited by its maintenance-intensive piston engines. Conroy built on the experience to develop the turboprop Super Guppy, and Airbus later applied similar thinking to its supersized A300-600ST Beluga.

Engines: 4 Pratt & Whitney R-4360-69 Wasp Major radial piston engines
Horsepower: 3,500 each
Maximum speed: 320 mph
Wingspan: 127 ft.

- First flight: September 19, 1962
- Number built: 1
- Logged about 25,000 air hours
- Fuselage size created drag that slowed landing speed somewhat
- Eventually scrapped

12.8.1962
BELL 206 JETRANGER

A RELIABLE MAINSTAY

The Bell 206 JetRanger and LongRanger family of two-blade, single- and twin-engined crafts has been a smashing success in law enforcement, medical evacuation, and military observation and training. Few helicopters are more user-friendly to fledgling students and old, bold pilots alike. A bit long-in-the-tooth technology-wise in today's fast-changing world, the utilitarian 206 is gradually being supplanted by newer rotorcraft.

Engine: 1 Allison 250-C20B turboshaft engine
Horsepower: 317 shaft
Maximum speed: 138 mph
Main rotor diameter: 33 ft. 4 in.

- First flight: December 8, 1962
- Trainer versions: Navy TH-57 SeaRanger, Army TH-67 Creek
- With H. Ross Perot Jr., completed the first helicopter round-the-world flight in 1982

10.7.1963
LEARJET

THE BULLET-SHAPED JET
THAT STARTED IT ALL

The most famous executive bizjet is the handiwork of American Bill Lear, deriving design features from the Swiss P-16 fighter, and (since 1990) the product of a Canadian planemaker, Bombardier. The Learjet's styling, performance, and innovative technologies set the standard. The Learjet is long in the tooth now, no longer coming off the assembly line, but in more than a dozen versions, in civilian and military use, it paved the way for every executive jet in the air today.

Engines: 2 Garrett TFE731-2-3B turbofan engines
Thrust: 3,500 lb. each
Maximum speed: 530 mph (Mach 0.81)
Wingspan: 39 ft. 6 in.

- First flight: October 7, 1963
- Number built: 738 Learjet 35 models
- Capacity: 8 passengers, 3,153 lb. of cargo
- Popular with private, corporate, and air taxi operators

CESSNA A-37 DRAGONFLY

ADDING ATTACK MUSCLE TO A TAME TRAINER

The A-37 Dragonfly is sometimes mistaken for its cousin, the T-37 Tweet trainer, but the A-37 is bigger, has bigger engines, and has a different mission—not training, but air-to-ground attack. By adding muscle and power to the basic T-37 design, Cessna and the US Air Force re-invented a solid aircraft for close support of ground troops by American and South Vietnamese pilots. Later, many Latin American air forces adopted the A-37 as a small, affordable air-to-ground weapon.

Engines: 2 General Electric J85-GE-17 turbojet engines
Thrust: 2,850 lb. each
Maximum speed: 507 mph
Wingspan: 35 ft. 11 in.

- First flight: October 22, 1963
- Number built: 616 (39 were A-37A, 577 were A-37B)
- Side-by-side seating; usually flown by a single pilot
- 1 is airworthy in the United States today

CURTISS-WRIGHT X-19

SOMETIMES IT DOESN'T LOOK RIGHT —AND IT ISN'T

If a big transport could take off and land straight up and down, we wouldn't need airports and that would be good, right? It's a goal yet to be attained, and it was the goal of the Curtiss-Wright Corp.—which has not had a successful aircraft design since World War II—when it made the proposal that became the X-19 research aircraft. This was a bold risk-taking on the part of designers, including the decision to have two full-sized wings on the aircraft—no one referred to it as a "biplane," although technically, it was—but the gamble produced only limited results. Costly and cumbersome to operate in tests, the X-19 contributed to knowledge but did not produce a practical transport aircraft.

Engines: 2 Avco Lycoming T55-L-5 turboshaft engines
Horsepower: 2,200 shaft each
Maximum speed: 454 mph
Wingspan: 19 ft. 6 in. (forward); 21 ft. 6 in. (aft)

- First flight November 20, 1963
- Number built: 2
- Cost: $3.9 million for X-19 program
- 1 crashed; no one was hurt

12.17.1963

LOCKHEED C-141 STARLIFTER

NOT PRETTY, BUT A VENERABLE VETERAN

The Lockheed C-141 Starlifter had a decades-long love affair with pilots, navigators, and loadmasters who didn't care that the aircraft lacked glamour or pizazz: They loved the United States' first jet-powered strategic transport, unconditionally. They girdled the globe in it, hitting every brushfire trouble-spot along the way. These cargo haulers of the 1960s (C-141A) held so much growth potential, the US Air Force "stretched" 270 of them to add payload volume in the 1970s (C-141B) and added digital avionics to 63 of them in the 1990s (C-141C).

Engines: 4 Pratt & Whitney TF33-P-7 turbofan engines
Thrust: 20,250 lb. each
Maximum speed: 500 mph
Wingspan: 160 ft.

- First flight: December 17, 1963
- Number built: 285
- Retired: May 6, 2006
- Comparable to: Ilyushin Il-76 (Soviet Union)
- C-141 "Hanoi Taxi" brought US prisoners of war home from North Vietnam, 1973

NORTH AMERICAN XB-70 VALKYRIE

A HIGH-TECH BOMBER WITH THAT SCIENCE-FICTION LOOK

It was futuristic, which was fitting for the bomber of the future. The XB-70 Valkyrie was the planned replacement for the B-52 Stratofortress, which was starting to grow old in the 1960s. It was to be the nuclear-armed, deep-penetration bomber for the Strategic Air Command, ready on alert for trans-polar atomic war with the Soviet Union. It was one of the fastest military aircraft ever built but had been designed with little thought to the potency of new generations of surface-to-air missiles. Delays, cost issues, the missile problem, and a horrible fatal crash all conspired to keep the XB-70, despite excellent performance, from winning a production contract. And the B-52? It lasted a little longer.

Engines: 6 General Electric YJ93-GE-3 turbojet engines
Thrust: 28,000 lb.
Maximum speed: 2,056 mph (Mach 3.1)
Wingspan: 105 ft.

- First flight: September 21, 1964
- Number built: 2
- Cost: $750 million per plane in 1964
- Retired: 1969
- 1 crashed

9.29.1964
LTV XC-142

WEIRD, WONDERFUL, AND POTENTIALLY VERY USEFUL

It's exciting to visualize this vertical takeoff and landing research aircraft in Vietnam, whisking flyers in and out of jungle clearings. The LTV (Ling-Temco-Vought) XC-142 was built to investigate vertical/short takeoff and landing air transport. Unlike today's V-22 Osprey, which has *rotors* that tilt 90 degrees, the XC-142 employed an entire *wing* that rotated, but the result was the same: it could take off and land like a helicopter and fly as an airplane. It was overpowered and was the fastest turboprop vertical-takeoff transport of its era. Pilots found control of the craft during the ascent stage to be intricate because propeller pitch determined the aircraft's roll characteristics.

Engines: 4 General Electric T64-GE-1 turboprop engines
Horsepower: 2,850 each
Cruising speed: 288 mph
Wingspan: 67 ft. 6 in.

- First flight: September 29, 1964
- Number built: 5
- Capacity: Fuselage volume adequate to carry 32 armed troops
- Fuselage similar in shape to the Chinook helicopter
- Made 488 flights totaling 420 hours
- 1 survives

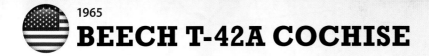

BEECH T-42A COCHISE

A FRIEND TO SKY-BORNE SOLDIERS WITH MULTI-ENGINE CREDS

The T-42A Cochise was the US Army's twin-engine instrument and transition trainer from 1966 to 1993. Many ex-military T-42As are flying in private hands today. The aircraft is a military derivative of the Beech Baron general-aviation aircraft. It provided an affable, comfortable way to learn twin-engine flying. Thousands of army aviators cut their teeth on the T-42A and liked it more than the bigger planes they flew later. Thousands more were pilots or passengers on the many occasions when the T-42A pulled double duty as an executive transport. The T-42A is no longer in uniform today, but some are operated by military flying clubs.

Engines: 2 Continental IO-470-L piston engines
Horsepower: 260 each
Cruising speed: 235 mph
Wingspan: 42 ft. 10 in.

- First flight: 1965
- 65 built for the US Army, five for the Turkish Army
- As a transport, carried pilot plus 4 passengers
- Not replaced; army no longer does fixed-wing, multi-engine training

AERO SPACELINES SUPER GUPPY

THEY USE IT TO CARRY BIG STUFF

The Aero Spacelines Super Guppy looks like a bloated steel whale. And, yes, it swallows stuff up. It's a huge, wide-bodied, cargo aircraft used for hauling outsized items of freight. It follows the piston-engine Pregnant Guppy and was built in two turboprop-powered versions (SG and SGT), generically dubbed the Super Guppy. Conceived by aviation pioneer Jack Conroy, all Guppy transports are built upon the architecture of the Boeing Stratocruiser, the military C-97 transport, and KC-97 tanker. One purpose for these outsized transports is to carry wing and fuselage components of Airbus aircraft to their final assembly plant—a job the Super Guppy performed brilliantly until being replaced at the turn of the century by the Airbus A300-600ST Beluga (ending the irony of a plane based on a Boeing design serving arch-rival Airbus). Super Guppies haul giant rocket fuel tanks and space-station components for NASA.

Engines: 4 Allison 501-D22C turboprop engines
Horsepower: 4,680 each
Maximum speed: 288 mph
Wingspan: 156 ft. 3 in.
Interior: 25 ft. tall, 25 ft. wide, 111 ft. long

- First flight: August 31, 1965
- Number built: 5 (1 was the SG, 4 were SGTs)
- Hinged nose opens 200 degrees so oversized cargoes can be slid in and out

5.21.1966
DAVIS DA-2

LOOKS LIKE A PACKING CRATE
BUT FLIES LIKE AN AIRPLANE

With a fuselage shaped more or less like a cinder block and a distinctive V-tail, the strange little Davis DA-2 is a home-built aircraft that turns heads. No, airplanes are not supposed to be square, but in spite of its boxy appearance the DA-2 and its close cousin the DA-2A are aerodynamically sound and perform well in flight. While many home-builts have a reputation for demanding too much know-how for an amateur pilot, the DA-2 and DA-2A are user-friendly and easy to fly. The manufacturer also produced a single DA-3, which expanded the plane's carrying capacity from two people to four.

- First flight: May 21, 1966
- Cost: About $2,300 in 1971
- Side-by-side seating for pilot and passenger

Engine: 1 Continental A65 piston engine (typical)
Horsepower: 65
Maximum speed: 120 mph
Weight: 1,125 lb. (gross)
Wingspan: 19 ft. 3 in.

10.2.1966
GRUMMAN GULFSTREAM II

CORPORATE COMFORT IN
A TIME OF TRANSITION

The first jet to bear its iconic name, the Grumman Gulfstream II offered spacious accommodations and long-range capability at a time when other bizjets were eclipsing the turboprop Gulfstream I. During its time in production, its assembly line moved from Bethpage, New York, to Savannah, Georgia, and its manufacturer underwent two corporate changes: Of 256 built, 121 came from Grumman, 106 from Grumman American, and 29 from Gulfstream American. The Gulfstream II could easily fly New York to Los Angeles (2,445 miles) against headwinds and with fuel reserves.

Engines: 2 Rolls-Royce Spey Mk 511-8 turbofan engines
Thrust: 11,000 lb. each
Maximum speed: 511 mph
Wingspan: 68 ft. 10 in.

- First flight: October 2, 1966
- 1 served in the US Coast Guard (VC-11A)
- Customer deliveries began December 1967

HAFE CH-1

IS IT IN A GARAGE SOMEWHERE?

The Hafe CH-1 is a two-seat, single-engine aircraft with retractable landing gear that appears to have been designed with recreation as the builder's top priority. It wasn't meant to be supersecret like the SR-71 Blackbird or the U-2 Dragon Lady, but very little information about the aircraft is circulating in the aviation community. It's a one-of-a-kind biplane that was a hit at air shows in the 1970s and 1980s. In 2002, it was for sale after a hard landing in which the propeller was bent and the fuselage was damaged. If it was sold, the buyer may not have intended to fly. It has since been deregistered, which means it's no longer airworthy. And it looks like it was a lot of fun, too.

Engine: 1 Lycoming O-520 radial piston engine
Horsepower: 100
Cruising speed: 85 mph
Wingspan: 22 ft. (estimated)

- First flight: 1967
- Number built: 1
- Builder appears to have been the only owner
- Logged 1,545 hours of air time

5.25.1968

NORTHROP GRUMMAN EA-6B PROWLER

AN ELECTRONIC INTRUDER ON STEROIDS

The EA-6B Prowler has been, from the Vietnam war onward, the US Navy's principal electronic warfare aircraft, replaced only recently by the Boeing EA-18G Growler. It's developed from the A-6 Intruder attack plane, but it's bigger, bulkier, and a little too slow to keep pace with a formation of warplanes on a strike mission. It carries anti-radiation missiles designed to take down a foe's radar sites. The EA-6B carries a pilot and three electronic countermeasures officers.

- First flight: May 25, 1968
- First service: July 1971
- Number built: 170

Engines: 2 Pratt & Whitney J52-P-408A turbojet engines
Thrust: 10.400 lb. each
Maximum speed: 651 mph
Wingspan: 53 ft.

6.30.1968

LOCKHEED C-5 GALAXY

WHEN "BIG" REALLY MEANS BIG

The C-5 Galaxy holds more cargo and travels farther than any other US cargo plane, even the much newer C-17 Globemaster III. The early C-5A overcame cost-overrun issues and hauled supplies in and out of Vietnam. A second production run gave the US Air Force—the only user—the upgraded C-5B model. Many of the latter are now being upgraded to C-5M standard with new engines and flight deck, and will be in service in the US strategic airlift fleet for many years to come.

- First flight: June 30, 1968
- First service: 1970
- Number built: 131
- Called "FRED" for "Fantastic Ridiculous Economic Disaster"

Engines: 4 General Electric TF39-GE-1C turbofan engines (C-5B)
Thrust: 43,000 lb. each
Maximum speed: 579 mph (Mach 0.79)
Wingspan: 222 ft. 9 in.

2.9.1969
BOEING 747

IN A CLASS BY ITSELF

A giant of the skies, the Boeing 747 revolutionized travel by carrying more people farther at lower cost than any previous aircraft. Called the jumbo jet because of its wide body, it's one of the most readily recognized aircraft and is credited with changing the world by opening air travel to the masses. Freighter versions are fast and efficient and have a large cargo capacity. The 747-400—the most numerous passenger version and the model with the longest range—is among the fastest airliners in service with a high subsonic cruising speed of Mach 0.855 or 570 miles per hour. The 747-400 model dispenses with a flight engineer and has just two pilots, who use advanced electronics and digital instruments and technology. "The perfect plane," one airline captain said, and the description fits. The 747-8 model slated for service in 2016 will exceed the current models' performance.

Engines: 4 Pratt & Whitney JT9D or Rolls-Royce RB211 turbofans (typical)
Thrust: 50,000 lb. each
Range: 8,350 mi. (747-400)
Wingspan: 195 ft. 8 in.

- First flight: February 9, 1969
- Number built: 1,487 as of April 2014
- Partially a double-decker, with a hump-shaped upper deck
- The wingspan of a 747 equals the distance covered by the 1903 Wright flyer's first flight

8.26.1969
FAIRCHILD METROLINER

A LONG, CRAMPED TUBE
THAT NEEDS A LITTLE LOVE

The Metroliner is a nineteen-passenger transport first produced by Swearingen and later by Fairchild (both now defunct). It's primarily a regional airliner although the US Air Force acquired several under the designation C-26 and the Swedish Air Force operates a VIP transport version called the Tp.88. In the same class as the Beech 1900, but not nearly as popular, the Metroliner served in several versions on airline routes before being replaced by jets. The Metroliner is considered claustrophobic by passengers and tricky to handle by pilots, and has a below-average safety record. The manufacturer had difficulty selling some of these. The Metroliner can be rated a modest success, but most have now been retired.

Engines: 2 Garrett AiResearch TPE-331 turboprop engines
Horsepower: 1,100 shaft each
Cruising speed: 355 mph
Wingspan: 57 ft.

- First flight: August 26, 1969
- Number built: 703
- Crew: 2 pilots

BELL 214ST

A MILITARY AND CIVILIAN "HUEY ON STEROIDS"

The Bell 214, called the "Huey Plus" during early development, began as a single-engine upgrade of the Vietnam-era Bell 205, or UH-1H Huey, using advanced technology of the pre-digital era. Delivered to the army of Iran in 1975, later assembled by Isfahan Aircraft (and still flying in post-revolutionary Tehran today), the 214 morphed into the twin-engine 214ST, where the "ST" suffix at first meant "Super Twin" and was later re-styled as "Super Transport." This is the heaviest hauler in the Huey family—a machine with mighty muscle.

Engines: 2 General Electric T700-T1C turboshaft engines (typical)
Horsepower: 2,250 shaft each
Cruising speed: 161 mph
Weight: Up to 13,100 lb. (gross)
Main rotor diameter: 50 ft.

- First flight: October 11, 1970
- Civil versions widely used to support offshore oil platforms
- Military users include Brunei, Peru, Thailand, Venezuela, and Oman

LOCKHEED L-1011 TRISTAR

BIG IN SIZE (500,000 POUNDS), SMALL IN NUMBER (250 BUILT)

The Lockheed L-1011 TriStar is a robust and sprightly jetliner built to meet an American Airlines requirement but sold only to other carriers. It served widely and well but must be viewed the loser in the "wide body war" of the 1970s where it competed with the Boeing 747 and Douglas DC-10. American's reluctance to buy, 1970s financial woes on the part of Rolls-Royce, and a bribery scandal in Japan all undermined the L-1011 sales effort. Pilots and flight engineers liked the L-1011 and often asked to be assigned to it.

Engines: 3 Rolls-Royce RB211-524V4 turbofan engines
Thrust: 50,000 lb. each
Cruising speed: 597 mph
Wingspan: 164 ft. 4 in.

- First flight: November 11, 1970
- 3 still airworthy in 2014
- Produced in 2 fuselage lengths—164 ft. 3 in. and 177 ft. 9 in.
- Orbital Sciences used a TriStar to launch Pegasus rockets into orbit
- 9 served the Royal Air Force as tankers and transports

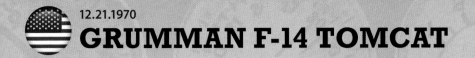
THE "TOP GUN" OF ITS ERA

The Tomcat shot down four Libyan fighters in two real-life battles, but many will remember this great navy fighter for its role on celluloid, in the hugely successful Tom Cruise film of 1986, *Top Gun*, named for the US Navy's Fighter Weapons School. The F-14 was a superb performer, but all versions were handicapped by not having enough power. It was touted as the US Navy's best carrier-based fighter, but land-based Iranian pilots racked up most of its aerial victories during the Iran–Iraq War. It inspired a generation of would-be naval aviators, thanks partly to Maverick and Goose, yet it was retired at a time when many believed the Tomcat still had more good years ahead.

Engines: 2 General Electric F110-GE-400 turbofan engines with afterburners (F-14D)

Thrust: 16,000 lb.

Maximum speed: 1,564 mph (Mach 2.37)

Wingspan: 64 ft. spread, 38 ft. swept

- First flight: December 21, 1970
- Number built: 712 from 1969 to 1991
- An effective reconnaissance plane using an external TARPS pod
- Replaced in the US fleet by the F/A-18E/F Super Hornet
- Except for the B-1B Lancer, the only US warplane with variable geometry wings

8.3.1971

FIFI

"THIS AIRCRAFT IS A TRIBUTE TO ALL WHO FLY AND FIGHT"
—Carl Barthold, B-29 veteran

FIFI is not so much an aircraft as a state of mind. The world's only airworthy B-29 Superfortress heavy bomber (as of 2014), *FIFI* is operated by the Commemorative Air Force, and tours air shows offering excitement to crowds and an unforgettable experience to those who book a ride. The CAF retrieved the bomber from a target range in California, restored it during the 1970s, and gave it a new restoration between 2006 and 2010. *FIFI* may be the best-known restored military aircraft, or warbird, in the world, and is a kind of aerial ambassador, celebrating the sacrifice of military aircrews and the joys of aviation.

Engines: 4 custom-built Wright R-3350-26WD/95W Duplex Cyclone radial piston engines
Horsepower: 3,750 each
Cruising speed: 357 mph
Wingspan: 141 ft. 3 in.

- First flight: August 3, 1971 (after recovery)
- Refurbished a second time, 2006 to 2010
- Resumed flying: August 5, 2010
- Typically visits a dozen air shows each summer

LOCKHEED S-3 VIKING

CARRIER-BASED, ANTI-SUB JET

The S-3 Viking was the last US fixed-wing aircraft to fly from carrier decks on an anti-submarine mission, patrolling at long distance while the Sikorsky SH-60F Ocean Hawk helicopter stalked enemy U-boats at closer range. The ES-3A Shadow (sixteen built) was an electronics intelligence version. With the end of the Cold War, S-3 Vikings flew conventional bombing missions in the 1991 Persian Gulf conflict. The Navy put the Viking to pasture reluctantly, largely as a cost-saving measure, and now does the job with helicopters and drones.

Engines: 2 General Electric TF34-GE-2 turbofan engines
Thrust: 9,275 lb. each
Maximum speed: 493 mph
Wingspan: 68 ft. 8 in.

- First flight: January 21, 1972
- Number built: 188
- Crew: 4

5.10.1972

FAIRCHILD REPUBLIC A-10 THUNDERBOLT II

UGLY, SLOW, LETHAL—AND AN ENDANGERED SPECIES

Built around an enormous nose gun, a 30mm GAU-8/A cannon, the A-10 was designed to kill Soviet tanks, became a close air support ace in Iraq and Afghanistan, and almost from its inception repeatedly proved itself while the Pentagon brass tried to find ways to retire it. Infantry troops love the A-10 for its eyes-on, in-your-face close air-support prowess, but the Air Staff never liked the fact that it lacks a pointed nose and isn't very fast. Participating in every US conflict since its earliest days, the A-10 remains popular with the grunt and the junior airman and disliked by strategists and generals. Oh, and the controls? This plane handles really well. It's nimble and responsive.

Engines: 2 General Electric TF34-GE-100 turbofans
Thrust: 9,065 lb. each
Maximum speed: 439 mph
Wingspan: 57 ft. 6 in.

- First flight: May 10, 1972
- Number built: 716
- Cost: $11.8 million per plane in 1994 dollars

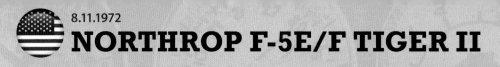

8.11.1972

NORTHROP F-5E/F TIGER II

SIMPLE, SENSIBLE, AND SERVING EVERYWHERE

The International Fighter Aircraft program of 1970 was intended to develop a fighter the United States could export economically—the intended first customer being South Vietnam. The Northrop F-5E/F Tiger won the Pentagon's IFA competition and soon reached overseas users, some of whom had operated the earlier F-5A/B Freedom Fighter. The F-5E (single-seat) and F-5F were delivered to seventeen countries, all of which wanted a small, light, versatile combat plane. Upgraded versions remain popular today from Mexico to Iran, but a planned successor, the F-20 Tigershark, never won a production contract. Proponents say this is what a fighter should be—a no-frills hot-rod of the skies.

Engines: 2 General Electric J85-GE-21B turbojet engines with afterburners
Thrust: 5,000 lb. each
Maximum speed: 1,050 mph (Mach 1.63)
Wingspan: 26 ft. 8 in.

- First flight: August 11, 1972
- Number built: 1,377 (1,144 F-5E, 233 F-5F)
- Cost: $31 million in 1978
- Armament: 2 20mm cannons in the nose
- First US fighter built explicitly for export

1973

GARRETT STAMP

OKAY, YOU CAN'T ACTUALLY FLY THIS ONE BECAUSE THEY NEVER BUILT IT, BUT . . .

There's nothing not to love about the Garrett STAMP (Small Tactical Aerial Mobility Platform), which makes you wonder if Scotty is getting ready to beam you up, even though it's not a teleportation chamber but a ducted-fan aircraft. At the height of the Vietnam era some of that love came from the US Army and Marine Corps, which wanted greater mobility for the infantryman on the ground. They loved the ducted fan, which produced thrust that could be vectored, or steered, by two nozzles. Engine exhaust was discharged through movable vanes at the rear of the aircraft, substituting for a horizontal stabilizer. An incomplete test article made one tethered flight in a hangar at Marine Corps Air Station, El Toro, California, on December 21, 1973, but soldiers and marines ended up not being bullish, and the complete aircraft was never flown.

Engines: 2 Garrett-AiResearch TFE 231 turboshaft engines driving ducted fans
Thrust: 1,050 lb. (via fan)
Maximum speed: 75 mph (expected)
Width: 7 ft. 6 in. (approximately)

- Design work done in 1973
- Crew: 2 (side-by-side enclosed seating)
- Power arrangement was similar to the Harrier "jump jet"
- Expected range was 30 miles

9.21.1973
BEECH T-34C TURBO MENTOR

PROVEN TRAINER TURBOPROP POWER

When Walter Beech's best-known piston trainer was mated with a gas turbine engine, the Beech T-34C Turbo Mentor was the happy result. The turbo "C model" replaced the T-34B and spent four decades schooling US Navy aviators and flight officers. It was replaced only in a new century by the Beechcraft (a corporate name change from Beech) T-6A Texan II. Navy pilots lined up in droves to get prized tours of duty instructing in the T-34C, while students lapped up the Turbo Mentor's nimbleness, power, and ease of handling.

- First flight: September 21, 1973
- Number built: 355
- Final US Navy flight: June 22, 2005

Engine: 1 Pratt & Whitney Canada PT6A-25 turboprop engine
Horsepower: 715 shaft
Cruising speed: 246 mph
Wingspan: 33 ft. 4 in.

1.20.1974
LOCKHEED MARTIN F-16 FIGHTING FALCON

THE MOST SUCCESSFUL JET FIGHTER

The F-16 Fighting Falcon was conceived as a lightweight, hot rod fighter but has evolved into a heavier, more complex combat aircraft. In its era—marketers call it a "fourth generation" fighter—the F-16 is the most widely used warplane in the West. Pilots like its canted ejection seat, enabling them to sit at an angle and handle gravity forces during tight maneuvers. With its unusually high, clear canopy, the F-16 gives the pilot extraordinary, all-around vision. A wide variety of missiles and bombs provides the pilot with great flexibility in air combat.

- First flight: January 20, 1974
- Number built: 4,562 worldwide as of 2014
- Cost: $18.6 million in 1998

Engine: 1 General Electric F110 or one Pratt & Whitney F100 turbofan engine
Thrust: 29,500 lb.
Maximum speed: 1,500 mph (Mach 2.0)
Wingspan: 32 ft. 8 in.

NORTHROP YF-17

SOMETIMES SECOND BEST CAN BE PRETTY GOOD

The pointy-nosed YF-17 lost out in the US Air Force's Lightweight Fighter Program competition that produced the spectacularly successful F-16 Fighting Falcon. This was through no fault in the design of the YF-17, which proved an agile and reliable dogfighter. Many pilots preferred the YF-17, which they saw as a hot rod of the skies, able to outmaneuver most other fighters handily. The US Navy chose to go its own way, not participating in the competition and giving only a little attention to a proposed naval version of the F-16 (never built) before enunciating its preference for the YF-17. As a result, the YF-17 design evolved into the McDonnell F/A-18 Hornet, which embodies many of the features of its forebear and continues to serve the navy with distinction.

Engines: General Electric YF-101-GE-100 turbofans with afterburners
Thrust: 14,400 lb.
Maximum speed: 1,116 mph (Mach 1.95)
Wingspan: 35 ft.

- First flight: June 9, 1974
- Number built: 2, both in museums today
- Together, logged 345.5 hours in 288 flights
- Able to sustain a 34-degree angle of attack in level flight
- Used a partial fly-by-wire control system

ROCKWELL B-1B LANCER

IT'S COOL AND IT'S POTENT—
BUT IT'S HIGH MAINTENANCE

The B-1B Lancer is one of the three current US bombers, along with the B-52 Stratofortress and B-2 Spirit, and is the only one of the trio no longer assigned the nuclear mission for which it was built. To those who balance the books, the B-1B is a maintenance pig that is difficult to keep in the air and costly to keep flying. The two pilots and two weapons officers in the B-1Bs love the comfort and roominess of this big aircraft, which includes an airline-style toilet, and say they can hit even the smallest target with pinpoint accuracy. Pilots like the fighter-style controls, which include a stick instead of a wheel.

Engines: 4 General Electric F101-GE-102 turbofan engines with afterburners
Thrust: 30,780 lb. each
Maximum speed: 830 mph (Mach 1.25)
Wingspan: 137 ft. extended, 79 ft. swept

- First flight: December 23, 1974
- Number built: 100
- Only plane in service with variable-sweep wings
- Troops call it the "Bone"

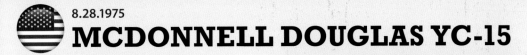

MCDONNELL DOUGLAS YC-15

A TACTICAL TRANSPORT CONCEPT FOR TIGHT SPACES

The Douglas YC-15 was a short takeoff and landing (STOL) test ship. It was designed for the US Air Force's Advanced Medium STOL Transport (AMST) competition, competing with the less orthodox Boeing YC-14. The YC-15 was a cargo and troop carrier intended to get in and out of tight spaces near the battle lines. Both competing aircraft performed well in the AMST contest, but neither was produced because the air force shifted its focus to long-range, strategic airlift. The YC-15 was a direct descendant of, and strongly influenced by, the Douglas C-17 Globemaster III, which became a Boeing product in the 1990s when Boeing acquired its AMST competitor.

Engines: 4 Pratt & Whitney JT8D-17 turbofan engines
Thrust: 16,000 lb. each
Maximum speed: 590 mph
Wingspan: 110 ft. 4 in. (typical)

- First flight: August 28, 1975
- Number built: 2
- Capacity: Crew of 3 (2 pilots, 1 loadmaster) and capacity for 150 fully armed troops
- 1 survives at a museum

BOEING AH-64 APACHE

FUTURISTIC YET FUN: THE PERFECT COMBINATION

It kills tanks. It fights insurgents. But watch your step. It's difficult to climb into—especially the front cockpit, which requires precarious footsteps on a narrow surface—but it's also one of the most enjoyable to fly. The Apache combines seat-of-the-pants flying with high technology in a perfect mix. Yes, it's a weapon of war and its infrared sensors, radar, and other gear enable it to fire lethal missiles and cannon shells, but the Apache is also a responsive and maneuverable platform that's simply fun to fly. Pilots sometimes live in a video-game-like world in darkness and at other times fly their Apache around the sky in brilliant daylight. The US Army's plan is to be operating 690 Apaches in 2027 and the Apache is expected to be delighting pilots for a long time to come.

Engines: 2 General Electric T700-GE-701C turboshaft engines
Horsepower: 1,890 each
Maximum speed: 227 mph
Main rotor diameter: 48 ft.

- First flight: September 30, 1975
- Number built: Almost 2,000 for all users (US, Egypt, Greece, Japan, Israel, Netherlands, Singapore, UK)
- The worldwide Apache fleet had accumulated 4 million flight hours by 2014
- Armament: Includes 30mm Hughes M230 Chain Gun (cannon)

8.9.1976

BOEING YC-14

A BOLD NEW APPROACH TO TACTICAL TRANSPORT

Looking at the YC-14, you might ask whether planemakers are willing today to take risks to explore new ideas as they were in the 1970s. The Boeing YC-14 was a short takeoff and landing (STOL) test ship and was one of two aircraft designed for the US Air Force's Advanced Medium STOL Transport (AMST) competition, the other being the Douglas YC-15. Both competing aircraft performed well, but no production order for either was forthcoming. The AMST competition and the test work conducted in this program strongly influenced the design of the Douglas C-17 Globemaster III, which became a Boeing aircraft in the 1990s when Boeing acquired its AMST competitor.

Engines: 2 General Electric CF6-50D turbofan engines
Thrust: 51,000 lb. each
Maximum speed: 504 mph
Wingspan: 129 ft.

- First flight: August 9, 1976
- Number built: 2
- Capacity: Crew of 3 (2 pilots, 1 loadmaster) and capacity for 150 fully armed troops
- Used a "powered lift" concept developed by NASA
- Both survive in Arizona

12.1.1977
LOCKHEED HAVE BLUE

"BEST KEPT SECRET SINCE THE ATOMIC BOMB"
—Pentagon spokesman Dan Howard, 1988

Have Blue was the code name—itself secret—for the flying testbed that paved the way for the F-117 Nighthawk stealth fighter-bomber. Its plate-like, faceted shape, designed to deflect electromagnetic waves, prompted some to call it the "Hopeless Diamond." Its sole purpose was to test the ability of an aircraft to evade radar detection. A product of Lockheed's Skunk Works division, flown in extreme secrecy at Groom Lake, Nevada—Area 51 to conspiracy buffs—*Have Blue* performed as expected and was considered a success even though both prototypes were lost in crashes. All aircraft that incorporate stealth features today derived some benefit from *Have Blue*.

Engines: 2 General Electric J85-GE-4A turbojet engines
Thrust: 6,200 lb. each
Maximum speed: 600 mph
Wingspan: 22 ft. 6 in.

- First flight: December 1, 1977
- Number built: 2
- Flown only by Ken Dyson and Bill Park
- No. 1 crashed in 1978, badly injuring Park
- No. 2 lost in 1979; Dyson ejected safely
- Originally dubbed "Experimental Survivable Testbed" (XST)

6.28.1978

DURAND MK V

A SUPER SHIP FOR ZIPPING AROUND THE SKY

The Durand Mk V is a really neat and very-different-looking home-built sportplane designed by William H. Durand. The all-metal aircraft features a unique negative stagger to its biplane wings. It uses spoilers instead of ailerons for control during turns. It looks unorthodox, but the basic design is straightforward. The canopy slides forward, making it easy to get in and out of. This is, simply, a very cool aircraft that is relatively easy to build and a joy to fly. Durand sold plans to ninety-one potential homebuilders. Although only about half a dozen Mk Vs were ever listed as airworthy at any one time, as late as 2014, sport pilots were still building these planes at home. One current operator is the designer's grandson, Chris Durand.

Engine: 1 Lycoming O-320 piston engine
Horsepower: 150
Cruising speed: 135 mph
Weight: 8,140 lb. (gross)
Wingspan: 24 ft. 6 in.

- First flight: June 28, 1978
- Cost: $800 for tooling and drawings, used, in 2014
- Capacity: 2 (pilot, passenger)
- Wings are braced with "I" struts

8.10.1979

BELL 412

A POPULAR AND VERSATILE ROTORCRAFT

The first Bell helicopter with a four-bladed rotor (the "4" in "412"), this beefy helicopter was also the first to make a move in the middle of its production run from Bell's Dallas, Texas, plant to its present-day assembly facility in Mirabel, Quebec. Of 900 built, AgustaWestland manufactured 260 under license. Military and civilian versions of the 412 are noted for their versatility and adaptability.

- First flight: August 10, 1979
- Pulls military duty in 37 countries
- 412EPI model introduced a "glass" cockpit and upgraded engines
- Backbone of the Los Angeles County Fire Department's air unit

Engines: 2 Pratt & Whitney Canada PT6T-9 Twin-Pac turboshaft engines (412EPI)
Horsepower: 900 shaft
Cruising speed: 144 mph
Main rotor diameter: 46 ft.

10.18.1979

MCDONNELL DOUGLAS MD-80

A FAMILIAR, FRIENDLY, AND VERY BUSY JETLINER

The McDonnell Douglas MD-80 family of narrow-body jetliners (including MD-81, MD-82, MD-83, MD-87, and MD-88) evolved from the proven and popular Douglas DC-9 and has become a mainstay of airlines with household names. It operates all over the world with various seating configurations but always the same, stalwart JT8D engines. Pilots see it as a gas guzzler but with amiable cockpit features and handling qualities. The MD-80 receives few headlines but has hauled tens of millions of passengers and given countless airline captains an easy working day.

- First flight: October 18, 1979
- Number built: 1,191
- Capacity: 130 to 172 passengers
- First user: Delta airlines, 1988

Engines: 2 Pratt & Whitney JT8D-200 turbofan engines
Thrust: 16,400 lb. each
Cruising speed: 504 mph
Wingspan: 107 ft. 8 in.

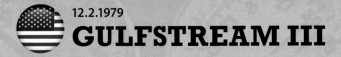

12.2.1979

GULFSTREAM III

A FLYING MOTOR HOME WITH GREAT PERFORMANCE

The Gulfstream III is one of the most successful in this series of VIP transports. In addition to many civilian users, it serves the US Air Force (C-20A, B), Navy (C-20D), and Army (C-20E). Three supersecret C-20Cs served the White House as war emergency aircraft until retirement in 2013. Gulfstream IIIs perform a variety of military and civilian missions and have even been associated with Central Intelligence Agency "rendition" of terrorism suspects. Pilots find the long-legged Gulfstream III easy and fun to fly. Production ended only because the better Gulfstream IV came along.

Engines: 2 Rolls-Royce Spey Mk 511-8 turbofan engines
Thrust: 11,000 lb. each
Maximum speed: 511 mph
Wingspan: 77 ft. 10 in.

- First flight: December 2, 1979
- Number built: 206
- Cost: $37 million in 1985
- Deliveries ended in 1986

4.12.1981

SPACE SHUTTLE

UNIQUE, HISTORIC, AND ALMOST EXTRAORDINARY

A manned spacecraft that was deemed a marvel when it appeared, the shuttle was launched vertically on the backs of rocket boosters, coasted into orbit, and operated like an eighty-one-ton glider when descending through the atmosphere to land. The pilots applied aerodynamic braking to help slow the vehicle down. *Enterprise* (which never flew in space), *Columbia*, *Challenger*, *Discovery*, *Atlantis*, and *Endeavour* completed 133 flights—the longest, by *Columbia* in 1996, lasting 17 days, 15 hours—in a spectacularly successful space effort that was marred by two fatal losses, *Challenger* in 1986 and *Columbia* in 2003. The successes have been unmatched by any other nation or space program.

Engines: 2 orbital maneuvering system (OMS) rocket engines
Thrust: 12,000 lb. each
Maximum speed: 18,000 mph in orbit
Wingspan: 23 ft. 9 in.

- First flight: April 12, 1981
- Final flight: July 21, 2011
- Carried 53,500 lb. of cargo to low Earth orbit
- 4 surviving shuttles now on museum display

6.18.1981

LOCKHEED F-117 NIGHTHAWK

"WE NEVER CALLED IT ANYTHING BUT 'THE BLACK JET'"—Dale Zelko, F-117 pilot

The F-117 is the only warplane ever to be fielded in squadron strength—and not in just one squadron but in two—while the public did not yet know its existence. Revealed in 1988 more than a decade after a Lockheed Skunk Works engineering team designed it, the F-117 used faceted surfaces to achieve stealth, the ability to evade radar detection. It was often called the "stealth fighter," but was always a fighter-bomber and never intended for air-to-air combat. The F-117 made its combat debut in Panama in 1989, achieved great success in the 1991 Persian Gulf War, and participated in every US conflict until its retirement—premature, in the opinion of many—on August 11, 2008.

Engines: 2 General Electric F404-F1D2 turbojet engines
Thrust: 10,600 lb. each
Maximum speed: 617 mph (Mach 0.91)
Wingspan: 43 ft. 4 in.

- First flight: June 18, 1981
- Number built: 59
- Final F-117 delivered July 3, 1990
- Pilots' slogan: "We own the night"
- Maintainers' nickname: "the Cockroach"
- Serbian forces shot down an F-117 on March 22, 1999; pilot was rescued

2.1982
NORTHROP TACIT BLUE

"I COULD TELL YOU, BUT I'D HAVE TO KILL YOU"—Pentagon officer, 1985

Cloaked in a "deep black" program so secret that only a few in Congress were told of it—and no one in the press or the public—*Tacit Blue* was designed to test stealth. With its low radar return signal, this aircraft proved that an aircraft could operate undetected close to the battlefield to monitor enemy forces and relay targeting information. It operated clandestinely at the supersecret Groom Lake, Nevada, base, also called Area 51 or Dreamland. The end of the Cold War and of the Soviet threat put *Tacit Blue* out of a job, and it's on museum display today, but even the existence of this technology testbed was revealed only a decade after it flew, and many details remain hush-hush.

Engines: 2 Garrett ATF3-6 high-bypass turbofan engines
Thrust: 7,000 lb. each
Maximum speed: 380 mph
Wingspan: 48 ft. 2 in.

- First flight: February 1982
- Number built: 1
- Logged 135 flights and 250 hours
- Only 5 pilots flew it
- Called "the Whale" by pilots
- Used a digital, fly-by-wire control system

9.3.1982

BEECH 1900

A KING AIR THAT ISN'T ON A DIET

The Beech 1900 is a nineteen-passenger transport. It's primarily a regional airliner although the US Air Force acquired four under the designation C-12J. It's a fattened derivative of the Beech 200/300 Super King Air with a later model of the same engines and redesigned fuselage and wings. The 1900, 1900C, and bulkier 1900D models are optimized to carry passengers in all weather conditions from airports with short runways. It is among the most popular aircraft in its class and until 2011 remained in production from the company now renamed Beechcraft. Today, many users are replacing their turboprop 1900s with jets. Peter Jensen, who flew the author of this book in a 1900C in Alaska, called it "a really nice, purring machine that does what you want."

Engines: 2 Pratt & Whitney Canada PT6A-67D turboprop engines
Horsepower: 1,280 shaft each
Cruising speed: 322 mph
Wingspan: 57 ft. 9 in.

- First flight: September 3, 1982
- Number built: 605
- Crew: 2 pilots

9.8.1982

BOEING 767

THE GOLDILOCKS JETLINER

Although officially called a widebody, the Boeing 767 is in some ways an odd size for an airliner, being not nearly as roomy on the inside as other commercial jets in its class. The US Air Force deemed it not too big, not too small, but just the right size to become an air refueling tanker and is acquiring 179 KC-46A Pegasus versions to be filling stations in the sky. Passengers generally find the 767 just right, too, but may feel the twin aisles a bit cramped. The flight deck and cockpit instruments of the 767 are identical to those of the 757 and are user-friendly toward pilots.

Engines: 2 Pratt & Whitney PW4056 turbofan engines (typical)
Thrust: 63,300 lb. each
Cruising speed: 530 mph
Wingspan: 156 ft. 1 in.

- First flight: September 8, 1982
- First widebody to exceed 1,000 planes built
- The first widebody to be "stretched" twice: the 767-300ER by 21 ft. and the 767-400ER by another 21 ft.
- 767s have made 16.2 million commercial flights
- It takes 28 minutes to put 23,790 gallons of fuel aboard a 767-300ER
- There are 125 miles of electrical wiring in a 767-400ER

10.6.1983

BELL OH-58D KIOWA/OH-58F KIOWA WARRIOR

A BELOVED ASSET TO AMERICAN SOLDIERS ON THE BATTLEFIELD

The distinctive mast-mounted sight inside a ball atop the main rotor on the OH-58D Kiowa Warrior will become history if the US Army can get congressional approval to retire its OH-58D and OH-58F battlefield helicopters. Soldiers will be unhappy. Beginning in the 1980s, the Kiowa Warrior—an armed version of the OH-58A/C Kiowa scout—has won a special place in the hearts of army aviators and of troops on the ground. Critics want the army to keep the Kiowa Warrior on duty until a replacement can be available, but the army has twice failed in efforts to develop a replacement and none is currently on the horizon.

Engine: 1 Rolls-Royce T703-AD-700A or 250-C30R3 gas turbine engine
Horsepower: 650 shaft
Maximum speed: 138 mph
Main rotor diameter: 35 ft.

- First flight, OH-58D: October 6, 1983
- First flight, OH-58F: April 26, 2013
- Armament: Minigun, grenade launcher, and missiles
- First combat: Operation Desert Storm, 1991
- 820,000 combat hours as of 2014
- 363 in inventory in 2014

GRUMMAN X-29

YOU'VE GOT TO BE KIDDING, RIGHT?

Swept-*forward* wings? Get out of here! Didn't the Germans try that in World War II and decide it didn't work? Based in part on research from exactly that source, the two Grumman X-29s were experimental aircraft intended to test a forward-swept wing and canard control surfaces. Each was built around the fuselage frames of a Northrop F-5A Freedom Fighter but with entirely new cockpit, nose section, engine, flight controls, and avionics. The X-29s made an enormous contribution to aeronautical knowledge, but so far no one has built an operational aircraft with swept-forward wings.

Engine: 1 General Electric F404 turbofan engine
Thrust: 16,000 lb.
Maximum speed: 1,100 mph (Mach 1.8)
Wingspan: 27 ft. 2 in.

- First flight: December 14, 1984
- 242 flights between 1984 and 1991
- First aircraft with forward-swept wings to fly supersonic
- Both X-29s are in museums today

4.2.1985
KAMAN SH-2G SUPER SEASPRITE

IT WAS OFTEN ON THE SIDELINES, BUT FOR A LONG TIME

The final manned aircraft from aviation pioneer Charlie Kaman, the SH-2G Super Seasprite is also the final model in a large family of single- and twin-engined rescue and anti-submarine helicopters operated from US Navy warship decks since Vietnam. An early UH-2A Seasprite flown by Cmdr. Clyde Lassen on a risky, behind-the-lines mission produced the most-decorated helicopter crew in history—the Medal of Honor for Lassen, and the Navy Cross for three crewmembers. The US Navy made use of the SH-2G anti-submarine version for only a few years, but examples remain in service in Peru, Poland, and New Zealand. Most versions had insufficient power and handling characteristics that were difficult to like, but Seasprites and Super Seasprites have chalked up a fine record of prolonged service.

Engines: 2 General Electric T700-GE-400/401C turboshaft engines
Horsepower: 1,725 shaft each
Maximum speed: 160 mph
Weight: 13,500 lb. (a bit of a heavy helo)
Main rotor diameter: 45 ft.

- First flight: April 2, 1985
- Crew: 3 (pilot, co-pilot, sensor operator)
- Cost: $26 million each in 1985

9.19.1985
GULFSTREAM IV

IT JUST KEEPS GETTING BETTER AND BETTER

With greater speed, range, and carrying capacity than planes that bore its famous name before it, as well as a stretched fuselage, the Gulfstream IV followed tradition by serving not just in the corporate world but in the US Army (C-20F), Navy (C-20G), Marine Corps (also C-20G), and Air Force (C-20H). In civilian-speak, long after it was a ubiquitous sight on the world's airways, the Gulfstream IV was renamed the G450, but airport operators and pilots still use the original term.

Engines: 2 Rolls-Royce Tay 611-8 turbofan engines
Thrust: 13,000 lb. each
Maximum speed: 581 mph (Mach 0.88)
Wingspan: 77 ft. 10 in.

- First flight: September 19, 1985
- Number built: About 550
- About 300 flying today

5.16.1987

AIR FORCE ONE

"IT'S LIKE A CRUISE SHIP, WITH THE WAY IT'S PROPORTIONED, AND WITH THE MAHOGANY IN THE CONFERENCE ROOM."
—Maj. Gen. James Hawkins,
Air Force One pilot

"Air Force One" is the radio call for any air force aircraft carrying the American president, but in practice that aircraft is usually one of two VC-25A models, military versions of the Boeing 747-200B, stationed near Washington, DC. Although the public associates Air Force One with glamour, the real-life Flying White House is neither at the cutting edge of technology nor unreasonably luxurious. It doesn't begin to compare with a 747 owned by a Middle East potentate that boasts a gold-plated bathtub. It's mostly a military aircraft with a wartime mission—a flying headquarters for the commander-in-chief. It's also an executive transport with global reach and superb communications.

Engines: 4 General Electric F103-GE-180 (CF6-80C2B1) turbofan engines
Thrust: 56,750 lb. each.
Cruising speed: 630 mph (Mach 0.91)
Wingspan: 195 ft. 89 in.

- First flight: May 16, 1987 (VC-25A)
- First president to use the VC-25A: George H. W. Bush (1990)
- Interior floor space: 4,000 sq. ft.
- Exterior paint scheme designed by Raymond Loewy
- Typically logs 350 to 450 flight hours annually
- No, there's no escape capsule

3.19.1989
BELL-BOEING V-22 OSPREY

A HELICOPTER, A PLANE—
AND, AT LAST, A SUCCESS

The Bell-Boeing V-22 Osprey is the world" first tilt-rotor aircraft. It takes off and lands with engine nacelles vertical and 38-foot blades functioning as rotors. In flight, the engines tilt forward, rotating 90 degrees in about 12 seconds, and the blades become propellers, pulling the Osprey through the sky. The Osprey had a troubled beginning and years of development difficulties. There were fatal crashes, and the entire program was cancelled at one point. Still, it survived to become operational with the US Air Force (CV-22) and Marine Corps (MV-22). Israel and Japan are expected to become the first overseas users. Pilots say making the transition to a tilt-rotor cockpit is intuitive, instinctive, and comes easily.

Engines: 2 Rolls-Royce Allison T406-AE-1107C turboshaft engines
Horsepower: 6,150 each
Maximum speed: 316 mph
Wingspan: 45 ft. 10 in.

- First flight: March 19, 1989
- Number built: About 200 as of 2014
- Capacity: Carries 24 to 30 troops
- Popular for special-operations missions
- Carries one M240 machine gun on ramp (typical)

1990
AIR TRACTOR FAMILY

FAMOUS AND UBIQUITOUS AG PLANE

The Air Tractor family of agricultural aircraft has been spraying, seeding, fertilizing, and firefighting since founder Leland Snow designed his first ag plane in 1951. One of the latest models, the AT-802 (pictured), is now tending farmland in countries around the world, and a handful, known as AT-802Us, have been adapted for light military duties. These big, hefty planes have now become the best-known agricultural aircraft in the world, and they offer pilots a strong, stable platform that handles beautifully even at treetop altitude.

- First flight: 1990
- World's largest single-engine aircraft (AT-802)
- Single-seat and two-seat models

Engine: 1 Pratt & Whitney Canada PT6A-65AG turboprop engine
Horsepower: 1,295 shaft
Maximum speed: 244 mph
Wingspan: 59 ft. 1 in.

4.29.1991
CESSNA CITATIONJET

A COLLEGIAL CONGLOMERATION OF CORPORATE JETS

The names Citation, CitationJet, and CJ cover several families of executive aircraft built by Cessna Aircraft in Wichita, Kansas. Seven distinct CitationJet versions have differing fuselage shapes, control surfaces, and engines. Some are relatively short ranged, while others are capable of nonstop coast-to-coast travel. The Citation X version is one of the fastest bizjets at about 580 miles per hour. Taken collectively, they give business aviation a downscale, affordable form of concierge travel for executives. A few serve in the military as VIP transports (UC-35) or, until recently, as navigator trainers (T-47B). The success of these families of bizjets is testimony to Cessna's determination to excel in the executive aviation market.

Engines: 2 Williams FJ44-1AP turbofan engines (typical)
Thrust: 1,955 lb. each
Cruising speed: 565 mph
Wingspan: 46 ft. 11 in.

- First flight: April 29, 1991
- Number built: About 400 so far
- Capacity: Typically, 2 pilots and 9 passengers

7.5.1991
RAYTHEON T-1A JAYHAWK

THOUSANDS EARNED THEIR WINGS

The Raytheon T-1A Jayhawk is the US Air Force's standard multi-engine trainer. It's based on the Beechjet 400A, which in turn is a version of the Mitsubishi MU-300 Diamond used for executive travel by business people around the globe. The T-1A is a joy to fly and has one of the best safety records of any military aircraft.

- First flight: July 5, 1991
- First service: 1993
- Cost: $4.1 million in 1992
- Number built: 180

Engines: 2 Pratt & Whitney JT15D-5B turbofan engines
Thrust: 2,700 lb. each
Cruising speed: 528 mph
Wingspan: 43 ft. 6 in.

9.15.1991
BOEING C-17 GLOBEMASTER III

A LATECOMER TO SUCCESS

The C-17 Globemaster III shares the "strategic airlift" mission—long-range cargo hauling—with the C-5 Galaxy. When it was new, cost and technical issues led crews to start calling it Buddha: "It's very big, it's very fat, it never moves, and everybody stands around and worships it." Since then, the C-17 has proven itself on trans-oceanic supply missions. Pilots like its inherent flexibility, fighter-style head-up display, and "glass" cockpit with a wealth of control and navigation instruments.

- First flight: September 15, 1991
- Crew: 3 (2 pilots, 1 loadmaster)
- Maximum takeoff weight is 585,000 lb.

Engines: 4 Pratt & Whitney F117-PW-100 turbofan engines
Thrust: 44,000 lb. thrust each
Cruising speed: 390 mph
Weight: 585,000 lb. (maximum takeoff weight)
Wingspan: 169 ft. 10 in.

1995

GENERAL ATOMICS MQ-1 PREDATOR

BEST-KNOWN DRONE

Predator. The name evokes and provokes. It's small, slow, sluggish, vulnerable, and universally feared. To advocates, it's the tip of the spear in an unmanned aerial vehicle revolution. To detractors, it's the anonymous strike-from-the-sky in a targeted killing program operated not by the armed forces but by the Central Intelligence Agency. To the world, the Predator is a drone, although the official US government term is unmanned aircraft system (UAS)—except in the air force, which calls it a remotely piloted vehicle (RPA). Armed and unarmed versions are in widespread use, although production ended in 2013. The crew of two—pilot and sensor operator—controls a Predator remotely from thousands of miles away. Predator pilots say their experience is almost exactly like being in a cockpit.

Engine: 1 Rotax 914F turbocharged piston engine
Horsepower: 115
Maximum speed: 135 mph
Wingspan: 48 ft. 8 in.

- First flight: 1995
- Number built: 360 (285 RQ-1, 75 MQ-1)
- Cost: $4.03 million per unit in 2010
- Can fly a mission lasting 14 hours
- Civilian uses include border enforcement and scientific studies

11.28.1995

GULFSTREAM V

HIGHER, FASTER, AND FARTHER— IN COMFORT

When the Gulfstream V made its debut at the turn of the century, it introduced new superlatives to intercontinental travel. It cruises above commercial air lanes at 51,000 feet and can travel from Washington, DC, to Belgrade, Serbia, nonstop. The planemaker produced a few military C-37 models and improved versions dubbed Gulfstream 500/550, but pilots of both still use the original name. Until the Gulfstream VI arrived in 2009, the Gulfstream V was the pinnacle.

- First flight: November 28, 1995
- Number built: 191
- Capacity: 16 people in standard seating mode

Engines: 2 Rolls-Royce BR710A1-10 turbofan engines
Thrust: 24,750 lb. each
Maximum speed: 589 mph (Mach 0.89)
Wingspan: 93 ft. 4 in.

1996

COMP AIR 8

A LITTLE NOSEY BUT A SWELL RIDE FROM POINT A TO POINT B

It has a distinctive proboscis and a modern-day sleekness about it, but otherwise it's a straightforward, kit-built, tailwheel aircraft highly suited to recreational flying. It's the ideal build-it-yourself plane for the pilot who wants the ability to carry four people plus full fuel and baggage. Comp Air, Inc., formerly Aerocomp, Inc., owned by Ron Lueck, is doing great things in the world of upscale, home-built aircraft. This is a serious, sensible design popular with pilots and builders.

- First flight: 1996
- Cost: Typically about $150,000 used
- All-composite construction protects from corrosion

Engine: 1 Walter M601 SER turboprop engine
Horsepower: 657
Cruising speed: 160 mph
Wingspan: 33 ft.

4.5.1996
LOCKHEED MARTIN C-130J SUPER HERCULES

"A WORKHORSE READY FOR ANY MISSION, ANYWHERE, ANYTIME" —Lockheed Martin

The C-130J Super Hercules continues the saga of the C-130, which dates to 1954 and has been in service longer than any other airlifter. In the 1990s, Lockheed Martin sought to harness new technology and apply it to the existing C-130 design. The result introduces a digital "glass" cockpit, dispenses with a navigator and flight engineer, and uses new-generation turboprop engines. Only the Israeli version is called the "Samson," but pilots in many countries acknowledge that the C-130J is both mighty and muscular.

Engines: 4 Rolls-Royce AE 2100D3 turboprop engines
Horsepower: 4,637 shaft (C-130H)
Maximum speed: 417 mph
Wingspan: 132 ft. 7 in.

- First flight: April 5, 1996
- First service: 1999
- Used extensively in Afghanistan and Iraq
- 300 delivered as of 2014

1.1.1997
COMP AIR 10

NOT EASY TO RECOGNIZE BUT A BALL TO FLY

Show up in this at a new airport and even the aviation experts won't know what it is, but the CompAir 10 is a fun airplane with a unique and nifty shape that always grabs attention, emanating from a bright new company on the kit-plane scene. This oddly pretty and distinctly utilitarian aircraft can be customized for your needs. Making the transition is easy because the cockpit design is simplicity itself, and the handling characteristics are out of this world.

Engine: 1 Walter 601D turboprop engine
Horsepower: 657
Cruising speed: 185 mph
Wingspan: 35 ft. 10 in.

- First flight: about January 1, 1997
- Cost: About $150,000 fully equipped in 2014; roughly $2 million in restored condition today
- Ideal for ranchers, outfitters, and fish camp operators

LOCKHEED MARTIN F-22 RAPTOR

STEALTHY, SLEEK, FAST, COSTLY, AND CONTROVERSIAL

The F-22 Raptor was the first air-to-air fighter designed from the outset to use stealth—coated surfaces and rounded contours—to evade radar detection. It is one of the fastest combat aircraft ever built, but critics argue that at more than $200 million per copy, it costs too much. In 2009, then–defense secretary Robert Gates, who saw an aircraft designed to fight the Soviet Union in an era when US forces were battling insurgents, succumbed to the controversy surrounding the F-22's technical issues and its price tag. Gates halted production at 187 airframes rather than the 381 the air force wanted, leaving the United States with the world's most advanced dogfighter but not very many of them.

Engines: 2 Pratt & Whitney F119-PW-100 turbofans
Thrust: 35,000 lb. each
Maximum speed: 1,498 mph
Wingspan: 44 ft. 6 in.

- First flight: September 7, 1997
- First service: December 15, 2005
- Armament: M61A2 Vulcan cannon and other weapons internally
- Cockpit is considered cramped, especially for tall pilots, despite the great size of the F-22
- Has overcome problems with on-board oxygen system
- Capable of supersonic cruise to target

2.28.1998

NORTHROP GRUMMAN RQ-4 GLOBAL HAWK

A FAR-RANGING UNMANNED SURVEILLANCE PLATFORM

You fly this one from a ground control station, called a booth. The Global Hawk is an unmanned aerial vehicle designed for reconnaissance, anti-submarine work, and electronic warfare. The air force, unhappily and under pressure from Capitol Hill, plans to use the RQ-4B block 30 model to replace the U-2 "Dragon Lady" manned reconnaissance aircraft. The US Navy has introduced the MQ-4C Triton version for broad-area ocean surveillance. The Global Hawk is extremely impressive in sheer size, in technological heft, and in potential, but it has drawn criticism for program delays, technical glitches, and cost increases. Numerous future versions are planned, and advocates say all issues are being resolved.

Engine: 1 Rolls-Royce F137-RR-100 turbofan engine
Thrust: 7,600 lb.
Cruising speed: 357 mph
Wingspan: 130 ft. 10 in.

- First flight: February 28, 1998
- Number built: About 454 as of 2014
- Cost: $222.7 million each in 2013
- $49,089 per flying hour in 2013
- Flew 33.1 hours up to 60,000 ft. in 2008
- Set an unmanned distance record, California to Australia, in 2001
- First unmanned aircraft to traverse the Pacific Ocean

BEECHCRAFT T-6 TEXAN II

A SENSIBLE TURBO TRAINER AND ATTACK PLANE

The Beechcraft T-6 Texan II is a single-engined turboprop aircraft built by the Beechcraft Aircraft Company (formerly Raytheon, and formerly Hawker Beechcraft). It is a derivative of the Swiss Pilatus PC-9 and, despite the name inherited from a different World War II trainer, is manufactured in Kansas. The Texan II is training pilots in several air forces, and the manufacturer is now marketing it as a light attack aircraft. The author flew the T-6A from the front cockpit and was impressed with its roominess, quiet, and responsiveness.

Engine: 1 Pratt & Whitney Canada PT6A-68 turboprop engine (typical)
Horsepower: 1,100 shaft
Cruising speed: 320 mph
Wingspan: 33 ft. 5 in.

- First flight: July 1, 1998
- First service: 2000
- Number built: About 640 as of 2014
- Instructor in rear, student in front

7.26.1998

SCALED COMPOSITES PROTEUS

IT GOES WAY, WAY UP, GETS THERE, AND STAYS

It's okay to do a double take. The Proteus takes some getting used to. But despite its unusual contours and unorthodox, tandem-wing layout, the Proteus makes perfect sense. Burt Rutan's Scaled Composites LLC—which has introduced an average of one proof-of-concept vehicle per year since its inception in 1983—designed the Proteus to fly at extreme altitude for prolonged periods. The impetus was the need for upper-atmosphere telecommunications relay work. Because it can linger up to eighteen hours at the edge of space, Proteus has performed many other duties, including reconnaissance, atmospheric research, commercial imaging, and space launch. Northrop Grumman owns the Proteus, which is flown by Scaled Composites crews.

Engines: 2 Williams International FJ44-2E turbofan engines

Thrust: 2,300 lb. each

Maximum speed: 288 mph (Mach 0.42)

Wingspan: 77 ft. 7 in.; expands to 98 ft. with removable wingtips installed

- First flight: July 26, 1998
- Number built: 1
- Crew: 2; can be operated by a single pilot, and future versions may be unmanned
- Can orbit over a point at 65,000 ft. for 18 hours

9.8.1999

HELIOS PROTOTYPE

EXPLORING THE UNKNOWN WITH THE UNMANNED

The Helios Prototype was the fourth and final aircraft developed in a NASA-sponsored study of solar- and fuel-cell-system-powered unmanned aerial vehicles, piloted by a researcher-aviator on the ground. One purpose was to test the capability to loiter for prolonged periods at extremely high altitude to conduct surveillance. On August 13, 2001, the Helios Prototype piloted remotely by Greg Kendall reached an altitude of 96,863 feet, a world record for sustained horizontal flight by a winged aircraft. Sadly, after several more successes, the aircraft was lost on a remotely piloted flight over the Pacific Ocean near Hawaii on June 26, 2003. NASA is conducting electric-power research today with its GL-10 Greased Lightning aircraft.

Engines: 10 to 14 motors powered by batteries, solar cells, and a modified hydrogen-air fuel cell

Horsepower: About 28

Maximum speed: 40 mph

Wingspan: 247 ft.

- First flight: September 8, 1999
- Number built: 1 (lost in a crash)
- Contributed hugely to alternate-powerplant research
- Dubbed an "atmospheric satellite," able to look down from great heights

LOCKHEED MARTIN X-35

THE TEST SHIP THAT LED TO THE JOINT STRIKE FIGHTER

The Lockheed Martin X-35 was a technology demonstrator for the Joint Strike Fighter program, along with the Boeing X-32. Two X-35 airframes were evaluated: the conventional X-35A (which was modified to become the X-35B with a short takeoff, vertical landing, or STOVL system) and the X-35C, which evaluated a larger and broader wing design. In the hands of a test pilot on July 20, 2001, the X-35B STOVL aircraft took off in less than 500 feet, reached supersonic speed, and landed vertically. Lighter and more agile than its X-32 competitor—and a lot better looking—the X-35 was declared the winning design for JSF on October 26, 2001, and became the basis of the F-35 Lightning II JSF.

Engine: 1 Pratt & Whitney F135 turbofan engine (with lift system on X-35B)
Thrust: 18,000 lb.
Maximum speed: 1,200 mph (Mach 2.0)
Wingspan: 35 ft.

- First flight: October 24, 2000
- Number built: 2
- Cost: $38 million in 1994 (X-35C)
- Some features derived from F-22 Raptor
- Both in museums now

BELL AH-1Z VIPER

LATEST IN A LONG LINE OF MUCH-ADMIRED ATTACK HELICOPTERS

Today's AH-1Z Viper for the marine corps is the latest in a vast family of single- and twin-engined AH-1 battlefield helicopters operated by soldiers and marines from Vietnam onward, including the AH-1G Cobra, AH-1J Sea Cobra, and AH-1W Super Cobra. Where earlier versions had two rotor blades, the Viper uses a four-blade, bearingless, composite rotor system. Also called the "Zulu" for the phonetic version of its letter suffix, the Viper serves alongside the UH-1Y Venom, or "Yankee," the marines' latest take on the fabled Huey helicopter. The AH-1Z is a participant in current conflicts. The cockpit has been optimized for efficiency after the interior of the earlier AH-1W became cluttered with add-on equipment. This is a robust helicopter, with plenty of power and speed.

Engines: 2 General Electric T700-GE-401C turboshaft engines
Horsepower: 1,800 shaft each
Maximum speed: 255 mph
Main rotor diameter: 48 ft.

- First flight: December 8, 2000
- Crew: 2 (pilot in back, co-pilot/gunner up front)
- Armament: M197 "Gatling" 20mm cannon and a variety of rockets and missiles

SCALED COMPOSITES WHITE KNIGHT ONE

HAULING A SPACECRAFT TO THE EDGE OF THE ATMOSPHERE

The gangly White Knight One was a jet-powered mother ship designed to launch the SpaceShipOne manned suborbital vehicle. The carrier and the spacecraft were products of the pioneering savvy of Burt Rutan's Scaled Composites firm. White Knight One made seventeen flights with SpaceShipOne attached during 2003 and 2004, including thirteen mid-air launches. On October 4, 2004, White Knight One and SpaceShipOne won the $10 million Ansari X Prize for a reusable, privately financed, manned spaceship. In 2005 and 2006, White Knight One performed captive-carry and air-launch drop tests of the Pentagon's supersecret X-37 orbital spaceplane, including five launches from the air force's hush-hush Plant 42 in Palmdale, California. In July 2014, White Knight One flew to Paine Field, Washington, to be retired to Microsoft co-founder Paul G. Allen's Flying Heritage Collection.

Engines: 2 General Electric J85-GE-6 turbojet engines with afterburners
Thrust: 2,400 lb. each
Maximum speed: 430 mph
Ceiling: 52,000 ft.
Wingspan: 82 ft.

- First flight: August 1, 2002
- Presented to the media: April 18, 2003
- Has a range of 1,375 miles

5.20.2003
SPACESHIPONE

Ryan Mulhall/Shutterstock

THE FIRST PRIVATE SPACESHIP

SpaceShipOne is a suborbital vehicle that in 2004 made the first private spaceflight, and, later the same year, won the Ansari X Prize—a $10 million bounty for the first reusable, privately financed, manned spaceship. Burt Rutan's Scaled Composites LLC and Paul Allen's Mojave Aerospace Ventures jointly developed SpaceShipOne, which was carried aloft by Scaled Composites' White Knight One. The prize-winning achievement broke a tradition of five decades of spaceflight being managed by the government—mostly by NASA—and began an era when the private sector is a player. This sentiment prompted a sign reading, "SpaceShipOne, government zero." Because it had attained such an important milestone, SpaceShipOne was promptly retired.

Engine: 1 N2O/HTPB SpaceDiv hybrid rocket motor
Thrust: 7,500 lb.
Maximum speed: 2,170 mph (Mach 3.09)
Ceiling: 367,360 ft. (that's space)
Wingspan: 16 ft. 5 in.
Length: 28 ft.

- First flight: May 20, 2003
- Retired after making 17 flights

10.16.2004

QUEST KODIAK

FOR SHORT-FIELD FLYING IN THE BUSH, THERE'S NOTHING BETTER

The Quest Kodiak is a high-tech, sturdy aircraft ideal for bush flying and adaptable as a VIP transport when the "Summit Package" executive interior is installed. It can operate as a floatplane, and there's a skydiving version as well. The manufacturer, Quest Aircraft Company of Sandpoint, Idaho, is an up-and-coming leader in the utility aviation field; the company was launched in 2001, and the Kodiak is its first model. The aircraft fits nicely into a niche of its own, larger than most general-aviation and bush planes yet capable of landing and taking off in as little as 700 feet. This is an attractive aircraft that pilots like for its ruggedness and reliability.

Engine: 1 Pratt & Whitney Canada PT6A-34 turboprop engine
Horsepower: 700
Maximum speed: 211 mph
Wingspan: 45 ft.

- First flight October 16, 2004
- Number built: about 120 as of 2015
- Capacity: 1 pilot, up to 10 passengers
- Climbs at 1,300 feet per minute
- Operates on unpaved, bumpy, and wet surfaces

4.7.2006

BOEING X-37

THE BLACKEST OF BLACK PROGRAMS

What is it? On October 17, 2014, the X-37B landed from its third mission after spending *two years* in space (well, 674 days). It's an orbiter similar to the Space Shuttle, unmanned but capable of being configured for a human crew. Once launched from an aircraft, it is now boosted into orbit on an Atlas V rocket. Apart these basics, officials will say nothing. The X-37 began as a NASA project in 1999, but went black when the Defense Department took it over in 2004. NASA used the first vehicle (the X-37A) for hypersonic research. The air force employs the second and third (both designated X-37B) on classified missions of extreme duration. Theorists say the X-37 is a space bomber focused on China's Tiangong-1 space station module. For sure, it's an intelligence-gatherer with secret capabilities, but if you're ever in the Pentagon, don't ask. They won't tell.

Engine: 1 Aerojet AR2-3 liquid-fuel rocket engine
Thrust: 6,600 lb.
Orbital speed: 17,426 mph
Wingspan: 14 ft. 11 in.
Length: 29 ft. 3 in.

- First flight: April 7, 2006
- First X-37B orbital mission: April 22, 2010, to December 3, 2010
- Second mission: March 5, 2011, to May 30, 2012 (469 days)

BOEING EA-18G GROWLER

ELECTRONIC WARFARE AT HIGH SPEED

The EA-18G Growler is a carrier-based electronic warfare (EW) aircraft derived from the F/A-18F Super Hornet and intended to replace the Grumman EA-6B Prowler in US Navy service. With a pilot up front and an electronic countermeasures officer in the back seat, the Growler typically carries jamming pods instead of bombs. It's the first supersonic EW aircraft and the first with sufficient speed to stay with a strike force during a large aerial attack. The Growler—also identified by the radio call sign "Grizzly"—is an important weapon in defeating an adversary's air defense system. Pilots say the Growler handles exactly like the fighter that provided its basic design features.

Engines: 2 General Electric F414-GE-400 turbofan engines
Thrust: 14,000 lb. thrust each
Maximum speed: 1,190 mph (Mach 1.8)
Wingspan: 44 ft. 9 in. (with wingtip pods)

- First flight: August 15, 2006
- Number built: 105 as of 2014
- Only overseas user: Australia
- Only current US electronic warfare aircraft

12.15.2006

LOCKHEED MARTIN F-35 LIGHTNING II JOINT STRIKE FIGHTER

"IT'S A SUPER SHIP TO FLY"
—Col. Andrew J. "Drifter" Toth, F-35 pilot

Meant to do a little of everything, the F-35 Lightning II is being accused by critics of not being good enough at any single mission. Once operational, the F-35 will wage air-to-air combat and will also fly air-to-surface missions. Land-based (F-35A), short/vertical takeoff (F-35B), and carrier-based (F-35C) versions are above cost, behind schedule, and plagued with technical difficulties. Test pilots say these issues are typical of any new aircraft and can be overcome. Pilots also say that the high-tech cockpit and helmet-mounted cueing sight make the F-35 a dream to fly. Near the end of 2014, some 107 F-35s were flying, but none were yet fully operational.

Engine: 1 Pratt & Whitney F135 turbofan engine with afterburner
Thrust: 43,000 lb. each
Maximum speed: 1,200 mph (Mach 1.6)
Wingspan: 35 ft.

- First flight: December 15, 2006
- Armament: 2 internal weapons bays
- Cost: Target price of $83/4 million (F-35A)
- 2,443 planned for US use
- 12 partner nations buying or considering
- A stealth aircraft, meant to evade radar

BELL 429 GLOBALRANGER

AN ULTRA-MODERN AERIAL AMBULANCE AND POLICE CRUISER

Impetus for the high-tech, digital Bell 429 GlobalRanger came from the emergency medical services community, which wanted a helicopter with state-of-the-art technology. Medics and law officers wanted not just the latest capabilities but also a large interior cabin that would carry plenty and would be easy to work. They got a craft with four-bladed composite rotors, lifting power, and versatility. It's a single-pilot helicopter with a glass cockpit, capable of single-engine operation. The helicopter company founded by Larry Bell says the 429 outperforms everything in its class.

Engines: 2 Pratt & Whitney Canada PW207D1 turboprop engines
Horsepower: 730 shaft each
Maximum speed: 178 mph
Rotor diameter: 36 ft.

- First flight: February 27, 2007
- About 320 on order as of 2014
- Built at Bell's facility in Mirabel, Quebec
- Canadian coast guard ordered 15

SCALED COMPOSITES WHITE KNIGHT TWO

THE ULTIMATE IN SPACECRAFT MOTHERSHIP

It's bigger. It's uglier. It's even more outlandish, and it does a magnificent job at the cutting edge of technology. And there will be more of them. White Knight Two is the latest carrier ship from Burt Rutan's Scaled Composites LLC, and follows in the tradition of the one-of-a-kind White Knight One. Its fundamental purpose was to lift the SpaceShipTwo vehicle to the edge of the atmosphere for release, but White Knight Two has other goals, including carrying a civilian manned spacecraft aloft for Richard Branson's Virgin Galactic. Its maker is billing it as an all-purpose mother ship, suitable for a variety of tasks from reconnaissance to firefighting. Scaled Composites plans to build five White Knight Twos.

Engines: 4 Pratt & Whitney Canada PW308 turbofan engines

Thrust: 6,900 lb. each

Maximum speed: 396 mph

Wingspan: 141 ft. 1 in.

Length: 78 ft. 9 in.

- First flight: December 21, 2008
- The first White Knight Two is named *Eve*, for Richard Branson's mother
- World's largest all-composite aircraft

Eugene Berman/Shutterstock

11.11.2009
GULFSTREAM G650

SPEED AND GRACE PAIRED
WITH STYLE AND COMFORT

The Gulfstream G650, also called the Gulfstream VI, is the ultimate in executive air travel. It's the biggest, fastest, most luxurious, and most technologically advanced jet that Gulfstream has built. Although it's muscular and robust, the Gulfstream G650 is as economical on a seat-mile basis as other executive jets. The G650 offers the longest range and the most-advanced cockpit in the Gulfstream fleet, but its operating speed draws the most attention: It is the world's fastest non-military jet, brushing up against the speed of sound.

- First flight: November 11, 2009
- Cost: $59.9 million in 2014
- Capacity: Up to 18 passengers

**Engines: 2 Rolls-Royce BR725A1-12
turbofan engines**
Thrust: 16,100 lb. each
Maximum speed: 620 mph (Mach 0.92)
Wingspan: 93 ft. 8 in.

12.15.2009
BOEING 787 DREAMLINER

"PART PLASTIC PUPPY, PART VIDEOGAME"
—John C., Dreamliner captain

The 787 Dreamliner applies breakthrough technologies to an all-new airplane design and appears to have overcome early teething troubles to become a big success on the airways. Its extensive use of composite materials is both a challenge and a leap forward. Passengers like the double-wide feel of the fuselage. The two-person flight crew is endowed with the latest technology, but it's not so automated that they don't feel the personal rewards that come with "hands on" piloting.

- First flight: December 15, 2009
- Number built: 170 as of 2014
- Capacity: 210 to 335 passengers

**Engines: 2 General Electric GEnx-1B
turbofan engines**
Thrust: 64,000 lb. each
Maximum speed: 590 mph
Wingspan: 197 ft. 3 in.

SPACESHIPTWO

Jeff Foust/Creative Commons

LATEST COMMERCIAL SPACE VENTURE

SpaceShipTwo followed in the path of the record-setting SpaceShipOne. The suborbital spaceplane was designed by Scaled Composites to be launched in flight by its White Knight Two, and Richard Branson's Virgin Galactic became the owner and operator in 2012. Virgin announced plans to operate a fleet of five of these spaceplanes in a private passenger-carrying service, with future SpaceShipTwos being manufactured by the Spaceship Company; more than 575 people have ponied up $200,000 each to get on the passenger waiting list. The first SpaceShipTwo completed fifty-three test flights, but development was behind schedule because of issues with the hybrid rocket motor. During a test on October 31, 2014, the plane exploded and crashed, killing one of the crewmembers.

Engine: 1 RocketMotorTwo liquid/solid hybrid rocket engine
Thrust: 7,500 lb.
Maximum speed: 2,500 mph (Mach 3.42)
Ceiling: 367,000 ft. (space)
Wingspan: 27 ft.
Length: 60 ft.

- First flight: October 10, 2010
- Capacity: 2 pilots, 6 passengers

TEXTRON AIRLAND SCORPION

"THE WORLD'S MOST AFFORDABLE TACTICAL JET" —AirLand Enterprises

A rare thing in America: a private venture, initially launched in secret, to create a new warplane using the planemaker's own funds. After AirLand Enterprises came to Textron (owner of Cessna) with the idea, Cessna constructed the Scorpion prototype. Ironically, the Scorpion took to the air after what had once seemed a promising market for small, light attack aircraft—suitable for counter-insurgency warfare—was drying up. Pilots say the Scorpion is a smooth-flying, lethal weapon ideal for brushfire conflicts.

Engines: 2 Honeywell TFE731 turbofan engines
Thrust: 4,000 lb. each
Maximum speed: 518 mph
Wingspan: 47 ft. 4 in.

- First flight: December 12, 2013
- Cost: Less than $20 million
- Crew: Carries pilot (front seat) and observer
- Armament: 6 "hard points" for bombs and rockets

NASA GL-10
GREASED LIGHTNING

A RUBE GOLDBERG CONTRAPTION
WITH AN UNUSUAL POWER SOURCE

The GL-10 Greased Lightning is a hybrid diesel-electric tilt-wing aircraft operated by remote control and intended for research into alternate powerplants and vertical flight. The current aircraft is a half-scale prototype of a future version. The GL-10, a praying mantis look-alike with an evocative name, continues a tradition of NASA research that included the Helios Prototype aircraft. Power comes from a two-step propulsion system—diesels inside the fuselage that use a fuel derived from fryer oil (grease) generating electricity (lightning) for lithium batteries to power ten propellers. An expanding envelope of tests is planned through 2020.

Engines: 10 electric motors powered by batteries plus 2 diesel engines
Horsepower: Electric about 20 each; diesel 8 each
Maximum speed: 30 mph
Wingspan: 20 ft.

- First flight: August 19, 2014 (on tether)
- Planned flight endurance: 24 hours
- Being tested at NASA Langley Research Center in Virginia
- Called "really cool stuff" in *Popular Science* magazine

SIKORSKY S-97 RAIDER

"[IT'S] NOT ONLY GORGEOUS. IT'S ABSOLUTELY BADASS" —*Gawker*

In this era of tight budgets the appearance of a new aircraft is a dramatic event, especially when it's a bold, innovative design. Unveiled in October 2014, and leveraging new technologies found in a test ship that established speed records, the sleek S-97 was expected to fly twice as fast as conventional helicopters. The S-97 will feature coaxial counter-rotating main rotors and a 7-foot pusher propeller that will improve maneuverability and hover efficiency, and greatly increase speed. The ambitious goal is to offer a leap into the future for any military helicopter user interested in agility and lethality on the battlefield—but the S-97 looks a lot like a military aircraft in search of a mission. Its manufacturer is promoting the S-97 as a replacement for the OH-58D Kiowa Warrior, the armed scout helicopter the US Army is retiring but no longer plans to replace. A lightweight at 11,000 pounds, the S-97 will be limited in the number of troops it can carry, and may be years away from having integrated sensors and weapons. It holds great potential, and its makers fully expect it to redeem the promise it offers.

Engine: 1 General Electric YT706 gas turbine engine
Horsepower: 2,600 shaft
Cruising speed: 253 mph (projected)
Main rotor diameter: 34 ft.
Length: 35 ft.

- First flight: Planned by December 31, 2014
- Number built: 2 being built in 2014
- Capacity: Crew of 2 plus 6 passengers
- Range: 354 miles
- Uses a single-piece, all-composite fuselage

BOEING KC-46A PEGASUS

A STRATEGIC FILLING STATION IN THE SKY

The Boeing KC-46A Pegasus is the next-generation air refueling tanker for the US Air Force and is competing worldwide with the Airbus A330 Multi-Role Tanker Transport for overseas purchases. The KC-46A is a military derivative of the Boeing 767-200 jetliner. Planemaker Boeing says the KC-46 "can refuel all US, allied, and coalition military aircraft compatible with international aerial refueling procedures . . . and can carry passengers, cargo, and patients whenever and wherever needed." The KC-46A is scheduled to replace aging KC-135 Stratotankers, some of which date to the Eisenhower era.

Engines: 2 Pratt & Whitney PW4062 turbofan engines
Thrust: 63,300 lb. each
Maximum speed: 570 mph (Mach 0.86)
Wingspan: 157 ft. 8 in.

- First flight: 2015 (projected at press time)
- 179 to be ordered for the US Air Force
- Approved for export; being considered by South Korea
- First 18 scheduled for delivery by 2017

9.8.1968

SEPECAT JAGUAR

ALL OVER THE PLACE WITH CONVENTIONAL AND NUCLEAR DUTIES

The Jaguar was an Anglo-French fighter that emerged from Cold War tensions to serve in the air forces of Britain, France, Ecuador, India, Nigeria, and Oman. Jaguars fought in brushfire wars around the world while remaining ready to deliver tactical nuclear weapons for Britain, France, and India. The Jaguar turned in high reliability figures and low casualty rates during the 1991 Persian Gulf war, known as Operation Desert Storm. This is a conventional, single-seat, sweptwing, twin-engine warplane with very long range for its class. Twin-engine trainer versions introduced many pilots to high performance flying. The Jaguar was well liked by those who've retired it and by its only current user, India.

Engines: 2 Rolls-Royce/Turbomeca Adour Mk 102 turbofan engines with afterburners
Thrust: 7,305 lb. each
Maximum speed: 1,056 mph (Mach 1.6)
Wingspan: 28 ft. 6 in.

- First flight: September 8, 1968
- Number built: 543
- Cost: $8 million per plane in 1998
- Retired by France in 2005, Britain in 2007
- A few are in museums today

8.14.1974

PANAVIA TORNADO

A POINTY-NOSED, SWING-WING WEAPON OF WAR

When its switchblade wings are fully swept, the Panavia Tornado slices through the air with the ease of a finely sharpened knife. The Anglo-German-Italian Tornado looks like it's breaking the sound barrier even when it's sitting still. When flying, it's a spectacle of agility and performance. "Multirole combat aircraft" is a mouthful, but that's what the sleek, versatile Tornado is. Somewhat limited in size, duration, and range, it served brilliantly throughout the Cold War and afterward. It gave pilot and navigator a bumpy ride at low level but was otherwise snug and smooth.

Engines: 2 Turbo-Union RB199-34R Mk 103 turbofan engines with afterburners
Thrust: 17,270 lb. each
Maximum speed: 1,490 mph (Mach 2.2)
Wingspan: 45 ft. 7½ in. (at 25 degrees sweep), 28 ft. 2½ in. (at 67 degrees)

- First flight: August 14, 1974
- Number built: 992 from 1979 to 1998
- Crew: 2 (pilot and navigator)
- Armament: Built in fighter-bomber, electronic-warfare, and air-defense versions
- Replaced the Lightning and Phantom in the Royal Air Force
- Just 1 is privately owned—and it's not flyable

11.9.1978

BAE/MCDONNELL HARRIER II

IMPROVING ON AN ORIGINAL IDEA

The second-generation Harrier II (called the Matador II in Spain) offered improved power, range, and weapons-carrying capability over its predecessor and enabled its users, the US Marines among them, to continue operating in tight spaces without needing airfields or runways. The marines' AV-8B models proved especially useful in the 1991 Persian Gulf War but sustained higher losses than conventional warplanes. The Harrier II is difficult to fly, but pilots who master it speak highly of the flexibility it offers.

Engine: 1 Rolls-Royce F402-RR-408 Mk 107 vectored-thrust turbofan engine
Thrust: 23,500 lb.
Maximum speed: 673 mph (Mach 0.91)
Wingspan: 30 ft. 4 in.

- First flight: November 9, 1978
- Cost: About $30 million in 1985
- Three kinds of AV-8B: day, night, radar-equipped
- Two-seat versions 3 ft. 11 in. longer
- Planned AV-8D version not built

4.3.1982

AIRBUS A310

SPACIOUS MULTITASKER

The A310 was the second wide-body jetliner from Airbus, an international planemaker with an assembly plant in Toulouse, France. It offers several sizes and seating options to airline users, and performs military duty as an air refueling tanker. Even in today's elbow-to-elbow travel environment, the A310 passenger cabin is considered roomy and passenger-friendly. Typical of a new generation of twin-engine, two-crew airliners, the A310 has a roomy and well-designed flight deck with semi-automated controls and "glass," or digital, instruments.

Engines: 2 Pratt & Whitney PW4156A turbofan engines (typical)
Thrust: 56,000 lb. each
Cruising speed: 580 mph
Wingspan: 144 ft.

- First flight: April 3, 1982
- Called "Porky" by some pilots for its corpulent fuselage shape
- Military versions serve in 11 countries
- Long range makes it ideal for trans-Atlantic routes
- Variant A310 MRTT was ordered, but then canceled, by the US Air Force for use as the KC-45A tanker

ATR 42

A FRANCO-ITALIAN TREAT FOR REGIONAL FLIERS

The ATR 42 is a twin-turboprop regional airliner built in France and Italy by ATR—*Aerei da Trasporto Regionale* to Italians, *Avions de transport regional* to the French. No longer called "commuter" or "feeder" airliners, these short-range regionals bring satisfied travelers to thousands of airports that are off limits to big jets. The ATR 42 comes in several versions, including a freight-hauling variant and the enhanced-technology ATR 42-600. All models give passengers a panoramic view from large, rectangular windows, and pilots praise the plane's smooth-as-glass handling qualities.

Engines: 2 Pratt & Whitney Canada PW120 turboprop engines (typical)
Horsepower: 2,400 each
Cruising speed: 230 mph
Wingspan: 80 ft. 7 in.

- First flight: August 16, 1984
- First flight of ATR 42-600 model: March 4, 2010
- Number built: About 630 as of 2014
- Cost: Reportedly $12.1 million used

10.11.1990

ROCKWELL-MBB X-31

AN AGILE "AMUSEMENT PARK OF THE AIR"

It goes up. It goes down. It flies backwards. (Yes, backwards.) Well, not any longer, because it's retired, but in its heyday the X-31 performed maneuvers not possible for any other airplane. This research ship from an American-German team of Rockwell International and Messerschmitt-Bölkow-Blohm existed solely for the purpose of testing thrust vectoring technology to assist in the design of future fighters. One crashed in 1995 and the other is on loan for display at Purdue University, but when it was flying, the X-31 gave its pilot a thrill ride like no airplane before or since.

Engine: 1 General Electric F404-GE-400 turbofan engine
Thrust: 16,000 lb.
Maximum speed: 900 mph (Mach 1.28)
Wingspan: 23 ft. 10 in.

- First flight: October 11, 1990
- Number built: 2
- Did 500 test flights from 1990 to 1995
- First airplane to fly at 70-degree angle of attack

EUROFIGHTER TYPOON

AN AGILE DOGFIGHTER PACKED WITH SOPHISTICATED GEAR

Developed in a joint effort by Britain, Germany, Italy, and France (which dropped out of the program), the Typhoon is a twin-engine, canard delta-wing fighter with impressive maneuverability and a comfortable cockpit packed with the latest digital technology. Former US Air Force chief of staff Gen. John Jumper called it a Formula One racer of the skies—smaller and less complex than the costlier F-22 Raptor or F-35 Lightning II but feisty and formidable. Small and simple, with an impressive smoothness of handling, the Typhoon is a lethal adversary armed with a Mauser cannon and a flexible range of missiles.

Engines: 2 Eurojet EJ200 turbofan engines with afterburners
Thrust: 13,490 lb.
Maximum speed: 1,400 mph or Mach 2.0
Wingspan: 35 ft. 10 in.

- First flight: March 27, 1994
- Number built: About 415 as of mid-2014
- Cost: About $120 million each at the factory door
- Armament: Stealth technology features include low frontal radar cross-section and passive sensors
- Used by Australia, Britain, Germany, Italy, Saudi Arabia, and Spain
- Able to "supercruise"—travel to the target at supersonic speed

9.13.1994

AIRBUS A300-600ST BELUGA

"WORLD'S STRANGEST-LOOKING AIRPLANE"
—Miguel Ros, CNN, September 17, 2014

The A300-600ST Beluga or Super Transporter is a version of the familiar A300 airliner extensively rebuilt and vastly enlarged to become a massive freighter for outsized cargoes—primarily, large components used in aircraft manufacture. The name Beluga is used separately for a large white whale and for a sturgeon: what the two creatures have in common is that they are very large. In cargo-carrying volume, the Beluga is the second largest freighter in the world although it rates only fifth when measured in weight-carrying capacity. The Beluga's primary purpose is to help the Airbus company build other planes: this giant makes sixty flights each week to and from eleven sites, carrying fuselage sections and wings for Airbus programs.

Engines: 2 General Electric CF6-80C2A8 turbofan engines
Thrust: 26,000 lb. each
Maximum speed: 490 mph (Mach 0.82)
Wingspan: 147 ft. 1 inch

- First flight: September 13, 1994
- Number built: 5
- Can carry cargoes weighing up to 103,616 lb.
- Typically operates to a range of 900 miles

4.27.2005
AIRBUS A380

REALLY, REALLY BIG—SERIOUSLY, NO KIDDING

The Airbus A380 gives new meaning to big, as in B-I-G. This four-engined double-decker is a giant cruise ship of the air, the world's largest airliner—so big that many airports had to build new facilities to accommodate it. While most A380s haul people, a few are freighters, and one is an executive jet for an owner who can afford to keep his identity secret. Despite its size and the fact that there is no other aircraft quite like it, the A380 has a good safety record and is liked by pilots, who appreciate the semi-automated digital environment on the flight deck.

Engines: 4 Rolls-Royce Trent 900 or Engine Alliance GP7000 turbofan engines
Thrust: 40,000 lb. each
Cruising speed: 580 mph
Wingspan: 261 ft. 8 in.

- First flight: April 27, 2005
- Number built: 124 in service delivered as of August 2014
- Has 40 percent more floor space than the next largest airliner, the Boeing 747-8
- Total sales of 400 aircraft expected

AIRBUS A330 MULTI ROLE TANKER-TRANSPORT

AN EXCELLENT PLATFORM FOR PASSING GAS

The Airbus A330 Multi Role Tanker Transport, or MRTT, is a modern-day air refueling tanker in use in four countries and in competition with the Boeing KC-46A Pegasus for further overseas sales. The US Air Force had once issued a contract to purchase the A330 MRTT, calling it the KC-45A, but the purchase was canceled and Americans will fly the KC-46A instead. Of the two iconic competitors, the A330 MRTT is substantially larger and took to the air for the first time at least half a dozen years earlier.

Engines: 2 Rolls-Royce Trent 772B turbofan engines (typical)
Thrust: 71,000 lb. each
Maximum speed: 570 mph (Mach 0.86)
Wingspan: 198 ft.

- First flight: June 15, 2007
- Operated by Australia, Britain, Saudi Arabia, and United Arab Emirates
- Expected potential sales: 180
- 17 in service as of August 2014

12.11.2009

AIRBUS A400M ATLAS

A DIFFERENT SIZE IN
A PROMISING CARGO PLANE

The Airbus A400M Atlas is bigger than a C-130 Hercules-style tactical airlifter but smaller than a C-17 Globemaster-type strategic cargo hauler. Despite its awkward size and early history of technical glitches, eight nations have invested in the A400M as a military transport. Advantages include the ability to land on unpaved surfaces near the front lines. The flight deck is digital, as in other Airbus products, and pilots remark on the ease of making the transition and flying military supply missions.

Engines: 4 Europrop TP400-D6 turboprop engines
Horsepower: 11,060 each
Cruising speed: 485 mph
Wingspan: 139 ft. 1 in.

- First flight: December 11, 2009
- First operational mission: December 29, 2013
- About 200 on order in 2014
- Called the "Grizzly" by crews

PLANES BY MAKER

Aero Spacelines Pregnant Guppy, 240
Aero Spacelines Super Guppy, 248
Aichi E16A *Zuiun*, 43
Air Force One, 277
Air Tractor Family, 279
Airbus A300-600ST Beluga, 312
Airbus A310, 308
Airbus A330 Multi Role Tanker-Transport, 314
Airbus A340, 26
Airbus A380, 313
Airbus A400M Atlas, 315
Airbus Helicopters AS350 *Écureuil*, 21
Airbus Helicopters AS532 Cougar, 22
Airbus Helicopters EC135, 25
Albatros D.III, 27
Alenia C-27J Spartan, 41
Antonov An-225 *Mriya*, 61
Arup S-2, 99
ATR 42, 309
Autogiro Company of America AC-35, 106
Aviatik D.I, 8
Avro Canada CF-100 Canuck, 11
Avro Canada VZ-9 Avrocar, 12
Avro Lancaster, 77
Avro Vulcan, 82

BAE Systems Hawk, 87
BAE/McDonnell Harrier II, 307
Baldwin Red Devil, 91
Beech 1900, 273
Beech Bonanza, 157
Beech Model 17 Staggerwing, 99
Beech T-34C Turbo Mentor, 260
Beech T-42A Cochise, 247
Beechcraft T-6 Texan II, 286
Bell 206 JetRanger, 241
Bell 214ST, 253
Bell 412, 268
Bell 429 GlobalRanger, 297
Bell 47, 156
Bell AH-1Z Viper, 290
Bell H-12, 157
Bell OH-58D Kiowa/OH-58F Kiowa Warrior, 274
Bell P-39 Airacobra, 115
Bell P-63 Kingcobra, 134
Bell UH-1 "Huey," 224
Bell X-1, 158
Bell X-2, 219

Bell X-5, 194
Bell XP-77, 144
Bell XP-83, 151
Bell YFM-1 Airacuda, 110
Bell-Boeing V-22 Osprey, 278
Blackburn Buccaneer, 83
Blériot XI, 15
Boeing 707, 212
Boeing 747, 252
Boeing 767, 273
Boeing 787 Dreamliner, 299
Boeing AH-64 Apache, 264
Boeing B-17 Flying Fortress, 103
Boeing B-47 Stratojet, 175
Boeing B-52 Stratofortress, 198
Boeing C-17 Globemaster III, 280
Boeing C-97 Stratofreighter, 147
Boeing CH-47 Chinook, 238
Boeing EA-18G Growler, 295
Boeing KC-135 Stratotanker, 223
Boeing KC-46A Pegasus, 304
Boeing X-37, 294
Boeing XB-15, 112
Boeing XF8B-1, 148
Boeing YC-14, 265
Boeing/Stearman PT-17 Kaydet, 106
Bombardier Challenger 600 Series, 13
Bombardier E-9A Widget, 14
Bowlus-Nelson BB-1 Dragonfly, 167
Bristol F.2B, 69
Bücker Bü 131 *Jungmann*, 30

Caproni Ca.20, 38
Caproni Ca.36, 39
Caudron G.4, 17
Cessna 150, 225
Cessna 170, 180
Cessna 172 Skyhawk, 215
Cessna A-37 Dragonfly, 242
Cessna CitationJet, 279
Cessna T-37, 213
Chase C-122 Avitruc, 171
Chase XC-123A Avitruc, 193
Comp Air 10, 283
Comp Air 8, 282
Consolidated B-24 Liberator, 120
Consolidated B-32 Dominator, 133
Consolidated B-36 Peacemaker, 163

Consolidated PB2Y Coronado, 113
Consolidated PBY Catalina, 101
Consolidated XC-99, 174
Convair 880, 231
Convair 990 Coronado, 236
Convair F-102 Delta Dagger, 206
Convair F-106 Delta Dart, 225
Convair F2Y Sea Dart, 202
Convair Liners, 168
Convair R3Y Tradewind, 207
Convair XB-46, 169
Convair XF-92A, 179
Convair XFY-1, 209
Convair XP-81, 150
Convair YB-60, 199
Curtiss JN-4D "Jenny," 92
Curtiss Model D, 90
Curtiss Model L, 93
Curtiss P-36 Mohawk, 102
Curtiss P-40 Warhawk, 116
Curtiss SB2C Helldiver, 127
Curtiss XF-87 Blackhawk, 177
Curtiss XP-37, 109
Curtiss XP-55 Ascender, 137
Curtiss-Goupil Duck, 93
Curtiss-Wright X-19, 243

Dassault HU-25 Guardian, 20
Dassault *Rafale*, 23
Davis DA-2, 249
de Havilland Canada DHC-1 Chipmunk, 10
de Havilland Comet, 79
de Havilland Dragon Rapide, 72
de Lackner HZ-1 Aerocycle, 214
Deperdussin *Monocoque*, 16
DHC-1 Chipmunk, 10
Discovery Aviation Model 201, 62
Douglas A-1 Skyraider, 152
Douglas A3D Skywarrior, 202
Douglas A-4 Skyhawk, 210
Douglas B-66 Destroyer, 211
Douglas C-133 Cargomaster, 222
Douglas DC-3, 105
Douglas DC-4, 130
Douglas DC-6, 160
Douglas DC-7, 203
Douglas F3D Skyknight, 178
Douglas F4D Skyray, 192

Douglas F5D Skylancer, 222
Douglas RD-2 Dolphin, 98
Douglas SBD Dauntless, 122
Douglas X-3 Stiletto, 200
Douglas XA2D-1 Skyshark, 188
Douglas XB-42 Mixmaster, 145
Durand Mk V, 267

English Electric Canberra, 78
Erco Ercoupe, 111
Eurofighter Typhoon, 311

Fairchild C-123B Provider, 186
Fairchild Metroliner, 252
Fairchild Model 24, 98
Fairchild Republic A-10 Thunderbolt II, 257
Fairchild XC-120 Pack Plane, 190
Fairey Gannet, 80
Fairey Swordfish, 73
Farman FF 65 Sport, 19
Ficon, 196
Fieseler Fi 156 *Storch*, 32
FIFI, 256
Fisher XP-75 Eagle, 140
Focke-Achgelis FA 330 *Bachstelze*, 34
Focke-Wulf FW 190 Würger, 33
Fokker D.VII, 29
Fokker Dr.I *Dreidecker*, 28
Fokker F-27 Friendship, 48
Ford Tri-Motor, 95
Fulton Airphibian, 170

Garrett Stamp, 259
General Atomics MQ-1 Predator, 281
Gloster Gladiator, 74
Goodyear Inflatoplane, 221
Great Lakes Sport Trainer, 97
Grumman AF Guardian, 156
Grumman F-14 Tomcat, 255
Grumman F4F Wildcat, 108
Grumman F6F Hellcat, 132
Grumman F7F Tigercat, 139
Grumman Gulfstream I, 228
Grumman Gulfstream II, 249
Grumman OV-1 Mohawk, 233
Grumman SA-16 Albatross, 173
Grumman TBF Avenger, 129
Grumman X-29, 275

Grumman XF5F Skyrocket, 121
Gulfstream G650, 299
Gulfstream III, 269
Gulfstream IV, 276
Gulfstream V, 282

Hafe CH-1, 250
Hawker Hart, 71
Hawker Hurricane, 75
Hawker Siddeley Harrier, 85
Helios Prototype, 288
Hiller X-18, 235
Hiller XH-44 Hiller-Copter, 145
Hispano HA-1112 *Buchón*, 63
Hughes H-4 Hercules, 173
Hughes XF-11, 162
Hughes XH-17, 201

IAI C-38A Courier, 37
IAI *Kfir*, 36
Ilyushin Il-10 *Šturmovík*, 51
Ilyushin Il-18, 57
Ilyushin Il-2 *Šturmovík*, 50
Ilyushin Il-76, 58

Kaman HH-43 Huskie, 193
Kaman SH-2G Super Seasprite, 276
Kawasaki T-4, 46
Kugisho MXY-7 Ohka, 44

Learjet, 241
Lockheed C-130 Hercules, 212
Lockheed C-141 Starlifter, 244
Lockheed C-5 Galaxy, 251
Lockheed F-104 Starfighter, 207
Lockheed F-117 Nighthawk, 271
Lockheed F-80 Shooting Star, 142
Lockheed F-94 Starfire, 184
Lockheed Have Blue, 266
Lockheed L-1011 TriStar, 254
Lockheed Martin C-130J Super Hercules, 283
Lockheed Martin F-16 Fighting Falcon, 260
Lockheed Martin F-22 Raptor, 284
Lockheed Martin F-35 Lightning II Joint Strike Fighter, 296
Lockheed Martin X-35, 289
Lockheed Model 18 Lodestar, 119
Lockheed P-38 Lightning, 117
Lockheed R6O-1 Constitution, 166
Lockheed S-3 Viking, 257
Lockheed T2V-1 SeaStar, 206

Lockheed U-2 Dragon Lady, 217
Lockheed XF-90, 185
Lockheed XFV-1, 209
Lockheed XP-58 Chain Lightning, 146
Lockheed XV-4 Hummingbird, 239
Loening Ol, 94
Long Midget Mustang, 176
LTV XC-142, 246

Macchi C.205 Veltro, 40
Martin 4-0-4, 192
Martin B-26 Marauder, 125
Martin B-57 Canberra, 205
Martin XB-51, 186
McDonnell/BAE Harrier II, 307
McDonnell Douglas MD-80, 268
McDonnell Douglas YC-15, 263
McDonnell F-101 Voodoo, 213
McDonnell F2H Banshee, 167
McDonnell F3H Demon, 195
McDonnell F-4 Phantom II, 227
McDonnell XF-85 Goblin, 182
McDonnell XH-20 Little Henry, 170
McDonnell XP-67, 141
Mercury Air Shoestring, 181
Mercury Space Capsule, 237
Messerschmitt Bf 109, 31
Messerschmitt Me 262, 35
Meyers OTW, 107
Mikoyan MiG-29, 60
Mikoyan-Gurevich MiG-15, 52
Mikoyan-Gurevich MiG-17, 53
Mikoyan-Gurevich MiG-19, 54
Mikoyan-Gurevich Mig-21, 56
Mitsubishi A6M Zero, 42
Mitsubishi F-2, 47

Nakajima Ki-115 *Tsurugi*, 45
Nasa GL-10 Greased Lightning, 302
Naval Aircraft Factory N3N, 104
Nieuport 17, 18
Noorduyn Norseman, 9
North American A-5 Vigilante, 228
North American AJ Savage, 180
North American AT-6 Texan, 102
North American B-25 Mitchell, 124
North American B-45 Tornado, 168
North American F-100 Super Sabre, 204
North American F-82 Twin Mustang, 153
North American F-86 Sabre, 172
North American FJ-1 Fury, 164

North American P-51 Mustang, 126
North American P-64, 125
North American Sabreliner, 229
North American T-2 Buckeye, 226
North American X-15, 234
North American XB-70 Valkyrie, 245
Northrop F-15 Reporter, 154
Northrop F-5E/F Tiger II, 258
Northrop F-89 Scorpion, 181
Northrop Grumman EA-6B Prowler, 251
Northrop Grumman RQ-4 Global Hawk, 285
Northrop P-61 Black Widow, 131
Northrop T-38 Talon, 232
Northrop Tacit Blue, 272
Northrop X-4 Bantam, 183
Northrop XP-56 Black Bullet, 138
Northrop XP-79b, 155
Northrop YC-125 Raider, 187
Northrop YF-17, 261

Panavia Tornado, 306
Percival Provost, 81
Piasecki HRP Rescuer, 152
Piasecki HUP Retriever, 178
Piasecki PV-2, 136
Piasecki VZ-8 Sky-Car, 230
Pietenpol Air Camper, 97
Pilatus PC-12, 67
Pilatus PC-21, 68
Pilatus PC-6 Porter, 66
Piper J-3 Cub, 114
Piper J-5 Cub Cruiser, 118
Project Tip-Tow, 191

Quest Kodiak, 293

Raytheon T-1A Jayhawk, 280
Republic F-105 Thunderchief, 218
Republic F-84 Thunderjet, 161
Republic F-84F Thunderstreak, 189
Republic P-47 Thunderbolt, 128
Republic RF-84F Thunderflash, 197
Republic XF-12 Rainbow, 159
Republic XF-84H "Thunderscreech," 216
Republic XF-91, 185
Republic XP-72, 143
Rockwell B-1B Lancer, 262
Rockwell-MBB X-31, 310

Royal Aircraft Factory S.E.5, 70
Ryan FR Fireball, 147
Ryan Pt-20A Primary Trainer, 100
Ryan X-13 Vertijet, 220
Ryan XF2R Dark Shark, 165

Saab 37 *Viggen*, 64
Saab 39 *Gripen*, 65
Scaled Composites Proteus, 287
Scaled Composites White Knight One, 291
Scaled Composites White Knight Two, 298
Sepecat Jaguar, 305
Seversky P-35, 104
Short C-23 Sherpa, 88
Short SC.7 Skyvan, 84
Sikorsky H-34 Choctaw, 208
Sikorsky HH-52 Seaguard, 226
Sikorsky Ilya Muromets, 49
Sikorsky R-4 and HNS, 130
Sikorsky S-97 Raider, 303
SOCATA TBM 700, 24
Space Shuttle, 270
SpaceShipOne, 292
SpaceShipTwo, 300
Spartan 7W Executive, 107
Spirit of St. Louis, 96
Stearman/Boeing PT-17 Kaydet, 106
Stinson L-5 Sentinel, 129
Supermarine Spitfire, 76

Textron AirLand Scorpion, 301
Tupolev Tu-104, 55

Volmer Sportsman, 231
Vought F4U Corsair, 123
Vought F6U Pirate, 164
Vought F8U Crusader, 215
Vought OS2U Kingfisher, 114
Vought V-173, 133
Vought XF5U-1, 149
Vultee BT-13 Valiant, 118
Vultee XP-54, 135

Westland Lynx, 86
Wright Flyer, 89

Yakovlev Yak-52, 59

AFTER LANDING

Okay. Now you're taxiing in. You've been in the cockpits of some of the most sensational, bizarre, and outlandish aircraft in aviation history.

Now you've landed; but the flight's not over until the paperwork's done.

The words and pictures in this volume—those figurative flights you've just taken on weird and wonderful wings—reflect hard work by a lot of people. This page is for them.

This book reflects vision on the part of people who make books at Zenith Press, where Erik Gilg, Madeleine Vasaly, Steve Daubenspeck, Rob Chapman, and Nichole Schiele all did important stuff.

It also reflects great thinking by people who sell books, including Bill Dawson and Natalya McKinney.

Apart from the author, the strongest force behind this frolic of flying is John Gourley, a superb photographer and writer who assisted with the book from the start. John is one of those nutcases who can identify every antenna sticking out from the top of the fuselage. He is a virtuoso with a camera.

In addition to John, I'd like to express thanks to: A. B. Bradley, Warren M. Bodie, Robert L. Burns, Luigino Caliaro, Hunter Chaney, the Collings Foundation, the Commemorative Air Force, Bill Crimmins, Jamie Darcy, Ben Dunnell, the Experimental Aircraft Association, Bob Hafford, Jim Hawkins, André Jans, John Lackey/Fly By Photography, Steve Link, D. Miller, Jordan Patkin, Lynn Ritger, Larry Titchenal, Jim Winchester, and Matthias Winkler.

That's it. Fun's over. Time for the debrief.